For EAL/ESL/E2L students

# Geography

Dr Anne Williams
Fran Montgomerie

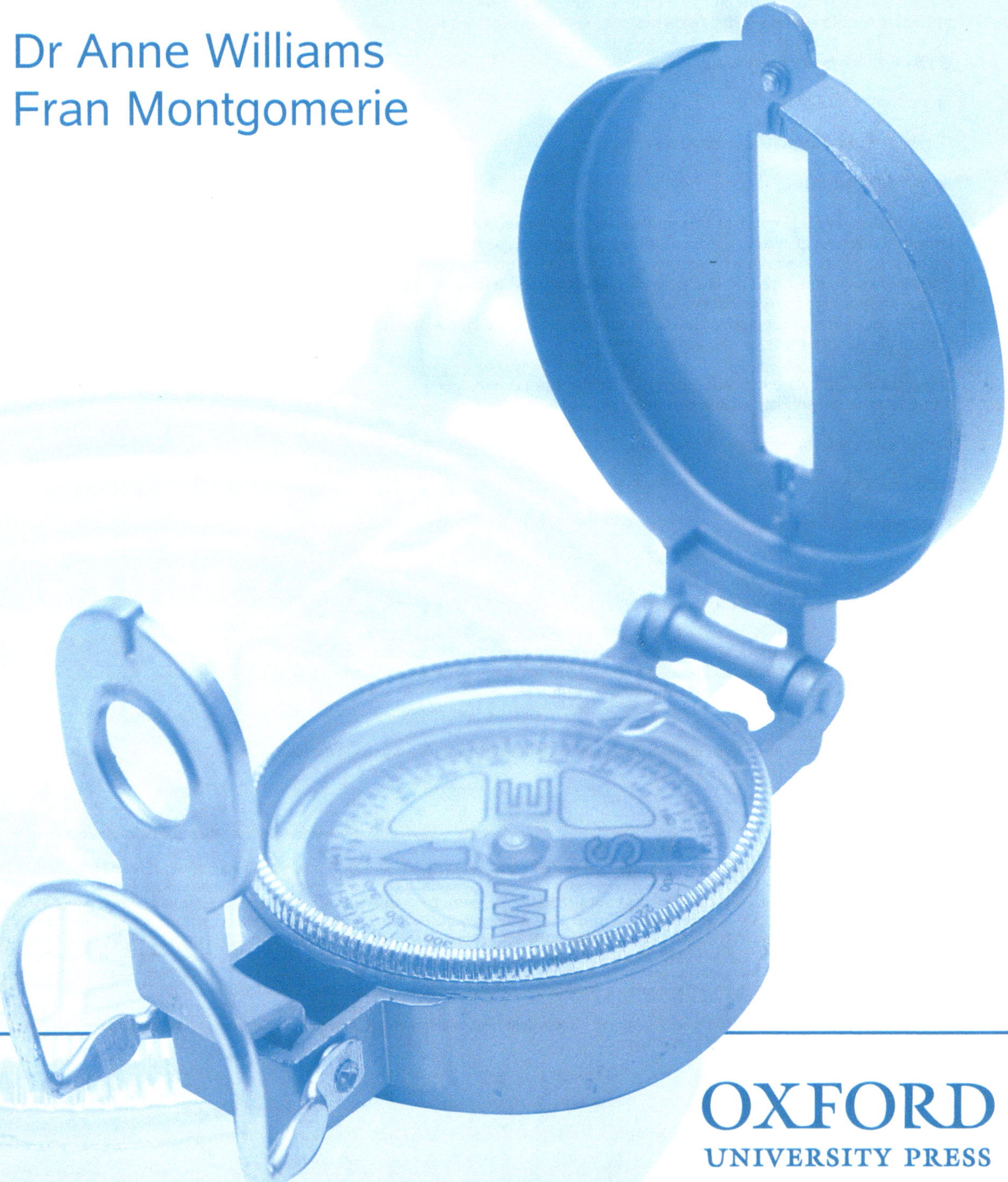

OXFORD CONTENT AND LANGUAGE SUPPORT

OXFORD
UNIVERSITY PRESS

Great Clarendon Street, Oxford OX2 6DP

Oxford University Press is a department of the University of Oxford.
It furthers the University's objective of excellence in research, scholarship,
and education by publishing worldwide in

Oxford   New York

Auckland   Cape Town   Dar es Salaam   Hong Kong   Karachi
Kuala Lumpur   Madrid   Melbourne   Mexico City   Nairobi
New Delhi   Shanghai   Taipei   Toronto

With offices in

Argentina   Austria   Brazil   Chile   Czech Republic   France   Greece
Guatemala   Hungary   Italy   Japan   South Korea   Poland   Portugal
Singapore   Switzerland   Thailand   Turkey   Ukraine   Vietnam

Oxford is a registered trade mark of Oxford University Press
in the UK and in certain other countries

© Oxford University Press 2010

The moral rights of the author have been asserted

Database right Oxford University Press (maker)

First published 2010

All rights reserved. No part of this publication may be reproduced,
stored in a retrieval system, or transmitted, in any form or by any means,
without the prior permission in writing of Oxford University Press,
or as expressly permitted by law, or under terms agreed with the appropriate
reprographics rights organization. Enquiries concerning reproduction
outside the scope of the above should be sent to the Rights Department,
Oxford University Press, at the address above

You must not circulate this book in any other binding or cover
and you must impose this same condition on any acquirer

British Library Cataloguing in Publication Data

Data available

ISBN 9780199135271

10 9

Printed in Great Britain by CPI Group (UK) Ltd., Croydon CR0 4YY

Paper used in the production of this book is a natural, recyclable product made
from wood grown in sustainable forests. The manufacturing process conforms to the
environmental regulations of the country of origin.

**Acknowledgements**
The authors would like to give special thanks to their families, without whom this work would not have been possible

Cartoons © Adrian Barclay

The publisher and authors would like to thank the following for their permission to reproduce photographs and other copyright material:

**Front cover photo**: Planner/Shutterstock; **p15**: Tim Graham/Getty Images; **p21l**: Photodisc/OUP; **p21r**: Xiao Xiong/Dreamstime; **p24**: Sai Yeung Chan/Shutterstock; **p31**: Dreamshot/Dreamstime; **p40**: Maria Predka/Dreamstime; **p41t**: Andrew Lever/Shutterstock; **p41m**: Cliff Parnell/iStockphoto; **p41b**: Andresr/Shutterstock; **p42t**: Konstantin Sutyagin/Shutterstock; **p42m**: Anantha Vardhan/iStockphoto; **p49ml**: Robert Estall/Corbis; **p49mr**: LianeM/Shutterstock; **p49bl**: Patricia Hofmeester/Shutterstock; **p49br**: Jim Lopes/Shutterstock; **p52t**: Gertfrik/Dreamstime; **p52m**: Bradcalkins/Dreamstime; **p57**: Jaggat/Dreamstime; **p64**: Joao Virissimo/Dreamstime; **p78**: Xavier Subias/Photolibrary; **p93**: EPS/Rex Features; **p105bl**: Corbis/Digital Stock/OUP; **p105bm**: Photodisc/OUP; **p105br**: Joyce & Frank Burek/Photolibrary; **p114**: Inigo Carrera/Photolibrary; **p117**: Frederic Soltan/Sygma/Corbis; **p125ml**: Pawel Toczynski/Photolibrary; **p125mr**: Bruce Amos/Shutterstock; **p125bl**: Jordan Tan/Shutterstock; **p125br**: Flight Images LLP/Photolibrary; **p129**: Yves Gellie/Corbis; **p136m**: Malgorzata Kistryn/Shutterstock; **p136b**: Dmitry Maslov/Dreamstime; **p141**: AFP; **p148**: Dr. Morley Read/Shutterstock; **p153bl**: Pascal Rateau/Shutterstock; **p153br**: JuNe74/Shutterstock.

Although we have made every effort to trace and contact all copyright holders before publication this has not been possible in all cases. If notified, the publisher will rectify any errors or omissions at the earliest opportunity.

# Contents

| | | |
|---|---|---|
| | About this book | 4 |
| | Study skills | 5 |
| 1 | Population | 11 |
| 2 | Settlements | 24 |
| 3 | Agriculture and food | 37 |
| 4 | Industry | 51 |
| 5 | Leisure and tourism | 61 |
| 6 | Energy and water | 74 |
| 7 | Plate tectonics | 86 |
| 8 | Weathering | 101 |
| 9 | Rivers | 109 |
| 10 | Marine processes | 122 |
| 11 | Weather and climate | 134 |
| 12 | Ecosystems and resource management | 147 |
| | Glossary | 159 |
| | Answers | 170 |
| | Index | 183 |

# About this book

This new series is designed for students whose first language is not English. The books include content and workbook style activities, with the intention that these activities are done in the students' own notebooks. They can be used alongside core textbooks, or outside of class as independent work. This title provides a useful resource for teachers in need of additional tasks and exercises which aim to reinforce the topics of the Geography syllabus, and to help students develop their linguistic control.

The content covers topics in both physical and human geography and introduces examples and case studies drawn from the international context.

The structure of each chapter follows the same pattern, making it easy for learners to navigate their way through each topic.

To facilitate the learning of key terms and concepts these are highlighted in boxes. Further key vocabulary is highlighted in bold throughout each chapter. Many of the terms recur so the students have the opportunity to see how they are used in different contexts, and also to assimilate their meanings. The extensive glossary provides an important resource for the acquisition of the terms and concepts introduced in the book.

Each chapter includes a range of exercises which aim to increase the students' confidence in the subject and in their ability to express themselves in the English language. At regular intervals there are exercises which focus on developing language skills. Other exercises aim to revise the geographical concepts. Many of these are based on examination skills such as graph and data interpretation, describing and using pictures, maps and photos, explaining cause and effect, and using comparatives to describe difference.

Studying Geography in English can be challenging, as well as fun, and it is our hope that this book makes the subject more accessible to students.

# Study skills

These good practices will help you to identify the key points and facts to improve your success in exams.

## Organisation

It is important that you keep control of the information presented to you in lessons and in this guide and to do this it is essential that you record key points, vocabulary and case studies in your own personal notebook or file.

Some students prefer to have a loose leafed file with dividers for each topic; others prefer to have a notebook in which they write down information as they learn it. Clear organisation in your notes will lead to clear organisation in your head! A section for recording vocabulary at the back of your file or notebook will save you time looking up recurring unfamiliar words.

Some students like to write on the right hand page only, so that they leave space to add more material such as short summaries or a list of the main points on the left hand page, opposite their main notes. This means they do not have to turn over a page to find the information they wish to work on.

In all cases it is a good idea to have an index at the front with a list of named sections, and page numbers of at least the first page of each section. By looking at the examination specification you can find the topics that you have to cover.

## Colour

Many students find it easier to recall the information that is relevant to a particular aspect of a topic by using a particular colour to highlight the related points. Highlighters make words stand out on the page and help you to identify the key points. (Beware of overdoing it though; otherwise your page will become a confusing sea of colours!)

## Visualisation

An image or diagram can sometimes be a quick reference for information e.g. a **nucleated** settlement can be represented like a nucleus in science, and the association will remind you that it is a settlement around a central point. 'Nucleated' is an adjective formed from the noun 'nucleus'.

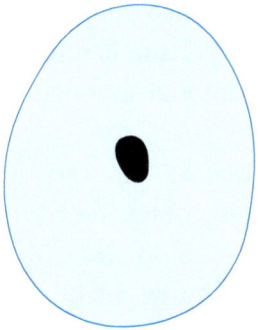

If you find it helpful to remember items in this way, make sure that you leave space for these diagrams and images in your notes.

## Reading

The ability to read quickly and efficiently is a vital skill in our world today. When you are given material to read, especially in examinations, you need to have a clear idea of what you are reading about and which pieces of information are important for the task that you have been set.

5

# Study skills

- **Focus in on the relevant information.** Look at the title, headings, sub headings and illustrations as these will help you to identify the subject.
- **Skim** through the text and check that the subject is what you expected – sometimes authors put a twist in the title to make it more interesting.
- **Look at the task** that you have been set, and identify which points you need to write a good answer. Highlight or underline these points if it helps you to keep them in mind.
- **Scan** the text carefully to pinpoint the sentences and phrases which contain the information you need. Mark the sections that contain the information so that you can refer to it quickly when you check your answers.
- Be ready to **infer** answers: this is used as a test of higher understanding, where you have the information needed to make a reasoned statement about something that is not directly stated in the text.

To follow an argument developed in a text, pinpoint the topic sentence of each **paragraph.** It can be the first sentence, but is not necessarily so. This is the sentence that moves the argument on to the next stage, and is often followed by examples or additional supporting facts.

> Take note of the 'markers' in the text which signal a **change of topic:** first; second; also; moreover; furthermore; in addition; however; but; nevertheless; finally; in conclusion; to sum up.
>
> **Identify different or opposing arguments:** look for 'markers' such as while; whereas; on the other hand.

- **Differentiate** between universally accepted facts, which are usually stated simply and objectively, and opinions which are often introduced with the idea of **some** people believing this and **others** believing something else. There are many different standpoints taken over the pressing issues of our world such as overpopulation, global warming, deforestation, over-fishing and climate change.

## Interpretation of data and diagrams

When data is presented in graph form you have to show that you understand the information and that you can interpret it accurately.

- The present simple tense is usually used.
- Different styles of graphs are used to show different information:
  - a line graph is used to indicate a trend or pattern which takes place over a period of time

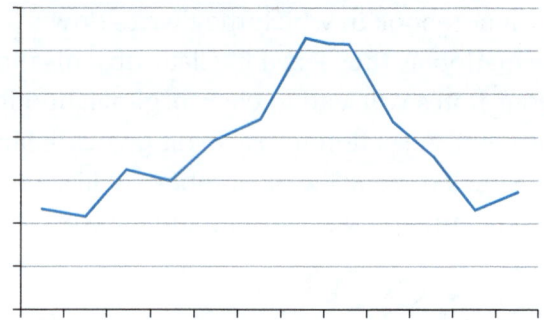

  - a bar chart compares data

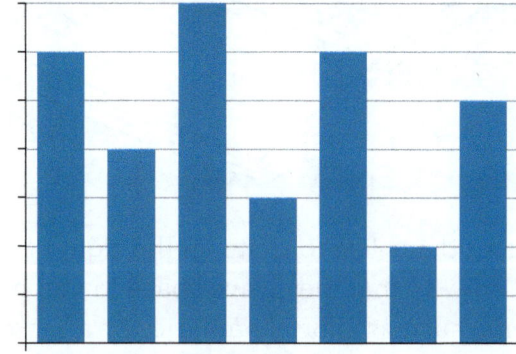

  - a pie chart illustrates how a given entity is divided up

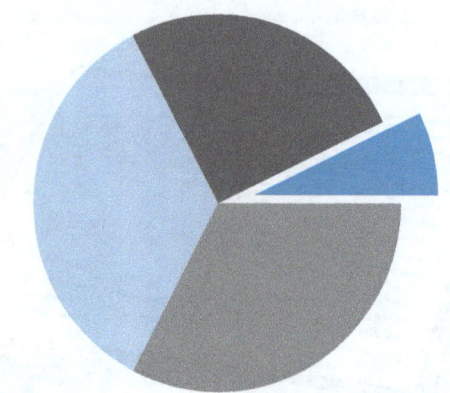

- State clearly what the graph is illustrating: 'This graph shows..............'. Make sure you mention the parameters covered by the graph.
- Identify the dominant trend or pattern.
- It is important to be factual in your description of the data: use percentages or clear indications such as 'just over half…; less than a third; almost all…'.
- Group similar data together.
- Indicate the most striking differences and similarities.
- Diagrams are often used to illustrate processes. Begin by stating the overall process being shown: 'This diagram shows how….'
- Identify where you wish to start your description and work through each stage logically. Be concise. - Use connecting words such as 'first; then; next; finally'.
- You may find that the **passive structure** is most suitable for focusing on the stages in the process rather than the agents causing or initiating the actions.

E.g. Water is carried downstream by the river; clouds are formed by the cooling vapour.

## Map reading

Maps show the location of places and the characteristics of the area.

Use compass directions to describe the location of a place on a map, e.g. It is south-west of the large city; it is east of the river.

Contour lines link points of equal height. The height of each contour is written on the line. Contours may be 5m, 10m or 50m apart. Use contours to tell the altitude of a place and also how steep the land is. Where lots of contour lines are very close together the land is very steep. Where contour lines are far apart the land is flat.

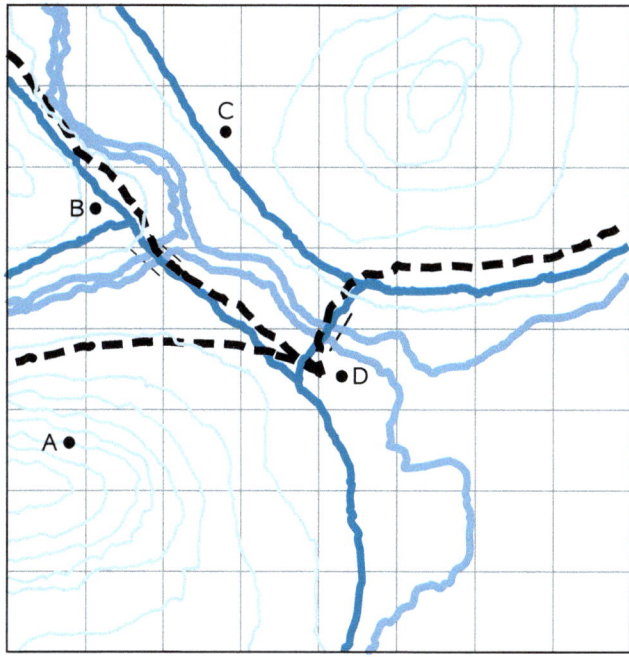

Map keys give the meaning of the symbols which show features on the map. Make sure you use the key to help you read the map, such as what services are provided in a settlement or what the land use is.

Make sure you read the scale on the map. This shows the distance measured on the map compared to that distance in reality e.g. 2cm on the map may be 1km on the ground. Maps often have grid lines to mark out distances e.g. 1km.

## Writing essays

Essay writing is the best chance that you have to show that you have fully understood the topic and that you can express yourself clearly in discussing it. They also carry a lot of marks compared with the short answer questions so it is important to include all the important points. Therefore, you should always make a plan so that you develop your ideas logically. You can either make a list of points that you wish to include or draw a mind map. By doing this preliminary work you avoid missing important facts out, or writing too much on one point. Remember to use paragraphs to help the reader to recognise when you are introducing another aspect.

Look at the title or task and decide what you want to say. Remember if you are putting forward an argument you should always consider the opposing position, and give your reasons for not agreeing. This strengthens your argument. The following outline can be adapted to most tasks:

| Introduction | state the purpose of your writing (and the conflicting viewpoints if it is a discussion.) |
| --- | --- |
| Development 1 | put forward the key facts (and your viewpoint) with good reasons and examples which support this view. |
| Development 2 | mention other points which influence the situation, perhaps in a different way. (Counter argument: Put the opposing viewpoint and reasons for it.) However/on the other hand, others think............. |
| Conclusion | come back to your position and restate it in a clear final sentence. Nevertheless/ on balance/ ultimately/ finally............. |

If the word limit is 150 words, aim to write 100 words on the development sections and 25 words each on the introduction and conclusion.

## Memory training

Your memory is crucial to your success, and, just like an athlete training for the Olympics, you can improve your performance by giving it plenty of exercise. Learning is an **active** process so involve yourself at every stage. Think about the material that you have just encountered and make sure that you understand it. Do some research using a dictionary, the library or the internet if you are unsure of anything.

- Be conscious of how you learn best – by seeing words on a page; by using mind maps; by imagining a picture with different elements; by associating items with colour; by using **mnemonics** (taking the first letter of key points and making them into a word); by using abbreviations e.g. CCTV/HF [Conurbation, City, Town, Village, Hamlet Farm] to remember the settlement hierarchy; by making up sentences which remind you of the initial letters of key points.

E.g. Naughty Elephants Squirt Water to remember the compass points.

- Associate certain facts with members of your family or your friends
- Make **notes** on your notes, perhaps reducing them to a list of key words.
- Link topics by adding an arrow in a different colour with the related topic written on it.
- Insert **images** which will trigger your memory.
- Write **cue cards** (small hand sized cards or post cards) on each topic with a question on one side and the important facts on the other.
- Put pictures with **labels** in big writing around your room so you see them whenever you are there.
- **Test yourself** when you are alone or travelling, and test your friends.

## Research

You may have to conduct research for course work or because you are unsure of a topic.

Use a **dictionary** to help you compile lists of words related to the topics you are studying. Divide your page so that you have one side for

the word and other words derived from it, and the other for its meaning and its use in context:
E.g.

| Urban | Relating to a town or a city |
| To urbanise urbanisation | The **urban** landscape is full of factories, high rise buildings, busy roads and power cables |

Go to a **library** if you want to read more about a topic. The librarian will direct you to the section that you need. The books and articles that you find on your topic may be too detailed or too simple, so check carefully to see if they are aimed at your level. Skim the contents and select the chapters that will be relevant to you. Make notes in the appropriate section of your own book or file. Record the author, the title and the date it was published.

> **Danger!** If you want to put part of the text directly into your work, you must acknowledge the source in a footnote or at the end of your work. Otherwise you will be guilty of plagiarism – claiming other people's work as yours.

The **Internet** offers you a huge bank of information but you should be careful to select the source to use carefully, as there is no 'quality control' on websites. Official sites and academic sites, magazines and newspapers are usually reliable. Look for sites with .ac .gov or .org as part of their address. Consider how to search for the information you want and type in your key words into the search engine. Make a note of the website address so that you can return there easily.

## Revision

It is best to plan your revision so that you allow yourself enough time to refresh all the topics you have covered.

Make a timetable of the days available before the examination and work out how many hours each day you will spend on this subject.

You know when you work best and how long you can concentrate on one topic.

Build in some relaxation and leisure time and do not spend too long on one topic.

Reward yourself at the end of a session.

> **Careful!** Merely reading through your notes is not enough! You should read a section, then try **actively** to reproduce it (in note form or by listing the key words), before moving on to the next section.

Ask family and friends to test you. You test your friends by giving them questions to answer.

Use questions from past papers to practise organising your answers and recalling the key facts.

## Examination techniques

Make sure that you know how the paper is set out: **how many questions** you need to answer from each section; **how many marks** are awarded for each answer; what equipment you may take with you into the examination; **how long** you can spend on each section – write down the time you should move on at the side of each question.

Read the rubric of the examination paper carefully and ask the invigilator if you do not understand what you have to do. It is better to ask questions at the beginning, before you get started.

Listen carefully to the instructions as there may be extra information sheets being handed out or corrections to the main paper to be made.

Skim through the whole paper quickly so you know what to expect.

Be ready to interpret the questions set by knowing what is expected when the following terms are used:

| **Analyse** | find out the different aspects so that you can understand it |
| **Calculate** | use given data to decide what will probably happen |
| **Compare** | look carefully at two or more aspects to find how they are similar |

## Study skills

| Describe | give details |
|---|---|
| Discuss | talk about the different aspects and decide how important they are |
| Estimate | make an informed guess about the possible outcome |
| Explain | give reasons for something happening |
| Identify | pick out the key factor(s) |
| List | make a brief list of points |
| Measure | use a ruler or compass to find the accurate amount/ length etc |
| Name | give the correct term |
| State | put into words (full sentences) |
| Study | look carefully at |
| Suggest | give a reasoned prediction or possible solution |
| Summarise | write a brief account |

Decide whether you want to do the short answers first or whether you would prefer to tackle the long questions while you have less pressure of time.

**Careful!** If you decide not to work through the questions in the order they have been presented you must be sure not to miss pages out. No answers = no marks.

Leave yourself enough time to read through your answers at the end so that you can check spellings and punctuation.

Good luck!

# 1 Population

**In this chapter you will answer...**
- What do we mean by 'population'?
- Why do death rates affect population growth?
- When is someone a migrant not a tourist?
- What is the difference between push and pull factors?
- Who migrates most?
- Where do most people live?

## 1.1 Natural population growth

The number of babies born each year per 1000 people is called the **birth rate**. The number of people dying per 1000 people each year is called the **death rate**. When the birth rate is greater than the death rate then the population will grow. This is called **natural increase**. Natural decrease in population occurs when the death rate is greater than the birth rate.

## 1.2 Population change over time

The world's population is growing rapidly. Death rates are decreasing as fewer people are dying each year and people's **life expectancy** increases. This is the average number of years a person is expected to live. Better food supplies, good healthcare and **vaccinations** mean people are now living longer. Traditions, poor education and lack of **contraception** (birth control) in many places, particularly Less Economically Developed Countries (LEDCs), mean many people still want to have large families. Therefore birth rates remain high. However, a country may have a high birth rate but many children may die before they reach one year old. This is the **infant mortality rate**. Therefore if the death rate is also high then the total number of people in the country may not change.

> **KEY WORD**
>
> **Population** means the number of people living in a place
>
> A country's population can grow in two ways:
>
> 1 When the number of babies being born is greater than the number of people dying.
> 2 When the number of people coming to live in the country is greater than the number of people leaving the country to live somewhere else.

> **KEY WORD**
>
> **Rate** how fast something happens, how often it happens or how much it happens

**Exercise**

**1** Match the phrases below with their consequences:

1 More babies being born          a Increase in infant mortality
2 More babies dying                b Increase of life expectancy
3 More people dying                c Natural increase
4 People living longer             d Rise in birth rate
5 The number of babies being born is    e Rise in death rate
  more than the number of people dying

11

## 1.3 Demographic transition model

Demography is the study of population. Transition means change. The **Demographic Transition Model** shows how birth and death rates affect population growth over time.

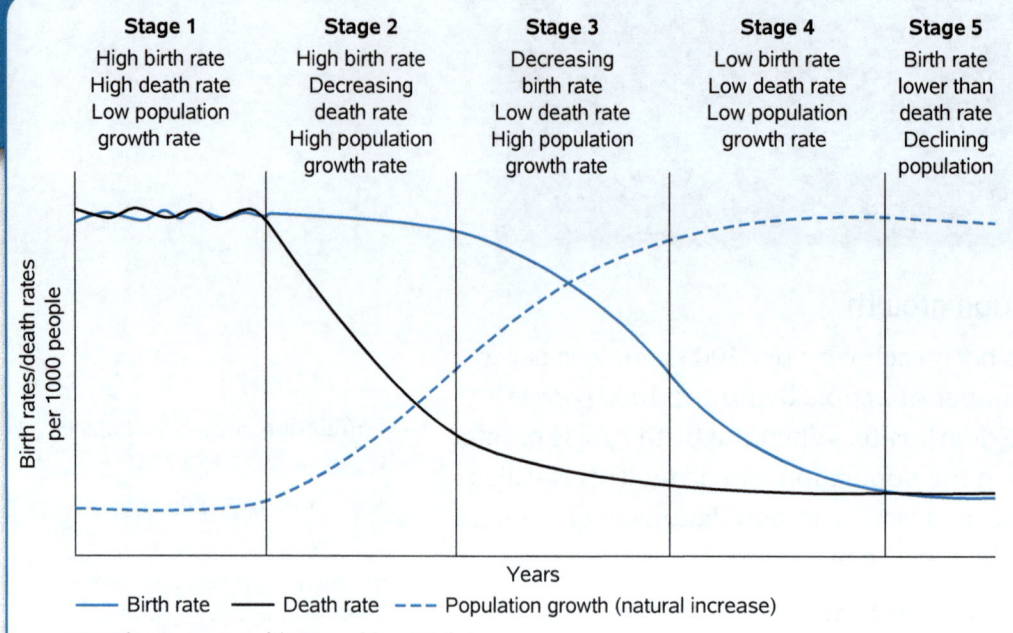

1.1 The Demographic Transition Model

**2 Complete the text below in your notebooks by choosing the correct options to describe the different stages in Figure 1.1.**

**Stage 1** Birth and death rates start *high/low* and *stable/changing*. A lack of medicines and lack of *clean/dirty* water mean *death/birth* rates are high. Birth rates are *high/low* because children are needed to help earn *money/cars* and there is a lack of contraception. There is *little/great* change in total population.

**Stage 2** Death rates suddenly *rise/drop* as more medicines and vaccinations become available. However *birth/death* rates remain *high/low*. Therefore population growth is rapidly *rising/tumbling*.

**Stage 3** Clean water and sewerage mean *birth/death* rates continue to *decline/increase* over time. Eventually the *birth/death* rates start to *fall/soar* as education improves, especially for girls, and there is greater use of contraception. Medicines mean fewer children die so there is less need for large families. The total population is still *growing/falling*.

**Stage 4** Over time the birth and death rates become *low/high*. More women have *careers/kitchens* so they start having children later in their lives. This means families are smaller. The rate of population growth is now *faster/slower*.

**Stage 5** In some places birth rates are *lower/higher* than death rates so the population is decreasing.

# Population 1

**Exercise**

**3** Which of the terms in the box below mean:
  a the same as 'increase'
  b opposite to 'increase'
  c the same as 'to stay the same'
  d opposite to 'to stay the same'?

| to tumble | to drop | to rise | to soar | to grow |
| to fluctuate | to stabilise | to accelerate | to dwindle | to decline |
| to fall | to decrease | to change | | |

## 1.4 Population structure

A country's population is made up of people of all ages. The **population structure** is the number of people in different age groups, male and female.

A country with a high birth rate will have lots of young people. The population aged 0–15 years are called the **young dependants**. At this age they usually depend on their parents. A country with a low death rate and high life expectancy will have more older people. The population aged over 65 years are called the **old dependants**. This is because they become too old to work and earn money. Therefore they depend on either their children or the government to help them in old age. The population aged between 16–65 years are called **economically active**. They work to earn money to support themselves and their families. They also pay taxes to the government.

A **population pyramid** shows the number of people in each age group. Each group is divided into males and females. A tall pyramid shows a high life expectancy, as more people live to a greater age. A wide base to the pyramid shows a high birth rate as there are more 0–4 year olds.

**KEY WORDS**

**Young dependants** the population aged 0-15

**Old dependants** the population aged over 65 years

**Economically active** the population between 16-65 years

**Structure** the way in which different elements fit together to form a whole

**Dependant** a person who relies on others for food, care, money and support

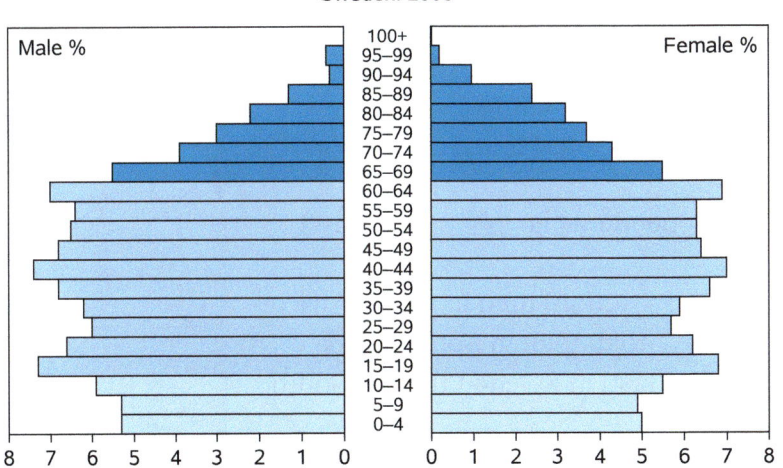

1.2 Population pyramid of Sweden 2008

13

## 1 • Population

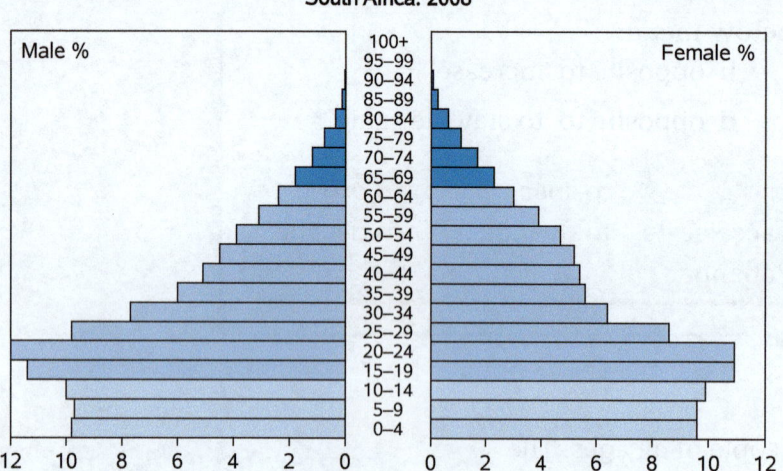

**1.3** Population pyramid of South Africa 2008

**KEY WORD**

**Proportion** the share or percentage of a whole number

**4** The following paragraph describes the population pyramid for South Africa above. Copy and complete the paragraph by using words from the box below.

The population _____ of South Africa shows a wide _____ but the largest age group are _____ years old. This is the _____ active population. There are more young _____ than _____ dependants. South Africa is probably in _____ three of the _____ transition model. Birth rates are _____ than death rates and population is still _____ rapidly.

| higher | base | old | economically | stage |
| demographic | pyramid | 20–24 | dependants | growing |

**5** Find the correct comparative for the word in brackets. Copy the correct sentences into your notebook. The first one has been done for you.

a In Sweden the proportion of people in the economically active age group is __larger__ (large) than the young dependants.
b The proportion of people living over 80 years old is _____ (great) in Sweden than in South Africa.
c In South Africa the proportion of old dependants is _____ (low) than in Sweden.
d In Sweden the life expectancy is _____ (high) than in South Africa.
e The population in Sweden are _____ (old) than in South Africa.
f The birth rate has decreased _____ (fast) in Sweden than in South Africa.
g There is a _____ (small) proportion of young dependants in Sweden than South Africa.
h The death rate is _____ (low) in Sweden than South Africa.

## 1.5 Government influence on population growth

In many countries governments have introduced policies to control population growth. **Pro-natalist** policies aim to increase birth rates in countries such as Sweden. **Anti-natalist** policies aim to decrease birth rates in countries such as China.

> **KEY WORD**
>
> **Policy** a formal plan of action which a person, group or government follows

### Comprehension

### China's many mouths

In the 20th century China experienced a huge rise in its population. This rapid growth can be described as a **population explosion**. The average number of children per couple reached 5.8. The birth rate had suddenly risen much higher than the death rate. This sudden population growth meant that the country was in danger of not being able to support its people. This would be a great **strain** on **resources** such as food, jobs and energy, and could tip the balance from **prosperity** to **poverty**.

To tackle this, the government introduced the One Child Policy in 1979. This was a system of financial and social rewards to encourage couples to have just one child per family. The couples who accepted the policy enjoyed free nursery care for their only child, education, cash payouts, and public recognition. Those who fought against it often lost their jobs and were criticised by their community. **Sterilization** and **abortion** were measures taken to ensure that the policy was carried out.

In urban areas the policy has been effective, as workers are often closely **monitored** by their employers. In rural areas, however, the traditional belief that many sons provide many hands for working in the fields meant that couples were more reluctant to obey. Indeed the policy now allows rural couples to have two children. The One Child Policy has been successful: in 2002 the population of China was 1.3 billion – about 400 million lower than predicted before 1979.

> **KEY WORDS**
>
> **Poverty** being poor and having a low quality of life
>
> **Prosperity** being well off and having a high quality of life
>
> **Resources** materials that can be used by a person or a country
>
> **Sterilization** an operation which makes a man or a woman unable to have children
>
> **Strain** pressure or demand that disturbs the performance of a person or system
>
> **To monitor** to watch and check the correct conduct or behaviour of people or processes

The 1979 policy has changed the structure and nature of Chinese society. The single children, who have been the sole focus of their parents, also inherit the 4-2-1 problem. They have to take on the responsibility for four grandparents and two parents as they reach middle age. The ageing population is dependent on the economically active population which is falling in number. The influence of Western attitudes means that for women, career development and an affluent life style can be more important than raising a family. The ratio of males to females (118 males to 100 females) also makes it impossible for all men to find wives. In 2009, concerns such as these led to Shanghai being the first city to start encouraging couples to have two children.

# 1 Population

**6** Comprehension questions:

a When was the One Child Policy introduced?
b Why did the Chinese government introduce it?
c How did the Policy encourage people to obey?
d Why was it more effective in urban areas?
e Did the Policy achieve its aim?
f Give two effects of the Policy on Chinese society.

**7** Find the adjectives from the following nouns used to describe the quality of life of a person or population.

| Noun | Adjective | Noun | Adjective |
|---|---|---|---|
| wealth |  | poverty |  |
| prosperity |  | affluence |  |
| riches |  | comfort |  |
| need |  | misery |  |

**8** Who said what? Decide which quote matches the options in the box below.

a "The proudest moment of my life was when I received my certificate for complying with the One Child Policy."

b "I have studied hard to get a good job so I am not going to throw it away to have a baby."

c "The increase in the birth of twins, triplets and even quadruplets shows that couples find ways to defy the policy."

d "I agree in principle with limiting the population for the sake of the nation, but for me many children means more help to make a living from the land."

e "My parents want to relive their hopes through me but I want to lead my own life."

f "We wanted to have another child but pressure from our employer and our neighbours was too great so we had to conform."

| a doctor in a rural community | 50 year old widow | a young couple with one child |
| an only child | a female graduate | a farmer |

# Population 1

## 1.6 The movement of people

> **Language**
>
> **Migration** the movement of people from one place to another
> **Immigration** the movement of people to a place
> **Emigration** the movement away from a place
> **Rural-urban migration** the movement from the countryside (rural areas) to the cities (urban areas)
>
> **Vocabulary building hint:** prefix **e/ex** adds the meaning of **out of/away**
> prefix **in/im** adds the meaning of **into/towards**
>
> *Examples:*    influx      exodus
> implosion   explosion
> include     exclude
>
> Note down other examples and check their meaning in a dictionary as you come across them.

**Migration** is the movement of people from one place to another. International migration is the movement of people from one country to another. A **migrant** usually stays in the new place for at least one year. A **tourist** is someone visiting a place for a shorter period of time and who will return home. The populations of cities, towns and villages have grown and declined as a result of migration. The population of a country or region changes as people move away from that country or enter it. **Emigration** is the movement away from a place. The people moving away are called **emigrants**. **Immigration** is the movement of people to a place. The people entering a country are called **immigrants**.

**Exercise**

**9** Imagine that you are doing a survey of people travelling through London Heathrow airport. Which category would you put the following travellers in? Copy and complete the table below.

a A university student flying to Beijing to take a 6-week language course.

b A businessman taking up a permanent job in Sydney.

c An 18 year old man seeking seasonal work in the vineyards of California.

d A 24 year old Polish graduate arriving to live with her aunt in order to find a job.

e A scientist from Oxford taking up a new post at the Space Research Institute in Florida.

f A retired couple who have sold their house in order to settle in Spain.

g A mother and three children from Jamaica coming to join the father in London.

h A young couple from New Zealand coming to visit relatives in the U.K.

| Immigration | Emigration | Tourism |
| --- | --- | --- |
|  |  |  |

# 1 Population

## 1.7 Types of migrants

Many people choose to migrate. These are **voluntary migrants**. Many are **economic migrants**. Economic migrants move from one place to another to find better jobs and higher incomes. These are usually the younger economically active people aged 25–40 years old. Most migrants of this age are men. Other voluntary migrants include older dependants who want to live somewhere warm and sunny in their retirement. However many other people have no choice and are forced to leave their homes. These are **involuntary migrants**. Their lives and homes may be in danger due to war or a natural disaster. These people are also called **refugees**.

## 1.8 Reasons for migration

People have many reasons why they might move from one place to another. **Push factors** are their own experiences of life in one place which might give them good reasons to leave it. People always have expectations of their destination. **Pull factors** are the expectations which attract them to the new place.

> **KEY WORD**
>
> **Factor** reason which influences people or situations and has an effect on outcomes

## 1.9 Internal migration

Huge numbers of people move within the same country from one region to another. In many countries the trend is to move from the countryside (rural areas) to the cities (urban areas) to find work and higher incomes. This is known as **rural-urban migration**. Push and pull factors influence their decisions.

**Exercise**

**10** Read the e-mails on the next page written by people who have moved away from their home. Are the following statements true, false or unknown?

a Tomo wanted to leave Tuvalu.
b Fishing catches are better from Wellington.
c Tomo believes that international aid will save his home.
d The rising sea levels are threatening to drown Tuvalu.
e Sergei is glad to have left Bosnia.
f Sergei wanted to find work in Italy.
g He was a soldier in the war.
h Juanita is enjoying city life.
i She wants to be an English translator.
j She enjoys her job in Rio de Janeiro more than her work on the family farm in Manari.
k Manuel plans to stay in Los Angeles.
l Working in the vineyards is exhausting but his wages allow him to send home money to his family.

# Population 1

### 📩 Talofa

Wellington, May 10th
Dear Cousin,

I arrived here in New Zealand from Tuvalu a month ago after a huge storm wrecked my fishing boat and my home. There was no way that I could survive as the water and crops that I had stored were ruined by the salty waves. Mum and Dad refused to leave as they say that the Chief is sure to get help for our islands but I am not so sure. I am too young to waste my life waiting for other people to act to save our nation. I want to return to my family and island paradise but unless the climate is better controlled there is no possibility of surviving there. I am working on a fishing boat, so can use the skills that you taught me.

Let me know how you are getting on in Sydney.
Your little cousin, Tomo

### 📩 Zdravo

Milan, August 3rd
Dear Sister,

I hope that you and my little brother are both well. The journey here from Sarajevo was full of dangers, but at least I am alive and free. Tomorrow I am starting work in a shoe factory – not my first choice - but I will earn enough to pay my way and with luck I should be able to send you some money soon. I still have nightmares about the war and the awful things that happened to friends and family who felt as I do, but I have been lucky and so now I have to build a new life here.

Write to me and give me all the news from home
Love Sergi

### 📩 Oi!

Rio de Janeiro, June 26th
Dear Mama and Papa,

How are you? I think about you all the time and will come back to see you soon.

Life here in the city is so different to Manari – no one seems to go to bed and you can hear music playing all night long. My workplace is quite near the seafront so I manage to get some fresh air during my lunch break. The work itself is interesting as I have to deal with phone calls from all over the world – my English teacher would be amazed at my progress! One day I will return for good but at the moment there is so much more happening here that I have decided to stay for a few years at least.

Love to you both and to all the family,
Juanita

### 📩 Hola

Los Angeles, September 29th
My dear Maria,

How hard it is not to be with you and the little ones. I am living in a hostel with other Mexicans so at least we can support one another. The work in the vineyards is back breaking and the day starts early and finishes late but we get a break in the middle of the day. The pay is not much but I am getting more than I did selling our produce in the local market so life will be easier. It is only for a few months so don't be sad. I will be home soon.

Send me all the news of the children and give them big kisses from me.
Your loving husband, Manuel

**1.4** Emails from migrants

**Exercise 11** Use an atlas to decide where the four writers moved from. Who moved from:
- a North to South?
- b South to North?
- c East to West?
- d West to East?

**1.5** Remember the compass directions – Naughty Elephants Squirt Water

19

# 1 Population

**Exercise 12** Use your language skills to choose the correct sentences from the options below.

1. a We arrived Hong Kong at 13.00pm.
   b We arrived in Hong Kong at 13.00pm.
2. a The coach came into the station fifteen minutes early.
   b The coach came the station fifteen minutes early.
3. a He entered the country illegally.
   b He entered into the country illegally.
4. a They got to the border at nightfall.
   b They got the border at nightfall.
5. a She went from her village to the city.
   b She went out of her village to the city.
6. a I set off from my hiding place at dawn to avoid enemy patrols.
   b I set off my hiding place at dawn to avoid enemy patrols.

Here are some verbs showing movement from and to places: to arrive at/to reach/to get/to come/to enter/to leave/to depart/to set off/to go.

Careful! Notice that some of these verbs need a **preposition** (at/in/into/out of/to/from) if the place is mentioned.

## 1.10 Where people live

The **population distribution** shows where people live in a country. It shows areas with high numbers of people crowded together and other areas which seem empty of people. The **population density** measures the number of people within a certain area, for example 1km².

### KEY WORDS

**Population distribution** where people live in a county

**Population density** the number of people within a certain area

**Choropleth map** uses shades of colour to show number values. The darker the colour, the higher the number.

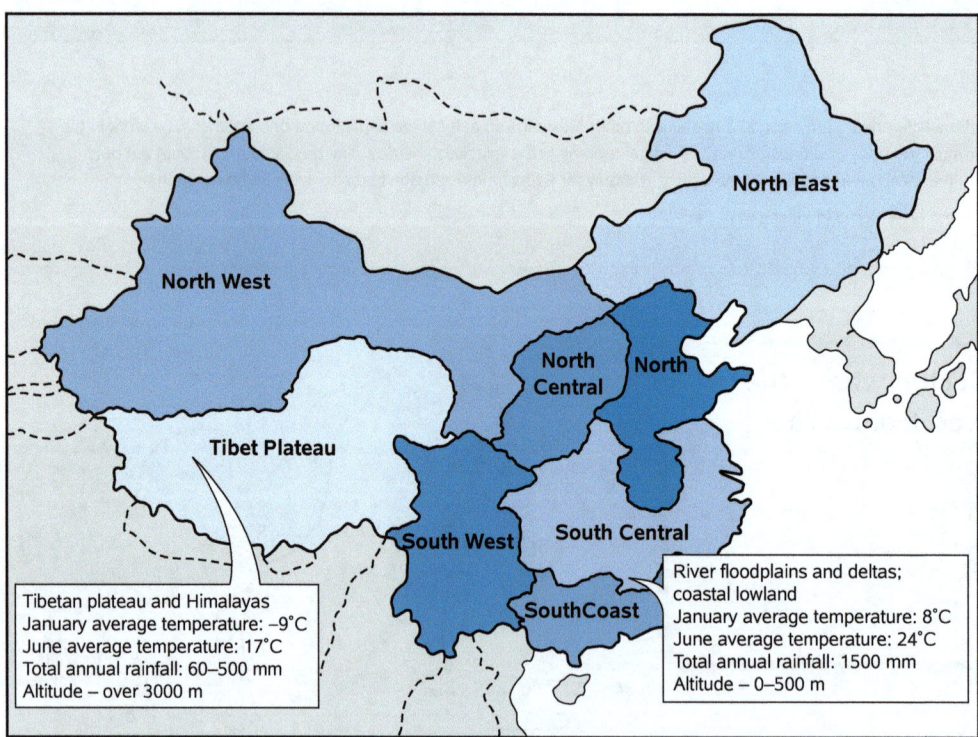

1.6 Choropleth map of population density in China

20

# Population 1

**13** Study figure 1.6 and use on the previous page. Use compass directions to complete the following sentences.

a The lowest population densities are found in the _____ of China.

b The highest population densities are found in the _____ and _____ of China.

c The population densities in the _____ are higher than in the _____.

**KEY WORDS**

**Distribution** the way in which something is spread across an area

**Density** the number of items, such as people, in a certain area

1.7 Shanghai – an area of high population density

1.8 Tibet – an area of low population density

**14** Use the information from figure 1.6 to find the correct comparatives below.

a The land to the west is _____ (high) and _____ (steep) than in the east.

b It is much _____ (dry) in the west and _____ (wet) in the east.

c In January it is _____ (warm) in the east than the west.

d In June the east is _____ (hot) than the north and west of China.

e The _____ (cold) and _____ (dry) climate in the west makes life there much _____ (hard).

f It is _____ (easy) to grow crops in the east as it is _____ (wet) and _____ (warm).

21

# 1 • Population

## 1.11 Influences on population distribution

**15** Copy the mind-map template below into your notebooks, and include the correct information from figures 1.6–1.8.

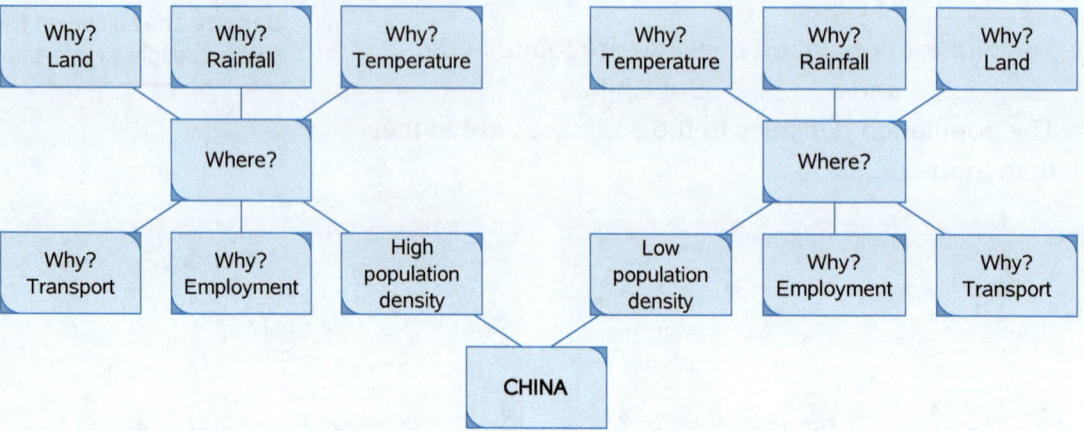

**1.9** Mind-map template to explain the population distribution in China

Write a short paragraph explaining the factors influencing the population distribution of China. Answer the questions as suggested in the mind-map.

### Extension

**16** What are the likely effects of the following events on the population? Copy and complete the table below in your notebooks.

| Events | Rise or fall in birth rate | Rise or fall in death rate | Total population growth or decline? |
|---|---|---|---|
| a  A period of economic growth | | | |
| b  A period of political stability | | | |
| c  An earthquake | | | |
| d  An epidemic of flu | | | |
| e  Several years of drought | | | |
| f  Forest fires which devastate crops and settlements | | | |
| g  Improved health care | | | |
| h  The outbreak of war | | | |
| i  The provision of wells to supply clean water | | | |

**17** From what you have learned in this chapter, determine the types of migrants below.

  a  Someone fleeing a war zone.
  b  Someone in search of work.
  c  Someone whose home has been destroyed in a big flood.
  d  Someone who wants to have more opportunities at work and in leisure time.
  e  Someone wanting to send money back to the family.
  f  Someone wanting to live in a better climate and enjoy a lower cost of living.
  g  Someone wanting to have to cheaper medical care in a different country.

**18** Fill in the gaps below using the key terms from the chapter and copy into your notebook.

  a  The number of people living in a town, an area, a country or a continent is called its _____.
  b  How people are spread across an area is known as _____.
  c  How many people live in a given area is known as _____.
  d  The study of population is known as _____.

### Talking points

What are the effects of a) population growth and b) population decline for a country?

Why might governments wish to control the population of their country?

Why would some countries want to have pro-natalist policies to increase birth rates?

How can population growth be controlled?

### Extension

Internet search: Find out about…
Population policy in your country of birth
Population explosion
Economically Active population

Think about the questions from the start of the chapter. Can you answer these now?

- What do we mean by 'population'?
- Why do death rates affect population growth?
- When is someone a migrant not a tourist?
- What is the difference between push and pull factors?
- Who migrates most?
- Where do most people live?

# 2 Settlements

**In this chapter you will answer...**
- What is a settlement hierarchy?
- Why do some towns grow into cities?
- Who lives in the suburbs?
- When do cities become too big?
- Where is the world's largest city?

**KEY WORDS**

A **settlement** is a group of buildings where people live and work.

**Urbanisation** is the process of increasing the number of people living in urban settlements

As a settlement grows different **land uses** develop

## 2.1 A settlement hierarchy

A **settlement hierarchy** puts settlements in a region or country in order of their size. At the bottom of the hierarchy are the **rural** settlements such as farms and villages. **Farms** are the smallest types of settlements. There are more of these than any other type of settlement. **Hamlets** are next in the hierarchy. These are groups of houses where people live but there are no services provided as there are not enough people living there. **Villages** are next up the hierarchy. These settlements have enough people living in them to have at least one service such as a shop. The **threshold population** is the minimum (lowest) number of people needed to keep a service in business.

Towns and cities are **urban** settlements. A **town** has a larger population than a village, so there are also more services. A **city** is the largest single settlement and is at the top of the settlement hierarchy. In a few countries, cities have grown so large that they have joined together to form **conurbations**, such as Tokyo-Osaka, Japan or Los Angeles-Long Beach, USA.

As you go up the settlement hierarchy from farms to cities the population of each settlement increases along with the number of services they provide.

**KEY WORDS**

**Settlement** a place where people live and work

**Settlement hierarchy** settlements in a region or country in order of their size

**Service** something providing goods or help to the population, for example shops, schools, doctors, places of worship

**Threshold population** the minimum number of people needed to keep a service in business

**Site** the land on which the settlement has been built

**Situation** the surrounding area of a settlement such as the roads, sea, other settlements, industry

**Function** the main purpose of a settlement

**Sphere of influence** the area around a settlement which it serves

**Rural** relating to the country

**Urban** relating to the town

2.1 Los Angeles is part of a sprawling conurbation

# Settlements 2

**Exercise**

1. Copy and complete the diagram below using the types of settlements given in the box. Start with the smallest settlement at the bottom. Colour the **rural** settlements green and the **urban** settlements red. One example has been done for you.

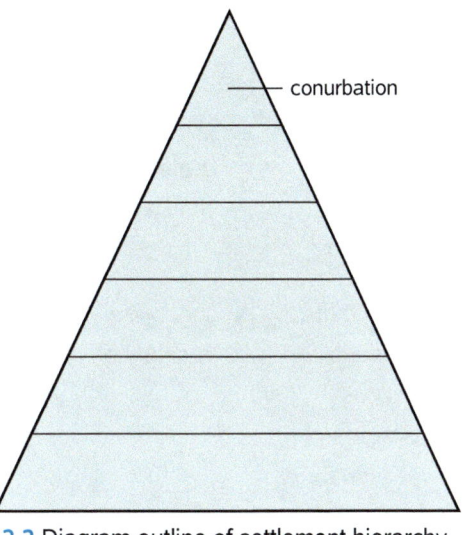

2.2 Diagram outline of settlement hierarchy

farm    conurbation    hamlet    village    town    city

2. Who lives where? Match the descriptions below with the settlements in your completed triangle.

a. "I know everyone who lives here. We go to school by bus but otherwise we have to go by car to do any shopping or to see the doctor as there are no services here."

b. "Our family has always lived and worked on this land. I love the peace and quiet, although in a harsh winter we can be isolated for days with no contact with anyone else."

c. "More and more people drive to out-of-town shopping centres to do their shopping so the future does not look good for our local small shops such as the butcher, post office and the newsagent."

d. "The advantage of living here is the variety of restaurants, bars and public transport close by, although I miss not having a garden."

e. "The countryside has been swallowed up by new developments, housing estates and factories. We used to be surrounded by fields and woods but now everything is covered in grey concrete."

25

## 2 Settlements

### 2.2 Rural settlement patterns

Buildings form patterns in small rural settlements. A **nucleated** settlement has buildings close to each other. In **linear** settlements the buildings are in lines which follow the line of a road, a river or a valley. A **dispersed** settlement has buildings scattered apart from each other.

### 2.3 Site of settlements

| Vocabulary | | | |
|---|---|---|---|
| Verb | Place | People | Adjective |
| To settle in | settlement | settlers | settled |
| To dwell in | dwelling | city/town dwellers | |
| To inhabit | habitation | inhabitants | inhabited |
| To reside in | residence | residents | residential |
| | city | citizens | |
| | village | villagers | |
| | | peasants | |
| To populate | | population | populated |
| | | (singular) | populous |

The **site** of a settlement describes the land on which the settlement has been built. The first settlers chose particular sites for good reasons. Most of today's settlements were originally started hundreds of years ago. The site may be:

- a **wet-point site** with a good fresh water supply such as a well or a river
- a **dry-point site** which avoids possible flooding
- high on a hill to *defend* the settlement from attack
- low in a valley to give **shelter** from the wind
- facing the *sun* to grow the best crops
- on *flat* or *gently* sloping land which is easy to build on

### 2.4 Situation of settlements

The **situation** of a settlement describes the surrounding area, for example the roads, sea, other settlements, industry. It is the settlement's situation which has meant some early settlements have grown from small farms into the large cities of today. Other settlements have remained very small and some have completely disappeared. A settlement's situation may change over time as new roads are built or an industry may close.

Many of the world's largest cities are located beside rivers or natural harbours. These have provided access for trade so encouraging the settlement to grow. The building of roads and railways has made these settlements even more accessible. The **sphere of influence** is the area around a settlement which it serves, and can be increased if accessible by a road or railway.

> **KEY WORD**
>
> **Situation** the characteristics of the location such as the area surrounding a settlement

Settlements 2

— Coast/river  — Main road  ▬ ▪ Railway  — Contours  ● Settlement
Scale – 1 square = 1km

**2.3** Map of settlements

**3** Study Figure 2.3 above. Which settlement on the map matches the **site** descriptions below?
  **a** It is a dry-point site on gently sloping land facing south-west
  **b** It is on flat land at the mouth of the river
  **c** It is a dry-point site above the **confluence** (join) of two rivers. The land slopes to the east.
  **d** It is on steep land on the north-facing slope. It is sheltered from the south-west wind.

**4** Settlement C is a linear settlement. Give two reasons why it has developed this pattern.

**5** Use the descriptions of the settlement **situations** below to decide which is a hamlet, village, town or city.
  **a** Settlement A is served by a single-track road. It has 5 houses but no services.
  **b** Settlement B is beside the junction of 2 main roads and is at the **bridging point** across the river. It has a secondary school, a large supermarket and a small cinema.
  **c** Settlement C is a linear settlement along a main road. It has 2 bars, a newsagent and a small grocery store.
  **d** Settlement D is beside a natural harbour and at the bridging point of the main river. It is a major port for large ships. It has many high and low order services. It is the terminus (end) for 3 railway lines.

27

## 2 Settlements

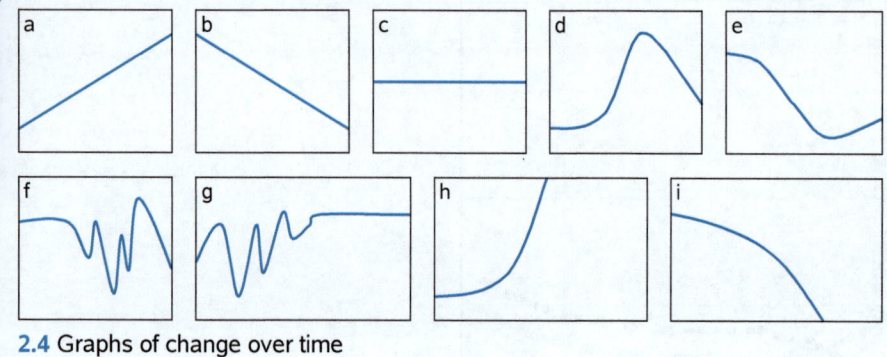

2.4 Graphs of change over time

**Change over time**
There are many words which describe *how things change over time*. Some words express a sudden and rapid change, others indicate a small and slow change, and some indicate that nothing much is changing, for example, rising, falling, increasing etc.

**6** Imagine that the graphs above follow the population of a village over a period of 20 years. Read the following sentences and choose a graph that matches.

a As young families moved into the village the population *grew steadily*.
b When the local mining industry closed the population *decreased* as people moved away to find new jobs.
c The building of a new industrial estate caused the population to *soar*; then it *dropped* as the construction workers moved on.
d When the new factory closed *suddenly* the population *tumbled* but the introduction of a new, fast railway service to the city made travel easy, and the lower cost of housing meant that the population rose.
e After a period of *stability* the population of the village *fluctuated* as new businesses came and went.
f After a few peaks and *troughs* the population remained *stable*.
g The absence of young families in the village caused the population to *dwindle*.

### 2.5 The function of a settlement

The **functions** of a settlement are its main purposes. The function of a small village may be farming or mining. A town's function may be its main industry such as car manufacture, or market trading. Cities may have many functions.

**KEY WORD**
**Function** purpose or use

**7** Match the terms to their meanings and copy the completed definitions into your notebook.

1 situation
2 site
3 function
4 threshold population
5 sphere of influence

a The purpose of a settlement
b The minimum number of people needed to keep a service running
c The characteristics of the area surrounding a settlement
d The area served by a settlement or service
e The natural characteristics of the actual location of the settlement

28

## 2.6 Services in settlements

A **service** provides goods or help to the population, for example shops, schools or places of worship. **Low order** services are used regularly by customers. They are cheaper and people will not travel far to use them. Examples of these are newsagents or small supermarkets. Low order services have a low **threshold population** so can be found in small villages. A city will have many low order services. **High order services** are not used so regularly. They are more expensive and people travel further to use them. They have a higher **threshold population** and are therefore more likely to be found in larger settlements e.g. a secondary school, a car showroom, or a cinema. A settlement with more high order services will have a larger **sphere of influence** as people will want to visit the settlement from further away.

**8** Find the 10 words relating to settlement in this word search:

| D | N | P | U | T | S | L | E | I | R | I |
|---|---|---|---|---|---|---|---|---|---|---|
| I | U | O | S | H | E | I | C | E | U | I |
| S | C | P | E | R | R | N | T | R | U | A |
| P | L | U | T | E | V | E | C | O | F | A |
| E | E | L | T | S | I | A | N | E | U | L |
| R | A | A | L | H | C | R | S | M | N | F |
| S | T | T | E | O | E | R | N | T | C | T |
| E | E | I | M | L | S | I | T | E | T | I |
| D | D | O | E | D | O | L | P | E | I | N |
| I | S | N | N | R | S | N | L | S | O | L |
| C | S | I | T | U | A | T | I | O | N | T |

settlement   population   dispersed   nucleated   linear
services     threshold    site        situation   function

## 2.7 The central business district

The **central business district** (CBD) is the middle of a town or city where the **higher order** shops, banks and offices are found. The main roads lead to the CBD and the main railway stations are here. This should make the CBD the most *accessible* part of the town.

The land is very expensive to buy or rent. Buildings are therefore very tall to fit more businesses onto a small area of land. Many people work in the CBD but very few people live in the CBD as the land is too expensive for houses.

### KEY WORDS

**Central Business District** the middle of a town or city where the higher order shops, banks and offices are found

**Suburb** the outer part of an urban settlement

**Rural-urban fringe** the open land on the edge of the city where the countryside begins

**Shanty town** areas of very high density housing built illegally on unused land

**Accessible** easy to reach

29

## 2 • Settlements

**9** Which words from the box below would best describe the CBD?

| quiet | busy | crowded | sparse | fresh |
|---|---|---|---|---|
| noisy | cheap | expensive | polluted | modern |

### 2.8 Urban residential areas in MEDCs

**Residential** areas are where people live. The **inner zone** is the residential area closest to the CBD. The houses are older and closely packed together. There are not many areas of open space or gardens. The inner zone has a high population density. Many people live in a small area in blocks of **flats or apartments**, or in rows of **terraced** houses. Residents use public transport services such as buses, metros and railways to travel to work.

**KEY WORD**

**MEDC** More economically developed country

The **suburbs** are the outer part of an urban settlement. In MEDCs there is a lower density of buildings and more open space. The land is cheaper as it is further from the CBD. This means houses are usually bigger. They are often **detached** or **semi-detached** buildings. There is less frequent public transport but a good road network so people are more likely to **commute** to work by car.

2.5 Examples of different dwelling places

**10** Which of the dwelling places in Figure 2.5 would you expect to find in the options below?

| mountains | suburbs | inner zones |
|---|---|---|
| countryside | shanty towns | |

**11** Are the following statements true or false for settlements in MEDCs? Copy the correct statements in your notebook.
  a Quality of life is higher in the suburbs than in the inner zone.
  b The houses in suburbs are older than the houses in the inner zone.
  c Car ownership is higher in the inner zone than in the suburbs.
  d Houses are larger in the inner zone than in the suburbs.
  e People are richer in the suburbs than in the inner zone.

# Settlements 2

## 2.9 Urban residential areas in LEDCs

The inner zones of cities in LEDCs often have larger houses and a lower population density than the suburbs. Many large settlements in LEDCs have **shanty towns**. These are areas of very high density housing. Shanty towns are often found in the **suburbs** or as **linear** settlements along railway lines and rivers, or beside industrial areas. The houses have been built by the people living in them. These people are usually poor and unable to afford to buy or rent houses in the city. They often lack basic services such as electricity, clean water and sewerage.

> **KEY WORD**
> **LEDC** Less economically developed country

## 2.10 Industrial areas

In many cities the industrial areas are found on the **rural-urban fringe**. This is the open land on the edge of the city where the countryside begins. There is more room for large buildings and the land is cheaper and the roads are less crowded. In cities in MEDCs the old industrial areas near the CBD are called **transition zones**. These are areas where land use changes, for example old industrial land becomes converted into houses or offices.

## 2.11 Urbanisation

Urbanisation is when more and more people live in towns and cities. Towns and cities grow in size by **rural-urban migration** and by **natural increase**. Tokyo in Japan is the world's largest city. In MEDCs most people live in urban areas. The fastest urbanisation is now happening in LEDCs. People move from poor rural areas to cities to find jobs, education and a better lifestyle. Some cities have grown so quickly that the **infrastructure** such as roads, sewers, electricity and water supply is struggling to keep up. This has caused problems such as traffic **congestion**, housing shortages and air **pollution**.

> **KEY WORDS**
> **Urban sprawl** when cities spread out into the countryside along main roads and railways
> **Pollution** harm to the natural environment
> **Congestion** roads overcrowded with traffic
> **Commuter** someone who travels from their home to their work place each day
> **Infrastructure** the parts of the built environment such as roads, sewers, electricity lines and water pipes

## 2.12 Managing urban problems

**Comprehension**

Mexico City is the world's second largest city. The modern city grew rapidly throughout the 20th century. Between 1960 and 1980 the population rose to 8.8 million as people fled the poverty of the countryside. By 2008 there were 19.5 million people living there. Skyscrapers, roads and factories now stretch far beyond the original settlement, putting severe pressure on the city's **infrastructure**.

Mexico City suffers from **air pollution**. It is situated in the Valley of Mexico, a large basin on the high plateau of central Mexico. The mountains to the north and south of the city reduce the flow of air. The smog caused by pollution from vehicles and factories hangs over the city.

2.6 Aerial photo of Mexico City

31

## 2 • Settlements

The average seven hours of tropical sunshine which the city enjoys encourages the **photochemical** reaction of sunlight with carbon dioxide ($CO_2$) emissions from vehicles. The high altitude (2,240 metres) reduces levels of oxygen, intensifying the effects of air pollution on the population.

In 2004 transport was found to be responsible for 84% of the city's air pollution. The huge increase in the numbers of people travelling to and from work, meant the need for a **sustainable** solution became pressing.

It was estimated that annually 2.5 million days were lost from work because of traffic congestion. Commuters spent on average 2.5 hours a day in traffic. Nearly 7,000 deaths were caused by respiratory disease and road accidents. Road accidents were the principal cause of death for children aged 5–14.

> **KEY WORDS**
>
> **Sustainable** meeting the needs of people today without harming the needs of people in the future
>
> **Smog** a mixture of smoke and fog

The Mexico City **metro bus** system was opened in 2005. 80 buses carry 250,000 passengers per day and 50 million per year. The buses run in bus lanes from north to south through the city, linking major roads and metro stops. Fares are low and tickets are prepaid to avoid delays when boarding, and boarding platforms enable passengers to get on and off quickly and safely. The time taken to cross the city has been reduced from over two hours to one hour. The system has been greeted with great enthusiasm. Along with the introduction of restrictions on private car use, productivity and health have improved, and it is predicted that $CO_2$ emissions will be halved.

**12** Comprehension questions:
  a What problems have been caused by the growth of Mexico City?
  b How do the surrounding mountains affect the quality of air in the city?
  c What are the problems if a city's transport system is inadequate?
  d Who benefits from the metro bus system? Explain why.

**13** Using the information above and on the previous page, make notes on Mexico City under the following headings:
  ◉ Site of Mexico City
  ◉ Growth of Mexico City
  ◉ Reasons for heavy air pollution in Mexico City
  ◉ Problems caused by transport before 2005
  ◉ The Mexico City metro bus system

**The Passive Voice** puts the focus of the sentence on the result of the verb, not the person or thing doing the action.

For example, 'The Aztecs founded the city' *becomes* 'The city was founded by the Aztecs'. Use 'by' to introduce the person or thing doing the action.

It is not necessary to include the person or thing doing the action when using the passive construction. An example of this is, 'They drained the lake to get more land' *becomes* 'The lake was drained to get more land'. Here, the main interest is in what happened to the lake, not who did the action.

# Settlements 2

Use the same tense as in the active sentence:
Present: is/are + past participle
Past: was/were + past participle
Present perfect: has/have been + past participle
Future: will be + past participle

**14** In your notebook, write the sentences below in the passive form. Which form do you think works better and why?

a High mountains surround Mexico City.
b The 4 million private cars in Mexico City cause high levels of air pollution.
c Waste water and sewage contaminate the city's drinking water.
d Better air quality improves the health of the inhabitants.
e They have reduced $CO_2$ emissions.
f People will save time travelling on the metro bus.
g They will buy tickets in advance.

**Tenses:** Use the Past Simple to talk about actions that happened in the past, [Regular verbs add –d or –ed to the infinitive, i.e. worked, lived, travelled]
For example, 'People settled on the island'.
To talk about past actions which occurred over a period of time but which no longer happen use the structure **'used to'**.
For example, 'The lake used to surround the town'. (It no longer does because the land has been drained to provide more living space).

**15** Put the following ideas into sentences using 'used to' to describe what life in Mexico City was like before the introduction of the Metro Bus.

a Private cars/cause/traffic congestion.
b Diesel buses/emit/$CO_2$ gas.
c Factories and vehicles pollute/air.
d Smog/hang over/valley.
e People/suffer/respiratory diseases.
f Children/die/traffic accidents.

## 2.13 Urban sprawl

**Urban sprawl** is when cities spread out into the countryside along main roads and railways. Car ownership allows people to live further from where they work so they **commute** to work. New roads have encouraged the residential suburbs to spread. As more roads are built the **rural-urban fringe** is used for industries, shopping centres and sports facilities. These attract more people and the suburbs grow.

Urban sprawl has caused harm to the natural environment. This is **environmental pollution**. Beautiful countryside has been destroyed in many places causing **visual pollution**. Wildlife habitats have been lost as roads and buildings have destroyed the countryside. The industries, motorways and airports cause **noise pollution**. The exhaust fumes from vehicles cause **air pollution**. Waste from industries and homes is pumped into rivers causing **water pollution**.

33

## 2 • Settlements

**2.7** Examples of urban pollution

> **Extension**
>
> **16** Look at Figure 2.7 then copy and complete the mind map below (Figure 2.8) in your notebooks. Some have been filled in already.
>
> You should include:
>
> **a** types of pollution      **b** the sources of pollution.

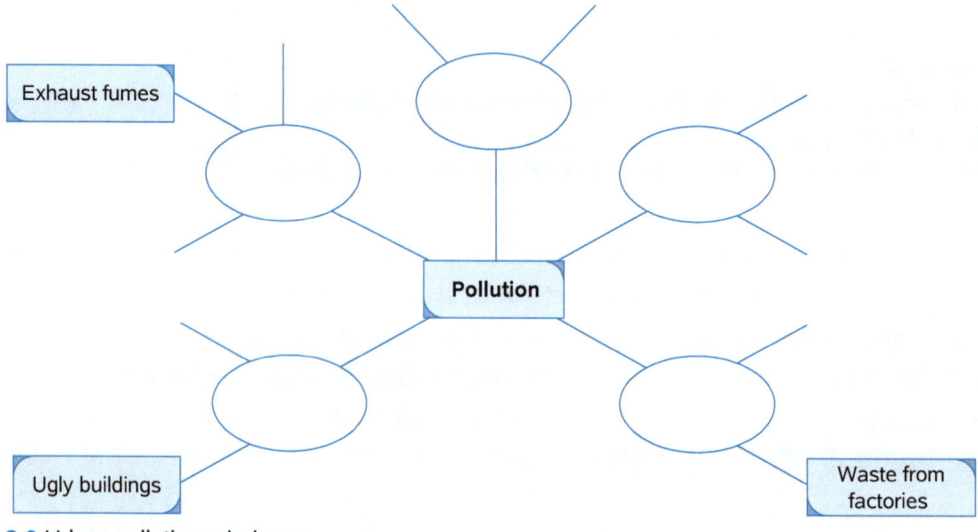

**2.8** Urban pollution mind map

**17** Reorganise the following sentences to make a balanced discussion of the advantages and disadvantages that rural-urban migration has to a city in an LEDC. Find the marker terms such as 'first', 'also' 'in conclusion' and highlight them in order to put the ideas into a logical sequence. The discussion starts with g.

> **a** Also, living in a town means that they can easily get to the shops by taking the bus or the tram, or they can walk to the local shopping centre, where they will find a wide variety of goods.
>
> **b** Families have to buy produce instead of growing it on their land or exchanging crops with their neighbours.

34

## Settlements 2

c First, there are many more opportunities to find employment in businesses and factories, and generally wages are higher.

d However, life can be very lonely and tiring, as many employees spend hours commuting to their place of work, and have little free time at the end of the long working day

e In addition, many of them live in cramped and squalid conditions in shanty towns, where disease spreads rapidly.

f In conclusion, life in a town or city is not always as exciting and as comfortable as people may expect.

g Life in a town or city has a lot to offer the people who live there.

h Second, there are lots more leisure facilities such as cinemas, cafes, restaurants and clubs where people can watch films, relax with friends, listen to music or do sport.

i Moreover, the cost of living is higher in town than in villages in the countryside.

j The water supply and the sewerage system cannot cope with the increasing numbers of people arriving from the countryside.

### Extension

**18** Solve the clues and fill in the missing letters. Then put the letters in the boxes together to find the mystery word. Give a definition for this term.

a A settlement that develops around a central point: n☐ _ _ _ _ _ _ _ _

b An adjective that describes the countryside: r _ ☐ _ _

c The area of a town or city where large shops, banks and businesses are found c _ _ _ _ _ _ / ☐ _ _ _ _ _ _ _ / _ _ _ _ _ _ _

d The poor level housing that grows up on the edge of cities: s _ ☐ _ _ _ / _ _ _ _

e The former industrial areas near town centres where houses and modern offices are being built: t _ _ ☐ _ _ _ _ _ _ / _ _ _ _

f Someone who lives in a place: ☐ _ _ _ _ _ _ _ _

g When a town spreads out into the countryside it is called: u _ _ _ _ / ☐ _ _ _ _ _

h The system of roads, water supply, electricity, schools and healthcare: I _ _ ☐ _ _ _ _ _ _ _ _ _

i Someone who travels to and fro to work in a city each day: c _ _ _ _ ☐ _ _

j A settlement that develops along a road or a river: l ☐ _ _ _ _

k A city which has grown so large that it merges with another city: _ _ _ _ _ _ _ _ ☐ _

l The problem caused by too many vehicles on the roads: c _ ☐ _ _ _ _ _ _

35

## 2 • Settlements

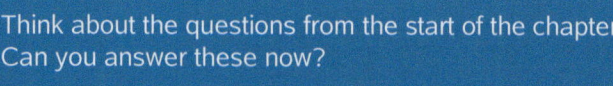

Why are most of the world's largest cities found in LEDCs?
What are the problems associated with living in mega cities?
Compare and contrast life in a city with life in a hamlet
How has the situation of your settlement changed over time?
How has this affected your settlement?

**Extension**

Internet search. Find out about...
Mega cities, such as Mumbai
Shanty towns
Rural migration

Think about the questions from the start of the chapter. Can you answer these now?

- What is a settlement hierarchy?
- Why do some towns grow into cities?
- Who lives in the suburbs?
- When do cities become too big?
- Where is the world's largest city?

# 3 Agriculture and food

**In this chapter you will answer...**
- What is an intensive subsistence farming system?
- Who are nomadic farmers?
- Where do food shortages occur?
- Why do famines happen?
- When did the Green Revolution happen?

## 3.1 Types of agriculture

**Agriculture** is the process of farming of **crops** and **livestock** (animals).

**Pastoral** farming is the rearing (growing) of livestock only such as sheep, goats, cows, pigs and horses. A **dairy** farm is an example of pastoral farming where cows are reared to produce milk. **Arable** farming is the growing of crops such as wheat, barley, potatoes and sugarcane. Many farms grow both crops and livestock and these are called **mixed** farms.

**Plantation** farming is the growing of tree crops such as tea, coffee, bananas and oil palms. These are usually very large farms and are most common in tropical countries. Most farms are **sedentary** which means they are fixed in one place. **Nomadic** farmers move around from place to place with herds of livestock such as goats, camels or cattle, to find fresh water and grass.

## 3.2 Aims of farmers

Most farms aim to produce food. **Commercial** farms grow crops or livestock to sell at markets. This makes a **profit** for the farmer and provides food for the population. Some commercial farmers produce 'non-food' crops which are used by industries, like oil palms for the soap industry. A **subsistence** farm produces crops/livestock just to feed the families that work on it. Very little, or none of the produce is sent to market. This is very simple farming.

## 3.3 The scale of farming

An **extensive** farming system uses large areas of land. This is possible in areas where there is a low **population density**. Cereal farming on the prairies in Canada is an example of extensive, commercial, arable farming. Pastoral farms are usually extensive as the animals need large areas of land to feed.

### KEY WORDS

**Pastoral** the rearing of livestock only

**Arable** the growing of crops

**Commercial** growing crops or livestock to sell at markets to make a profit

**Subsistence** growing crops or livestock just to feed the families that work on the farm

**Extensive** farming which uses large areas of land

**Intensive** farming which uses small areas of land

**Livestock** Animals kept on farms to produce food

**Crops** Plants which are grown to produce food

**Scale** the relative size of something

## 3 • Agriculture and food

Very large, extensive farms of sheep or cattle are called **ranches**, and can be found in countries such as Australia and Brazil.

An **intensive** farming system involves very small areas of land. This is more common where there is a high population density and **fertile** soil. If soil is fertile it can produce a lot of crops from a small area. Extensive and intensive farming can be commercial or subsistence, producing large or small amounts of produce.

> **KEY WORD**
>
> **Fertile** soil which has a lot of nutrients

**Exercise**

1 Complete the crossword by using the information above. Copy your answers into your notebook.

### Across

1. A farm which aims to sell most of its produce (10).
6. When the farming remains in one place (9).
7. When people move from place to place in search of food and water for their animals (7).
8. A farm which rears cattle for milk (5).
9. A collective noun for produce such as wheat, carrots, potatoes and sugarbeet (5).
10. The type of farming where only enough to feed the farmer and his family is produced (11).

### Down

2. A farm where livestock and crops are produced (5).
3. A farm which rears only animals (8).
4. An area planted with fruit trees which produce fruit such as apples, pears, plums and cherries (7).
5. A farm which covers only a small area (9).

## 3.4 Farming systems

A system is made up of: inputs, processes, stores and outputs. The **inputs** go into a farm to make things happen. Physical inputs include sunshine, water, soil and air. Human inputs include labour, money, tools or machinery, fertilisers and pesticides. **Stores** on farms are where things are kept. These include sheds for machinery, barns for livestock, silos for grain, a farmhouse and farm shops. **Processes** are the actions which are carried out by the farmer such as feeding livestock or harvesting wheat. The **outputs** of a farming system are the produce that is grown. The outputs of an arable farm are crops, for example, wheat. The outputs of a pastoral farm are livestock items such as meat, milk or wool, and any waste such as manure.

> **KEY WORD**
>
> **Yield** the amount produced, for example crops from farming

**Exercise**

2   Match the processes below with their correct definitions and copy into your notebook.

   1  To plough        a  To collect up the crops when they are fully grown
   2  To irrigate      b  To remove the unwanted husks from the grains of cereal
   3  To fertilise     c  To mix up the soil to prepare it for sowing crops
   4  To harvest       d  To cut the wool off a sheep
   5  To shear         e  To add nutrients to the soil
   6  To sow           f  To pull up unwanted plants from a field
   7  To herd          g  To give nutrients to livestock
   8  To weed          h  To add water to the soil
   9  To thresh        i  To put seeds into the soil
   10 To feed          j  To collect together livestock such as sheep

3   Copy and complete the table below by putting the words into the correct columns for the farming system of a sheep farm.

| Inputs | Stores | Processes | Outputs |
|--------|--------|-----------|---------|
|        |        |           |         |

sunshine   barn        feeding   wool        rainwater    shed
grass      mowing      labour    farmhouse   fertilising  meat
sheepdog   washing     fields    herding     shearing     machinery
profit     quad bike   money

## 3 • Agriculture and food

**Exercise**

**4** Are the following statements about the farming system in Exercise 3 true or false? Copy the correct statements into your notebook.

  a This is an arable farm.
  b This is a sedentary farm.
  c This is a commercial farm.
  d Sunshine is an output from this farm.
  e Herding the sheep is a process occurring on this farm.

**5** Use the corrected statements above to write a paragraph describing this sheep farming system.

**Exercise**

**6** Copy and complete the table below by matching the start and end sentences to find the factors influencing extensive cereal farming in Canada.

| | |
|---|---|
| Large areas of flat land ___ | ___ produces high yields of crops |
| Fertile prairie soil ___ | ___ helps farmers produce and harvest more cereal to make more profit |
| Warm, dry summer climate ___ | ___ allow machinery such as combine harvesters to be used easily. |
| Modern machinery such as combine harvesters ___ | ___ provides good conditions for the growing and ripening of the wheat |

3.1 Cereal farming on the Canadian prairie

**Exercise**

**7** Copy and complete the paragraph below by choosing the correct present passive verbs to describe an intensive subsistence farming system in India. The first one has been done for you.

Rice (is *grown*) on the floodplain of the River Ganges in India. The land (flood) by river water during the monsoon season and the soil (fertilise) by the silt from the river. The fields which (use) are less than 1 hectare in size because the soil is so fertile. The muddy fields (plough) using a wooden plough. This (draw) by an ox. The rice plants (sow) in the flooded fields. The rice crop (harvest) by the farmer and his family. It (dry) by the sun and (thresh) to remove the husks from the grain.

# Agriculture and food 3

## Comprehension

### Farmers' Forum: livelihoods on the line

*Profile*: Seth O'Malley; married with two teenage sons.

*Farm*: 485 hectares in Alberta, Canada.

*Output*: wheat

*Purpose*: export profit

*Labour input*: 3 full-time workers; seasonal labour and family at **harvest** time

*Machinery input*: tractor; seed drill; combine harvester; hired spreaders for fertiliser, pesticide and herbicide.

*Farm processes*: One harvest per year. Saving seeds to use the following year. Spraying fertilizers, pesticides and herbicides to improve the quality and quantity of the crop.

*Problem*: Large **transnational** companies want to introduce **genetically modified** seeds to the Canadian prairies. The foreign markets oppose this and there is a danger of **cross-contamination**. This would mean that his **livelihood** could be lost.

> **KEY WORD**
>
> **Harvest** the quantity of crops produced at the end of the growing cycle, usually in autumn

---

*Profile*: Kwame Otunga, single.

*Farm*: 86 hectares in Nyeri, Kenya.

*Output*: coffee beans

*Purpose*: export profit

*Labour input*: 68 employees and their families; casual labour at harvest times

*Machinery input*: truck for collection of harvest; tractor

*Farm processes*: two harvests per year; labour intensive care of the bushes: planting new stock; pruning; spraying with herbicide; picking.

*Problem*: Profits are low. Transnational companies have increased coffee bean production in other countries, causing a **glut** in the market (too much), so even the best quality beans are cheaper. Coffee is a **cash crop** so falling prices threaten the survival of the farm.

---

*Profile*: Colin Macgregor, married with two sons and a daughter.

*Farm*: 161 hectares near Christchurch, South Island, New Zealand.

*Output*: meat and wool from 4000 sheep

*Main outlet*: export profit

*Labour input*: family

*Machinery input*: **quad bike** for travelling to outer pastures; tractor; electric fences; **shearing** tools.

*Farm inputs and processes*: Sheep graze outside all year round; feeding hay and silage in winter; lambing in spring.

*Problem*: dry summers mean lighter weight lambs which sell for less. Competition with increasing number of beef farms also reduces prices. Transport costs are constantly rising. There is a drop in world market for lamb.

41

## 3 • Agriculture and food

*Profile*: Nils de Graaf, married with three daughters.

*Farm*: 8 hectares near Lisse, The Netherlands.

*Output*: Bulbs and cut flowers

*Purpose*: export profit

*Labour input*: family

*Machinery input*: tractor; **bulb** lifter

*Farm inputs and processes*: Annual spring harvest of bulb blooms; manual tending of the bulb fields; treating with pesticides; picking of the blooms; developing of new strains over several years.

*Problem*: large companies are buying up family businesses, and are undercutting profits. Costs of chemicals used are rising. Other countries are challenging the dominance of the Netherlands in the flower trade. Economic crisis affects sales of flowers as they are a luxury item.

---

*Profile*: Sanjiv Kutah, married, with 3 sons and 2 daughters.

*Farm*: 0.5 hectares in Bihar, India.

*Output*: rice

Purpose: family food with small amounts used for **barter** in local market

*Labour input*: family

*Machinery input*: wooden plough with **buffalo**,

*Farm inputs and processes*: three crops per year; planting and harvesting by hand. **Irrigating** fields by channels from the river.

*Problem*: frequent flooding from monsoon rains and the River Ganges bursting its banks, which ruins crops and stores. There is often not enough food for the family.

**8** Comprehension questions:
 a Which farm covers the largest area?
 b Which farm employs most people?
 c In your notebooks, highlight the inputs into each farm in one colour and the processes in another colour.
 d Whose problems do you think are mainly caused by climate?
 e Which farmers have similar concerns caused by transnational companies?

**9** Copy and complete the table below by choosing the categories which apply to the farms described.

| Farm location | Commercial/Subsistence | Extensive/Intensive | Pastoral/Arable/Mixed/Plantation |
|---|---|---|---|
| Canada | | | |
| Kenya | | | |
| New Zealand | | | |
| Netherlands | | | |
| India | | | |

## Agriculture and food 3

**Language**

Nouns which describe processes often end in -ation, or -ion if the verb ends in -ate.

For example, to urbanise: urbanisation.

If the verb ends in -ify, change the -y to -i.

There is more information on this process in chapter 12.

**Exercise**

**10** Copy and complete the following table in your notebooks.

| Verb | Noun naming the process | Noun | Adjective |
|---|---|---|---|
| To industrialise | _____ | industry | industrial |
| To purify | _____ | purity | pure |
| _____ | _____ | desert | desert |
| To irrigate | _____ | _____ | _____ |
| To contaminate | _____ | _____ | _____ |
| To modernise | _____ | modernity | modern |
| To fertilise | _____ | fertility | fertile |
| To diversify | _____ | diversity | diverse |

### 3.5 Food shortages

If the inputs to a farming system are reduced, then the size of the yield (outputs) may be reduced too. This may lead to a food **shortage**. 25,000 people die every day from hunger and related illnesses. Subsistence farmers may only produce enough food for their family to eat that year. If there is a decline in their yields then they will experience food shortages.

**KEY WORDS**

**Drought** a decline in the amount of rain over a long period of time

**Flood** when high levels of rainfall cause rivers to overflow their banks

**Malnutrition** when a person does not eat enough of a certain food group e.g. protein

**Famine** a widespread decline in the amount of food per person for a large number of people, leading to starvation

**Food aid** food given to governments or people who are experiencing food shortages

**Shortage** a limited amount of something that is needed

**Green Revolution** a period in the 1960s and 1970s when crop yields in some LEDCs rapidly increased

**Exercise**

**11** Which word does not fit into these word groups?
Copy the correct word groups into your notebook.
The first has been done for you.

a Drought: dry, parched, arid, desert, ~~lush~~ [adjectives]
b Flood: swampy, scorched, inundated, sodden, saturated [adjectives]
c Shortage: glut, dearth, lack, absence, scarcity [nouns]
d Exhaustion: tired, empty, fertile, finished, drained [adjectives]
e Nutrition: eating, feeding, consuming, nourishing, stunting [present participles – can be used as nouns or adjectives]
f Yield: produce, crops, harvest, debt, outcome [nouns]
g Famine: hunger, thirst, abundance, deprivation, malnourishment [nouns]
h Aid: help, assistance, support, relief, neglect [nouns]

## 3.6 Natural causes of food shortages

A **drought** is a decline in the amount of rain over a long period of time. This will cause the outputs of a farm to decline. Too much rainfall can also cause food shortages. **Flooding** is when high levels of rainfall cause rivers to overflow their banks. If farmland is flooded then both crops and livestock could be destroyed. **Tropical cyclones** bring strong winds and heavy rain. The Caribbean islands suffer particularly from cyclones destroying their plantations of crops such as bananas. **Storm surges** from cyclones cause salty seawater to be thrown onto land by the strong winds. Storm surges affect low-lying coastal areas where salt water can kill crops e.g. rice grown on the delta land in Bangladesh.

**Pests** are creatures such as locusts or rats which damage crops. Both locusts and rats breed in huge numbers and can completely destroy a crop in hours. Crops and livestock on a farm may become infected with **disease** which may destroy a farms output. **Soil exhaustion** occurs when each time a crop is harvested nutrients are removed from the soil and not replaced. Over time the yields of crops will decline as there are insufficient nutrients remaining in the soil. If a yield of grass declines then the quality of livestock will decline too.

### Ethiopia drought and food crisis

The failure of two previous rainy seasons has affected the grass pastures of southern Ethiopia. Lack of food and water has led to the death of livestock and now up to 15 million people face food shortages. Wells have dried up and stores of food have been exhausted.

### The Big Dry hits Australian farmers

More than 10,000 farming families are leaving their farms as the worst period of drought for a century is hitting the wheat farmers of Australia. Farmers are forced into debt and rural communities are suffering. The export of wheat has plummeted.

**12** Read the articles above and choose the correct statements from the options below.

a Drought has reduced output from farms in Ethiopia and Australia/Drought has increased output from farms in Ethiopia and Australia.

b The wheat farmers in Australia are extensive, arable, subsistence farmers/The wheat farmers in Australia are extensive, arable, commercial farmers.

c The people in Ethiopia are facing food shortages as they do not have enough food in storage/The people in Ethiopia are facing food shortages as they have large stores of food to use.

d In both Ethiopia and Australia the urban communities are suffering most/In both Ethiopia and Australia the rural communities are suffering most.

e Drought is more likely to lead to starvation and malnutrition in Australia than Ethiopia/Drought is more likely to lead to starvation and malnutrition in Ethiopia than Australia.

## 3.7 Human causes of food shortages

**Wars** cause food shortages. The number of people available to work on farms (labour input) is reduced and this may affect how much output can be produced. War creates problems in transporting the outputs to markets and this means some people will be unable to get food. **Capital investment** is money given to farmers by their governments to buy inputs to help them produce higher yields. Where governments do not invest in agriculture the farmers may struggle to produce enough to feed the population.

## 3.8 The effects of food shortages

When less food is produced by farmers then food becomes more expensive. This means that the poorest people may not be able to buy enough food to eat. In extreme cases the amount of food available per person may decrease so much that they become malnourished or starve. **Malnutrition** is when a person does not eat enough of a certain food group such as protein. This may lead to diseases such as kwashiorkor or rickets. **Starvation** is when people do not have enough food to give them energy to live. A **famine** is a widespread decline in the amount of food per person for a large number of people, leading to starvation. A country affected by both war and drought or flooding may suffer from serious food shortages causing famine.

**Exercise**

**13** Copy and complete the table below in your notebook.

| Noun | Verb | Adjective |
| --- | --- | --- |
| starvation | _____ | _____ |
| _____ | | exhausting |
| _____ | _____ | nourishing |
| malnourishment | _____ | malnourished |
| undernourishment | _____ | undernourished |
| _____ | feed | _____ |
| consumption | _____ | consuming |

## 3.9 Food aid

Sometimes **food aid** is given to governments who can then sell it to the people of the country. **Emergency food aid** is food given for free to people who are suffering from natural disasters such as droughts or war. Food aid is given by **donor** countries to **recipient** countries which are suffering from food shortages.

## 3 • Agriculture and food

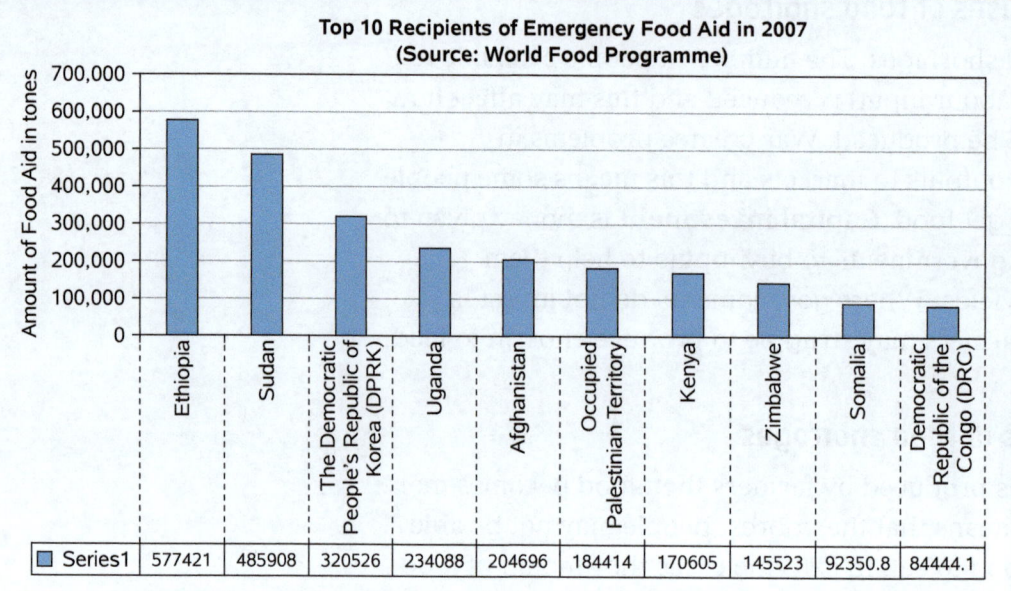

**Exercise**

**Top 10 Recipients of Emergency Food Aid in 2007**
(Source: World Food Programme)

| | Ethiopia | Sudan | The Democratic People's Republic of Korea (DPRK) | Uganda | Afghanistan | Occupied Palestinian Territory | Kenya | Zimbabwe | Somalia | Democratic Republic of the Congo (DRC) |
|---|---|---|---|---|---|---|---|---|---|---|
| Series1 | 577421 | 485908 | 320526 | 234088 | 204696 | 184414 | 170605 | 145523 | 92350.8 | 84444.1 |

Amount of Food Aid in tones

**3.2** Bar graph of recipients of emergency food aid

**14** Use the graph above to work out if the following statements are true, false or not possible to say? Copy the correct statements into your notebook.

 a Ethiopia received the most emergency food aid in 2007.
 b Uganda was the recipient of more food aid than Sudan.
 c Most of the top 10 recipients of emergency food aid are in Africa.
 d Only two of the top 10 recipients are in Europe.
 e Most of these countries have suffered from drought.
 f Afghanistan received 200,000 tons of emergency food aid in 2007.
 g Somalia received 100,000 tons less than Afghanistan.

### 3.10 The Green Revolution

The **Green Revolution** was a period in the 1960s and 1970s when crop yields in some LEDCs rapidly increased. This was a result of the input of modern technology to farming. This technology included farm machinery such as tractors, **irrigation** facilities, chemical **fertilisers** and **pesticides** and new seeds which produced high yields. These seeds were called **High Yielding Varieties** (HYVs) and were of the basic food crops – wheat, rice and maize. These seeds are **hybrids**. This means they were developed over many years of cross-breeding between individual plants.

> **KEY WORDS**
>
> **Revolution** a complete change from one system to another
>
> **Technology** modern methods which use machines and science to improve processes

46

> **Exercise**
>
> **15** Choose the correct definition for the following terms.
>
> a Green Revolution
> - ◎ The increase in grain production in Asia and Central America through the introduction of new farming technologies.
> - ◎ The increase in farm sizes to increase production of crops in Asia and Central America.
>
> b High Yielding Variety
> - ◎ A crop variety that has been genetically modified in a laboratory to produce high yields.
> - ◎ A crop variety that has been developed by cross-breeding of varieties of the same crop.
>
> c Irrigation
> - ◎ Drainage of soil to get rid of water.
> - ◎ Adding water to crops from river or groundwater through canals, sprinkler systems or wells.

## 3.11 The advantages of the Green Revolution

In the 1960s India experienced **famine** as **drought** and lack of **capital investment** in farming led to food shortages.

Since the introduction of the Green Revolution the number of malnourished people has decreased and India has become self-sufficient in wheat and rice production. The Green Revolution increased the output of wheat, maize and rice crops. These are the **staple food** crops of Asia and Central America. This has led to a reduction in food shortages in these regions.

> **KEY WORD**
>
> **Drought** shortage of water caused by lack of rainfall over a long period of time

## 3.12 The disadvantages of the Green Revolution

The Green Revolution increased **inequality** in countries between the rich farmers and the poor farmers in LEDCs. Rich farmers could afford to buy HYV seeds, new tractors and irrigation facilities and the fertiliser to help the crops to grow. However poorer farmers could not afford all these new inputs. Many poor farmers ran into **debt** as they borrowed money to buy inputs but were unable to make enough profit to pay back the loan.

Rich farmers became richer. Poor farmers became poorer. The natural **environment** is becoming polluted as a result of too much chemical fertiliser being used on fields. It is washed into rivers causing **algae** to grow. Algae removes oxygen from the water so killing other water life. **Groundwater** has been used for irrigation so much that wells are now drying up.

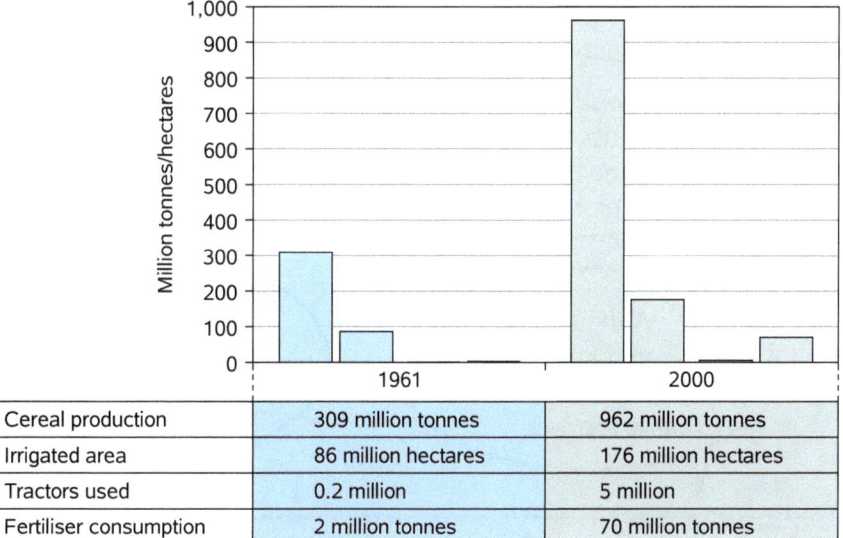

| | 1961 | 2000 |
|---|---|---|
| Cereal production | 309 million tonnes | 962 million tonnes |
| Irrigated area | 86 million hectares | 176 million hectares |
| Tractors used | 0.2 million | 5 million |
| Fertiliser consumption | 2 million tonnes | 70 million tonnes |

3.3 Table showing changes in agriculture in Asia

47

## 3 • Agriculture and food

**Exercise**

**16** Copy and complete the following paragraph using information from the Figure 3.3.

Between 1961 and _____ cereal production in Asia has nearly tripled from _____ tonnes to 962 million tonnes. This has been possible because the _____ area has doubled to 176 million _____ so water availability has _____. Machinery has also increased in use and there are now over 5 million _____ used compared to just _____ in 1961. Cereal production has also increased because of a huge increase in the amount of _____ which has been added to the soil to provide more nutrients.

**17** Find the *opposite* term from the alternatives given below.

| a | Donor | agent/user/recipient/importer |
| b | Flood | starvation/famine/inundation/drought |
| c | Shortage | lack/glut/need/provision |
| d | Irrigation | drainage/fertilisation/precipitation/cultivation |
| e | Revolution | development/change/continuation/regeneration |

**Extension**

Green Revolution technologies, along with food aid, have helped many countries suffering from food shortages.

**18** Read the following statements and decide which are advantages or disadvantages of food aid. What do you think are some other advantages and disadvantages?

"Food aid only leads to corruption and supports bad governments so they do not have to invest in agriculture"

"Food aid provides essential help to those people in greatest need"

"Food aid may not help a country get richer but it may allow people to live longer, healthier lives"

"Food aid helps countries but it cannot overcome their long term problems"

"Food aid does not always go to the people who need it most"

"It would be better to provide the means to grow crops rather than provide people with cheap food"

"Without food aid millions of people would die. Any other way would take too long"

"Providing continuous food aid simply stops people and governments having the incentive to make progress"

48

Agriculture and food  3

**19** What are the extreme consequences of:

a too little rainfall?
b too much rainfall?
c a total lack of nutritious food?
d not enough nutritious food?

Copy your answers into your notebook.

**20** Give suggestions how the above conditions could be **alleviated**.
Copy and complete the table below.

| Condition | Suggestion |
|---|---|
| a | |
| b | |
| c | |
| d | |

**21** Identify the type of farm in the sketches below.
Write down 4 inputs, 4 processes and 1 output for each.

3.4 Examples of farming

49

## 3 • Agriculture and food

**22** Find the words on Agriculture from the options in the box below. Write down the words you find in your notebook.

| N | A | A | F | A | D | I | P | E | E | S | S |
|---|---|---|---|---|---|---|---|---|---|---|---|
| P | D | I | A | I | N | A | A | L | C | E | U |
| L | E | D | M | N | U | A | S | T | E | D | B |
| A | G | R | I | C | U | L | T | U | R | E | S |
| N | E | O | N | F | L | O | O | D | E | N | I |
| T | B | U | E | T | P | E | R | O | A | T | S |
| A | F | G | E | F | S | A | A | L | L | A | T |
| T | R | H | A | O | N | L | L | C | S | R | E |
| I | L | T | M | I | X | E | D | A | G | Y | N |
| O | L | O | P | S | S | R | A | I | B | T | C |
| N | O | D | L | E | T | A | R | A | B | L | E |
| N | P | N | D | O | A | A | T | D | E | H | S |

agriculture   sedentary   mixed
pastoral      arable      aid
famine        drought     flood
cereals       plantation  subsistence

### Talking points

How can farmers survive when the market for their produce disappears?

How has farming changed as a result of scientific and technological progress?

Why do people move from the country to the town?

Why is there starvation when the world produces enough food for all?

Which farming systems will have the greatest impact on the environment?

Which farming systems are most/least affected by changes in global trade?

### Extension

Internet search: Find out about…

Agriculture in your country of birth

Organic farming

Sustainable farming

Think about the questions from the start of the chapter. Can you answer these now?

◎ What is an intensive subsistence farming system?
◎ Who are nomadic farmers?
◎ Where do food shortages occur?
◎ Why do famines happen?
◎ When did the Green Revolution happen?

# 4 Industry

**In this chapter you will answer...**
- Who works in primary industries?
- What are tertiary industries?
- Where are newly industrialised countries (NICs)?
- When does a country become a NIC?
- Why are transnational companies spread around the globe?

### KEY WORD
People work in **primary**, **secondary** or **tertiary industries**. The number working in each type of industry changes over time and is different in different countries

## 4.1 Types of industry

**Primary industries** remove **raw materials** from the earth. Raw materials are found naturally on earth. Rocks, plants and animals are all raw materials. There are four primary industries: **fishing**, **forestry**, **farming** and **mining**. Secondary industries use raw materials to make new things. These are manufacturing industries. **Tertiary industries** provide a service to a population. These are the service industries.

### KEY WORDS
**Primary** industries which remove **raw materials** from the earth

**Secondary** industries which use raw materials to manufacture new things

**Tertiary** industries which provide a service to a population

**raw material** something found naturally on earth

**Employment structure** the proportion of people working in primary, secondary or tertiary employment

**Industry** a commercial activity that many people are involved in

**Exercise 1** Copy and complete the table below by putting the following verbs in the correct columns.

| To remove | To make | To provide |
|---|---|---|
|  |  |  |

to give   to use   to extract   to manufacture
to mine   to process   to take out   to create
to supply   to construct

**Exercise 2** Match the definitions to the terms and copy the completed terms into your notebook.

1 Primary industry
2 Fishing
3 Forestry
4 Farming
5 Mining
6 Secondary industry
7 Tertiary industry

a A primary industry involving cutting down trees
b An industry providing a service to a population
c An industry which extracts nutrients from the soil to grow crops and livestock
d The removal of raw materials from the earth.
e An industry using raw materials to manufacture a finished product.
f An industry which extracts minerals from rocks such as coal, oil, gold, limestone.
g An industry where fish are caught from seas, lakes and rivers for food

# 4 Industry

> **Exercise**
>
> **3** Copy the table into your notebook and put the jobs below in the correct columns.
>
> | Primary industries | Secondary industries | Tertiary industries |
> |---|---|---|
> |  |  |  |
>
> Doctor    Banker          Steel worker     Farmer      Car maker
> Gold miner    Lumberjack   TV presenter    Fisherman   Engineer

## 4.2 Industrial systems

An industry is a system of **inputs, processes, stores** and **outputs**. The **inputs** to a secondary industry are the raw materials, labour, machinery and money.

**Processes** are the actions needed to change the raw materials into a finished product.

**Stores** are where inputs and products are kept and processes occur such as factories, mills, warehouses and sheds. **Outputs** are the finished products and any waste materials.

**4.1** A sheep being sheared

> **Exercise**
>
> **4** Copy the table below into your notebook and sort the following stages in the production of sheepskin boots into:
>
> | Inputs | Processes | Stores | Outputs |
> |---|---|---|---|
> |  |  |  |  |
> | Shearing the **fleeces** from the sheep | Sewing the pieces into boots | Warehouse for the finished boots | |
> | Sunshine | Sheep | Preserving the skins with salt | |
> | Packaging the boots | Rain | Cutting the wool from the skins | |
> | Grass | Gluing soles on to the boots | Applying the boot patterns to the skins | |
> | Fodder | Farm | Farm hands | |
> | Sheepskin boots | | | |

**4.2** Sheepskin boots

### KEY WORDS

**Employment** working for money

**Proportion** a part of the whole amount

**Majority** most of the people or things in a group

## 4.3 Employment structure

The **employment structure** of a population is the **proportion** of people working in primary, secondary or tertiary employment. This is the percentage (%) of people working in each type of employment.

In the poorest LEDCs the majority of people work in **primary** industries, particularly farming and fishing. In richer countries the majority of the population work in **tertiary** employment. Very few people work in primary industries. Machines replace people working on farms, mines, boats and in factories so fewer people are needed in those jobs.

**Employment structure in selected countries**

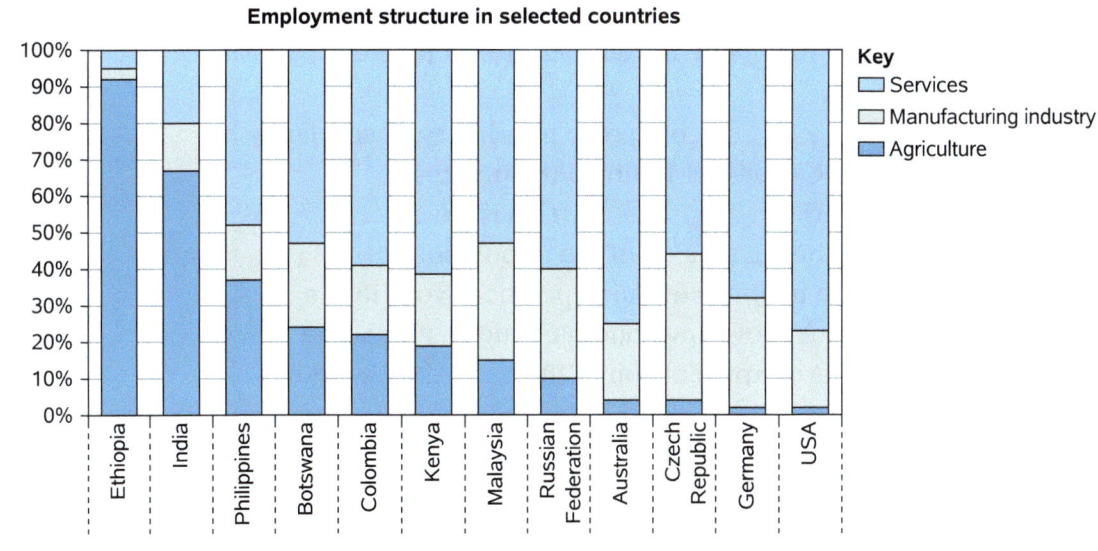

**Key**
- Services
- Manufacturing industry
- Agriculture

Countries (left to right): Ethiopia, India, Philippines, Botswana, Colombia, Kenya, Malaysia, Russian Federation, Australia, Czech Republic, Germany, USA

4.3 Bar graph and table of employment structure

### Exercise

**5** Look at Figure 4.3. Are the following statements true or false? Copy the correct statements into your notebook.

a India has the greatest proportion working in agriculture.
b Columbia has a higher proportion of people working in services than Botswana.
c The largest proportion of population working in manufacturing industry is in the Czech Republic.
d The proportion of population working in manufacturing industry is lowest in the Philippines.
e The richest countries have the smallest proportion of population working in agriculture.
f Germany is the richest country on the list and has the highest proportion of people working in services.
g The two countries with the largest proportion of the population working in manufacturing industry are in Europe.

## 4.4 Change in employment structure over time

People have always used raw materials for their own needs, such as providing food and shelter. This is **subsistence** use of raw materials. When a country sells its raw materials to make money an economy starts to develop. Many poorer countries earn most of their income from primary industries by exporting raw materials. If that country builds factories to process the raw materials it can make more money. This is secondary industry.

Manufactured products make more **profit** than basic raw materials. People will earn higher incomes by working in factories than in primary industries. This means the percentage working in secondary industries grows. People work in the **tertiary sector** to buy and sell the raw materials and manufactured products. If the profits made are invested in services such as education, healthcare, banking, leisure and tourism then the percentage of people working in the tertiary sector will grow.

## 4 • Industry

> **Exercise**
>
> **6** Copy the following paragraph into your notebook and fill in the blanks using the words below.
>
> The _____ structure is the _____ of people in primary, secondary and _____ industries. In LEDCs such as Ethiopia the greatest proportion of the population works in _____. This is a _____ industry. In the richest MEDCs the _____ of the population in agriculture is very _____. The majority of the population work in the _____ sector. Countries with growing economies such as Malaysia and the Czech Republic have a larger proportion of the _____ working in _____ industry.
>
> | employment | primary | secondary | agriculture | proportion |
> | small | tertiary | proportion | population | tertiary |

### 4.5 Industrial location

The **location** of an industry is very important for the success of the business. Usually the location is chosen to try to reduce costs for the business.

◎ **Raw materials**

An industry which needs large amounts of heavy, bulky raw materials as inputs is a **raw material oriented industry**. The industry chooses to locate closer to the raw materials to reduce the cost of transport. The outputs are smaller, lighter and cheaper to transport to markets.

◎ **Communications**

Raw materials need to be **imported** from primary industries to factories. The finished products are **exported** from factories to the markets. A location close to transport routes such as roads, railways, airports or ports is therefore essential.

◎ **Land**

Large factories and warehouses need large areas of flat land. A location in the **rural-urban fringe** has cheaper land and more space for expansion than within an urban area.

◎ **Labour**

An industry which needs a large number of workers will locate near to a large urban area. Hi-tech industries often require highly skilled labour and therefore many locate near to universities and training colleges.

◎ **Government**

Governments encourage industries to locate in certain places by offering **incentives**. **Enterprise zones** may provide tax-free land so it is cheaper for industries to locate there.

> **KEY WORDS**
>
> **Imports** something being brought into a country or region
>
> **Exports** something being sent out of a country or region
>
> **Subsidies** money given to a company to help reduce their costs
>
> **Enterprise zones** areas with reduced taxes to encourage businesses to locate there
>
> **Footloose** industries which can locate almost anywhere
>
> **Labour** the collective noun for the workers, especially manual workers, of a company, industry or country

Grants provide money to an industry. **Subsidies** make inputs cheaper. Governments may provide the **infrastructure** such as roads, railways and buildings to attract industries to an area.

◎ Markets

Industries which use smaller, lighter inputs to make a large, bulky finished product are **market oriented industries**. They locate closer to the market where the finished product will be sold so transport costs are reduced. Industries making **perishable** goods are also located close to their markets so the product can be sold before it rots.

> **7** Pick the correct statements from the options below and copy into your notebooks.
>
> 1. a A steel industry has inputs of heavy coal, iron ore and limestone so it is a raw material oriented industry
>    b A steel industry has inputs of heavy coal, iron ore and limestone so it is a market oriented industry
> 2. a Governments encourage industries to locate in certain places by offering instructions.
>    b Governments encourage industries to locate in certain places by offering incentives.
> 3. a Raw materials are exported from factories as the finished products.
>    b Raw materials are imported to factories to make the finished products.
> 4. a It is cheaper to locate an industry in the countryside than in the middle of a city.
>    b It is more expensive to locate an industry in the countryside than in the middle of a city.

## 4.6 Footloose industries

A **footloose industry** can locate almost anywhere. It can be in any country and may not need to be near raw materials, good communications or large populations.

## 4.7 Transnational Companies

Sony, Coca-Cola, Honda and Shell are examples of **transnational companies (TNCs)**. These companies have their **headquarters** in one country and offices, factories and stores in many other countries. This means they produce and sell their products globally.

The manufacturing centres are often located in LEDCs. There are often large populations in these countries which provide a large labour force. Labour is cheaper in these countries and therefore costs for the industry are lower. Jobs that require higher levels of skill are usually found in MEDCs. These parts of the business include the research and development of new products. The populations in these countries usually have more education and skills.

**KEY WORDS**

**Transnational companies** companies which have their **headquarters** in one country and offices, factories and stores in many other countries

**Newly industrialising country** a country whose economy has developed very quickly

**Pacific Rim** the countries around the edge of the Pacific Ocean

# 4 Industry

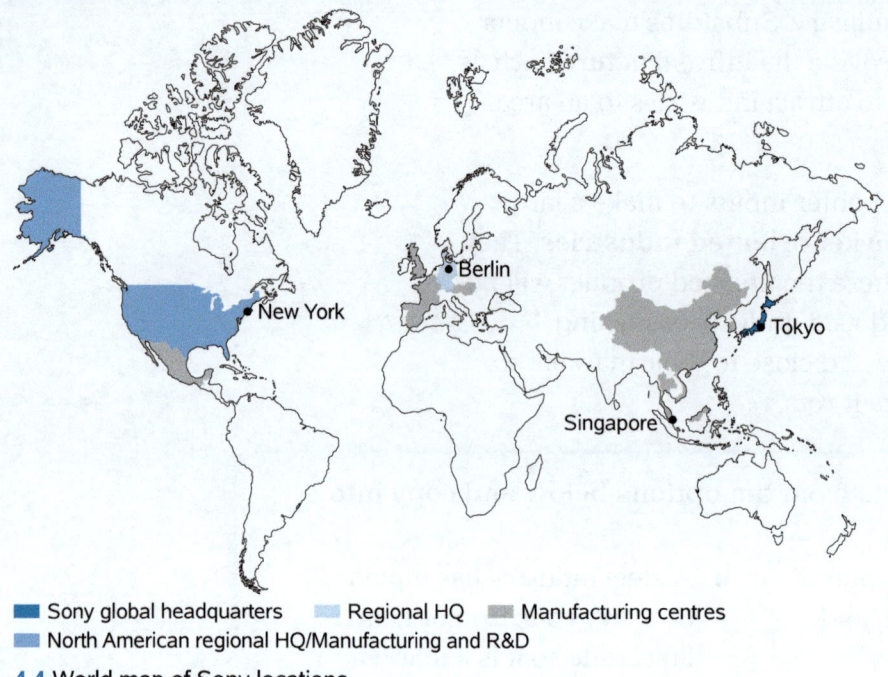

4.4 World map of Sony locations

- Sony global headquarters
- Regional HQ
- Manufacturing centres
- North American regional HQ/Manufacturing and R&D

**Exercise**

**8** Copy and complete the following paragraph using the words in the box below.

Sony is a _____ company with its headquarters in _____, Japan. It has regional headquarters in _____, _____ and Berlin in Germany. Sony has established manufacturing centres in _____ countries across three continents but most manufacturing occurs in _____. The countries of Asia have large populations and therefore the cost of _____ is low. Countries such as _____ have also set up 'free-trade zones' eg. Penang, where transnational companies are attracted by good _____ and _____ land. Research and Development occurs in the _____ and Europe where _____ labour with experience is available. Sony is a well-known brand in North America, _____ and the Asia-Pacific region so this is where its largest _____ are.

| 12 | transnational | infrastructure | Asia | USA | Europe |
| Malaysia | Singapore | tax-free | | markets | Tokyo | skilled |
| labour | New York | | | | |

## 4.8 Newly industrialising countries

Malaysia, Indonesia and China are all examples of **newly industrialising countries** (NICs). Most examples can be found around the **Pacific Rim** (the countries around the Pacific Ocean). The economies of these countries have developed very quickly since the 1970s. They have changed from having employment and trade mainly in the **primary sector** to producing and selling products using their own **raw materials**. This means the majority of their population are now employed in the **secondary and tertiary sectors**. These sectors now produce most money for the country.

**KEY WORD**

**NIC** newly industrialising country. A country which is rapidly developing its secondary sector and increasing its GDP.

# Industry 4

The rapid economic development in NICs has been helped by **foreign investment**. Transnational companies have set up manufacturing centres in the countries. The governments have attracted TNCs by providing **incentives** such as tax-free land and a good infrastructure of roads and airports. TNCs such as Toyota have set up manufacturing centres where there is also cheap labour. They have trained the labour force and provided new skills so workers earn a respectable salary.

## Comprehension

### Malaysia: a country in transition

Malaysia is a country in South East Asia. West Malaysia has a higher population and the capital city Kuala Lumpur. It is more developed than East Malaysia, which has more natural oil and gas resources, and more tropical rain forest. Traditionally, the **primary industries** of agriculture and mining have been key sectors in the Malaysian economy. The fertile coastal plains, river valleys and low hills of West Malaysia combine with the tropical climate to create an ideal environment for farming. In 1975 the production of rice, tropical fruits, palm oil, rubber and timber formed 28% of the GDP.

4.5 Kuala Lumpur, Malaysia

Malaysia's **raw materials** of tin, oil and gas have also been extracted for **export**. In 1980 crude oil formed 25%, rubber 18%, timber 15%, palm oil 10% and tin 9% of the exports. Manufactured goods formed the remaining 23%.

The transition from primary industries to **secondary industries** occurred mainly in the 1980s. The government provided incentives to **transnational companies** to invest in the country. By 1985 agriculture contributed only 19.3% to the GDP, in contrast to industry's 35.5%. The trend continued in 2004 with agriculture dropping to just 7.2%.

The **service industries** showed a significant increase from 40.7% in 1975 to 59.1% in 2004, reflecting the rising standard of living and improvement of the country's **infrastructure**. By 2007, manufactured goods formed 80% of exports, while crude oil and palm oil fell to 5% and 6% respectively, rubber was a mere 2% and liquid natural gas 4%. This change was accompanied by a population explosion in the capital city to 1.6 million by 2006, as people migrated from the countryside to the new factories in the city. Malaysia seems ready to take a leap into the future with plans to develop a multi-media business environment,

### KEY WORD

**GDP** the gross domestic product. This is the amount of money made by a country (not including foreign investments) over one year.

## 4 • Industry

Cyberjaya. The hi-tech infrastructure aims to attract foreign investment and establish Malaysia's place at the hub of transnational trade.

**9** **Comprehension questions:**
  a Which part of Malaysia is richer in natural resources?
  b Where does most farming take place?
  c In which part of Malaysia do most people live?
  d Which raw materials did Malaysia export in 1980?
  e Which sector's contribution to the GDP of Malaysia declined most between 1985 and 2004?
  f Why does the service sector expand as the standard of living improves?
  g Which sectors will expand with Malaysia's plans for the future?

**10** Use one of the expressions from the box below to complete the following statements.
  a Transnational companies are keen to establish manufacturing centres in Malaysia _____ its cheap labour force.
  b Malaysia has been able to rapidly develop its economy _____ its huge natural resources.
  c The flow of migrants from rural to urban areas is _____ the lack of income from subsistence farming.
  d The divide between town and country has increased _____ the lack of investment in rural areas.
  e More people are employed in the service industries _____ increased use of machinery and robots in factories.

| because of | thanks to | on account of | due to |
| as a result of | resulting from | | |

**11** Which of the statements below are advantages of TNCs setting up in NICs and which are disadvantages? Copy the completed table into your notebook.

| | Advantage / Disadvantage |
|---|---|
| The TNCs take business away from small local companies | |
| The TNCs provide more employment for the country | |
| The TNCs encourage governments to improve infrastructure such as roads, airports and electricity | |
| The country can become too dependent on the foreign business | |
| The TNCs bring more money to the country | |
| A lot of the money made by the TNC will go back to its headquarters in a different country **(leakage)** | |
| The TNCs train local people to learn new skills | |

### Extension

**12** Choose the activities from the table below which are typical for the four categories on the left. Copy your choices into your notebook.

| Secondary industry | Processing of raw materials<br>Mining raw materials<br>Exporting raw materials<br>Manufacturing goods from raw materials |
|---|---|
| Tertiary sector | Farming<br>Nursing<br>Teaching<br>Mining |
| Export | Selling tin to the USA<br>Buying cars from the USA<br>Using timber from the rainforest to build houses<br>Supplying DVD players to European market |
| Incentives | Grants to attract new industry<br>Taxes on new business<br>Subsidies to help new companies<br>Restrictions on construction of new factories |

**13** Read the following statements about industry and choose the correct term in each. Copy the correct sentences into your notebook.

a The *tertiary/secondary* sector provides services for the population.
b The *primary/secondary* sector extracts the raw materials which are processed in factories.
c The *secondary/primary* sector uses raw materials to produce goods
d Manufacturing generates *more/less* income than the extraction of raw materials.
e Enterprise zones *reduce/increase* the costs of **location** for new businesses.
f Governments use incentives such as grants and subsidies to *attract/discourage* foreign investment in less developed areas.
g Newly Industrialising Countries are mainly located in *Europe/on the Pacific Rim*.
h The employment structure of a country indicates where the majority of the population *works/lives*.
i Labour is *more/less* expensive in MEDCs than in LEDCs.
j A footloose company is largely *dependent/independent* of its location.
k As a country becomes more industrialised, its infrastructure *expands/contracts* to serve the needs of the population.
l The goods that a country *exports/imports* contribute to the wealth of that country.

## 4 • Industry

**Extension**

**14** Use the definitions to work out the anagrams below.
An anagram is a mixture of letters which make up a word.
- a RETITYRA – An industry providing a service
- b OFTOOSOLE – An industry which can locate almost anywhere
- c PROXET – A raw material or product sent away from a factory
- d YARMPIR – An industry extracting raw materials
- e URFICTERNATSUR – Roads, airports, electricity provided for industries
- f LARTAINSTANON – Companies that are spread out around the world
- g ARW TRAIMLEA – Rocks, plants and animals found naturally on earth
- h CORYDENAS – An industry using raw materials to make finished products.

**Talking points**

How has on-line shopping affected town centres?
Who benefits most from industrialisation?
Who suffers most when industries move away?
How have computers changed industries?

**Extension**

Internet search. Find out about…
TNCs
NICs
Employment in primary/secondary/tertiary sectors in the country of your birth

Think about the questions from the start of the chapter.
Can you answer these now?

- Who works in primary industries?
- What are tertiary industries?
- Where are NICs?
- When does a country become an NIC?
- Why are transnational companies spread around the globe?

# 5 Leisure and tourism

**In this chapter you will answer...**
- Who is a tourist?
- Where are the most popular tourist destinations?
- Why is tourism growing?
- What is seasonal employment?
- When were National Parks created?

## 5.1 Leisure time and tourism

**Leisure time** is when someone is not working during the day or week. Leisure time may be spent watching TV, meeting friends, playing sport or going on holiday. A **tourist** is someone travelling away from home in their leisure time. **Tourism** is a **tertiary industry** which provides services for tourists such as hotels, transport and activities. More and more people now choose to spend part of their leisure time as tourists travelling away from home on holidays.

## 5.2 The growth of leisure and tourism

Since the 1950s people have had more money and more leisure time. Transport has become easier, quicker and cheaper so more people are travelling away from home. As people have become wealthier they can afford to travel more often, for longer holidays and to more distant places. Many people go on **package holidays**. A travel agent organises their transport, hotel, food and some activities for the whole holiday. Cheap package holidays have encouraged more and more people to travel. In the 21st century the **internet** has made going on holiday even easier. People can find cheap deals and book hotels, transport and activities themselves without having to go to a travel agent.

**KEY WORD**

**Tourism** is the process of travelling away from home for a period of at least one night. As leisure time has increased so have the number of tourists. Tourism can have positive and negative impacts

**KEY WORDS**

**Leisure** free time when you do not have to work

**Tourism** travelling away from home for pleasure

**Tourist** someone travelling away from home for at least one night

**Destinations** the places people go to

**Honeypot** somewhere which attracts large numbers of people

**Package** a type of holiday where everything is organised for you in advance by the travel company

5.1 The growth of international tourist numbers

## 5 ◉ Leisure and tourism

**Exercise**

**1** Copy the table below. Describe Figure 5.1 by completing following paragraph using the options below.

The number of tourists has _____ by over 775 _____ since _____. In 1950 there were only _____ million tourists worldwide. There was a _____ growth between 1950 and 1985. Then the _____ increase has occured since _____ when numbers jumped from _____ to 806 million.

| | | | |
|---|---|---|---|
| 25.3 | 1950 | million | steady |
| 1985 | increased | greatest | 320.1 |

**Language**

**2** Copy the table below. Sort the following verbs into those that indicate something getting bigger and those that indicate something getting smaller.

| Getting bigger | Getting smaller |
|---|---|
| | |

| | | | | | |
|---|---|---|---|---|---|
| to contract | to decrease | to drop | to expand | to grow | to fall |
| to increase | to plummet | to rise | to shrink | to slow | to lower |

**3** Which of these adverbs would you use to show a surprising change in the number of tourists?

| | | | |
|---|---|---|---|
| gradually | dramatically | rapidly | slightly |
| suddenly | steadily | slowly | steeply |

### 5.3 Different types of tourism

A tourist is someone travelling away from home for at least one night. **Domestic tourism** is where people stay in their own country for their holiday. **City breaks** have become popular where people visit a city for a weekend or a few nights. This **urban tourism** often involves **sight-seeing** – visiting historic or cultural **attractions**. **Rural tourism** is when people spend time in the countryside.

**National Parks** are popular rural destinations. **Short-haul** holidays are spent within 4–5 hours flying time from home. **Long-haul** holidays are spent more than 5 hours flying time from home. Many people travel to see the different traditions and history of places – this is **cultural tourism**. **Adventure tourism** is travelling to different places to have new and exciting experiences. This may involve trekking, skiing, white-water rafting or bungee jumping. **Eco-tourism** is when tourists try to restrict the impact of their holiday on local environments and people, and is becoming increasingly popular.

**KEY WORDS**

**Attraction** a place or feature which people want to visit

**Culture** the shared knowledge, customs and beliefs of a community

**4** Match the following activities with the type of tourism below.
  a Paul lives in Sydney, Australia and spent his holiday on the Great Barrier Reef.
  b Joelle and Pierre decided to spend a romantic weekend in Venice.
  c Carmel enjoys visting art galleries, museums and historic buildings on her holidays.
  d Natasha flew 10 hours to spend her holiday in Shanghai.
  e Paulo and Lucia are having a cycling holiday to reduce their environmental impact.
  f Tomas will be trekking to the Everest base camp on his next exciting holiday.

| Eco-tourism | Domestic tourism | Cultural tourism |
| Adventure tourism | Longhaul travel | Short-break |

## 5.4 Tourist destinations

The destination is where the tourist travels to.

**Primary resources** are the basic attractions of a destination. This includes the weather (hot and sunny, good snow for skiing) and the landscape (mountains, sandy beaches, exciting cities). **Secondary resources** are provided for the tourists. These include accommodation, transport, footpaths, activities etc.

|  | International Tourist Arrivals in 2005 (millions) |
| --- | --- |
| France | 75.1 |
| Spain | 52.4 |
| USA | 46.1 |
| China | 41.8 |
| Italy | 37.1 |
| UK | 27.8 |
| Mexico | 20.6 |
| Germany | 20.1 |
| Russia | 19.9 |
| Austria | 19.4 |

5.2 World Top 10 tourist destinations

**KEY WORD**

**Destination** the place that you are travelling to

**5** Using the information in Figure 5.2 above copy the correct statements into your notebook.
  a In 2005 more people visited Germany than Russia.
  b In 2005 more people visited Austria than Germany.
  c There are more Asian countries in the top 10 tourist destinations than any other continent.
  d There are more European countries in the top 10 tourist destinations than any other continent.
  e Mexico is the only country in North America in the top 10.
  f There are no African countries in the top 10 tourist destinations.

## 5 Leisure and tourism

### Barbados: island of sun and fun

a Barbados is in the West Indies. Its western shores are lapped by the Caribbean Sea, while its eastern shores are pounded by the Atlantic Ocean. The name 'Barbados' or 'bearded ones' is said to come from the bearded fig trees which grow there.

b Most of the island is made of low lying coral limestone. The island is surrounded by coral reefs which protect its shores from erosion. Originally many areas were covered in tropical rainforest but much was cut down to make room for sugar plantations. Most of the **mangrove swamps** have been cleared to make way for hotels, but a few have been preserved and made into nature reserves.

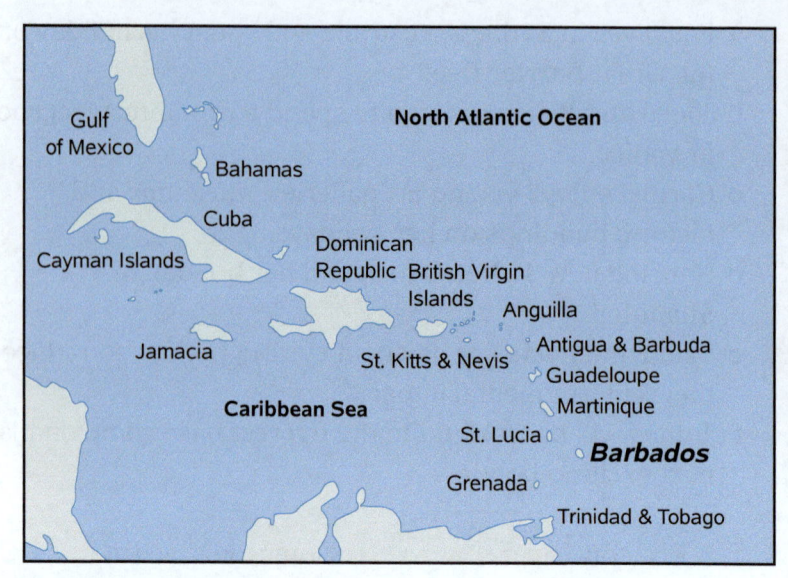

**5.3** Map showing Barbados, north coast of South America and the Eastern Caribbean

c The island enjoys a tropical climate. The brilliant white sandy beaches and clear blue sea make Barbados a dream holiday destination, despite the strong currents of the Atlantic coastline. The wet season runs from July to November, and the dry season runs from December to June. It is the most easterly Caribbean island and it rarely suffers hurricane damage.

**5.4** Beach in Barbados

d The island was uninhabited when Portugal and Spain discovered it in the 16th century. In 1627 England claimed the island as a colony. English remains the official language of Barbados.

e Settlers established tobacco, cotton and sugarcane plantations as cash crops. Slave labour from Africa was imported to work in the large sugar plantations. For the next 200 years the sugar cane industry in Barbados flourished. Sugar and its by-products of rum and molasses were Barbados's main exports.

f Barbados gained its independence from Britain in 1966. Its government made great efforts to **diversify** its economy from agriculture into other sectors. Light manufacturing, construction and financial services grew, but the greatest growth was in tourism.

g It is no surprise that tourism replaced sugar as the main industry. The natural attractions combined with the cultural **inheritance** and the well developed infrastructure make it a prime destination. **Package holidays** and cheaper flights have opened up Barbados to a wider market. The construction of a deep harbour allows huge cruise liners to dock in Bridgetown. Hotel complexes along the western coast provide accommodation, restaurants and entertainment for visitors from all over the world. Water sports such as surfing and scuba diving, golf, rainforest treks, shopping, music and the spectacle of the traditional 'crop over' festivities, not to mention the national sport of cricket, are popular pursuits.

h At the beginning of the 21st century the GDP of Barbados was estimated to be 6% agriculture; 16% industry and 78% services. This reflects the change in the economic growth of the island.

i There is a project to construct two artificial islands off Bridgetown: one is to be a national park and the other is planned as a high class tourist development. The low tax regime encourages **investment** by TNCs, for example international hotel chains.

**6** Choose the appropriate heading for each of the paragraphs about Barbados.

| Climate | Future | Location |
| Colonisation | Independence | Sugar |
| Landscape | Tourism | Economy |

**7** Find 3 primary and 3 secondary tourism resources of Barbados. Copy and complete the table below.

| Primary resources | Secondary resources |
|---|---|
|  |  |
|  |  |
|  |  |

Prepositional phrases: These are used to link elements in a description.
Surrounded by; lined with; situated in/near/on; located in/near/on; fringed with.

**8** Select an appropriate phrase to complete the following sentences and copy into our notebook.
   a  Barbados is _____ coral reefs.
   b  The beaches are _____ palm trees.
   c  Bridgetown is _____ Carlisle Bay on the south west coast of the island.
   d  The main avenue is _____ shops and restaurants.
   e  Barbados is _____ the easterly edge of the Caribbean Sea.

## 5 • Leisure and tourism

> **Language**
>
> Habitual actions in the past which no longer happen are often expressed by using **'used' [to do]** instead of the simple or continuous past.
>
> For example, 'Sugar cane **used to be** the backbone of the island's economy'. (It has been replaced by tourism)
>
> **9** Copy and complete the following sentences. Write the verbs in the correct form to show the reason why each situation has changed.
>
> a The first settlers in Barbados _____ tobacco and cotton as cash crops. [cultivate]
> b Plantation owners _____ slaves. [import]
> c Barbados _____ a British colony. [be]
> d Tropical rainforest _____ large areas of Barbados. [cover]
> e Most of the population _____ in the primary sector. [work]
> f The harbour at Bridgetown _____ too shallow for large ships and cruise liners. [be]

### 5.5 Honeypots

A tourist **honeypot** is somewhere which attracts large numbers of people (like bees to honey). A honeypot could be a single attraction such as the Taj Mahal, India or the Colosseum, Rome. A honeypot could also be a whole place such as Pompei, Italy or Mont-St-Michel, France. A city or a National Park may have many honeypots. Honeypots of London include Buckingham Palace, Trafalgar Square and the Tower of London.

> **KEY WORDS**
>
> **Honeypot** a place that attracts large numbers of tourists
>
> **Impact** the effect something has on something else

### 5.6 Positive impacts of tourism

Tourism is a **tertiary industry** which makes a lot of **money**. It is the most important industry for many countries such as The Maldives or Kenya. Tourist **services** such as hotels, transport, and activities make money for a country. Tourists visiting a country are also required to pay taxes or buy visas which brings **foreign exchange** to the **destination** country. Hilton and Sheraton are **transnational companies** which build and run hotels in different countries around the world. This **foreign investment** can be very important to a country's economy. The money from tourism is often used to improve **infrastructure** such as roads, airports, electricity and water supplies. These improvements will directly help the local population. The money is also used for **conservation** and **management** of tourist **honeypots**. The tourist industry provides **employment** opportunities for millions of people such as airline pilots, hotel owners and tour guides. Tourism also encourages a **multiplier effect** (Figure 5.5 below) in terms of jobs and other attractions.

```
                    ┌─────────────┐
                    │ HOTEL BUILT │
                    └─────────────┘
```

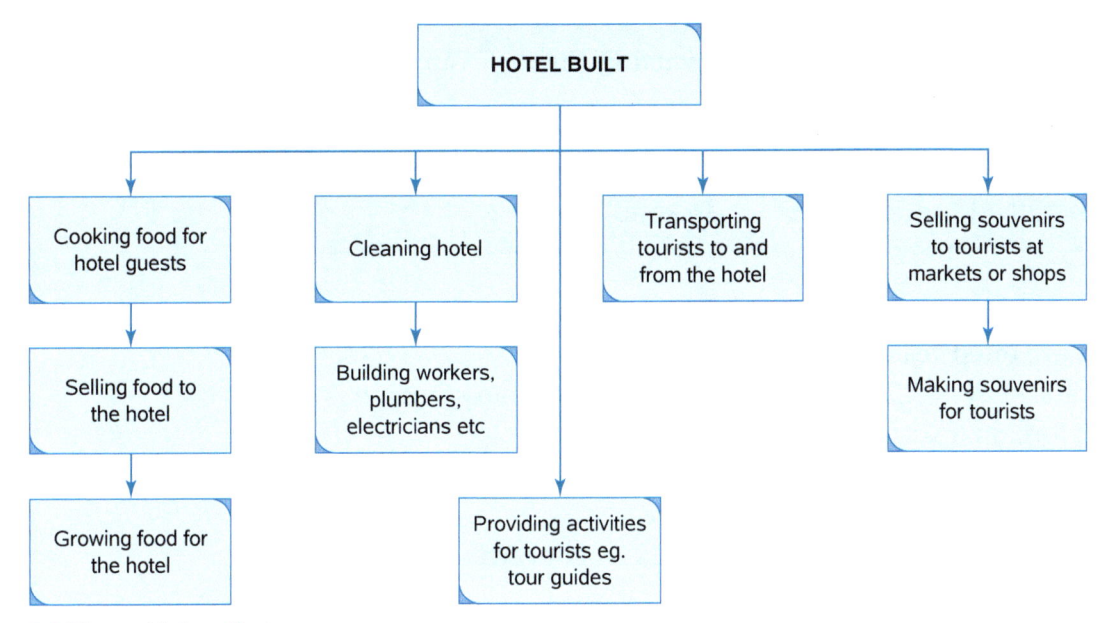

- Cooking food for hotel guests
- Cleaning hotel
- Transporting tourists to and from the hotel
- Selling souvenirs to tourists at markets or shops
- Selling food to the hotel
- Building workers, plumbers, electricians etc
- Making souvenirs for tourists
- Growing food for the hotel
- Providing activities for tourists eg. tour guides

5.5 The multiplier effect

## 5.7 Negative impacts of tourism

Tourism is **seasonal** in many places. Tourists visit these places only at certain times of the year for instance, ski resorts become popular in winter when the snow is best. Many places become most crowded with tourists in the **peak season** such as the school holidays. During the rest of the year – the **off-season** – the number of tourists might be very low. This means employment in the tourism industry is also often seasonal. Therefore it may be hard to depend on tourism for a livelihood.

The countries which depend on tourism for their GDP suffer badly when tourists are put off those destinations by international worries. Terrorist threats or natural disasters such as the 2004 tsunami can put off tourists from visiting those places. A sudden decline in tourists can lead to a **de-multiplier effect**. Many services at tourist resorts such as hotels are owned and run by foreign companies such as Hilton and Sheraton. Most of the money they make goes to the transnational hotel company rather than to the country the hotel is in. This is **leakage**. It means the country may lose a large amount of the money made by tourism.

At honeypot sites crowds of tourists on foot or in cars and coaches may cause **congestion** on paths and roads. Too many cars and coaches can increase the **air pollution** and **noise pollution.** Too many people on the paths around a honeypot site for example Machu Picchu, Peru, may lead to **erosion** by wearing away the paths. Tourists often have a cultural impact on the destination countries too as they introduce new languages, customs and dress.

### KEY WORDS

**Season** a part of the year, such as summer and winter

**Traditional** a way of life or a style which has not changed over the years

## 5 Leisure and tourism

**10** Copy and complete the sentences below using the appropriate word from the following options.

| Despite | Although | Although | On the other hand |
| On the other hand | However | Despite | |

a _____ tourism provides employment for millions around the world, these jobs are often seasonal.
b Leakage is caused by TNCs _____ these companies provide important foreign investment.
c Money from tourism supports local communities _____ large amounts of money are lost through leakage.
d Countries keep trying to attract tourists _____ concerns about terrorism.
e _____ the high levels of congestion in peak season, people keep visiting tourist honeypots.
f _____ tourists may have a cultural impact on a country, they also bring important foreign exchange.
g The big hotels in poor countries have running water and electricity _____ local villages may still depend on dirty rivers for their water supply.

**11** What are the positive and negative impacts of tourism on Barbados? Copy and complete the mind map below (Figure 5.6) with the ideas from the table below and also add your own ideas.

| More money made from tourism than sugarcane | Mangrove swamps are being cleared for hotels to be built. | Cruise liners bring many more people to Bridgetown. | Ecotourism helps conserve the rainforest |
| A new National Park is being made | Cruise passengers do not use local restaurants and entertainment. | International hotels allow leakage | |
| The economy becomes overdependent on tourism | More diverse economy | International hotel chains bring foreign investment | |

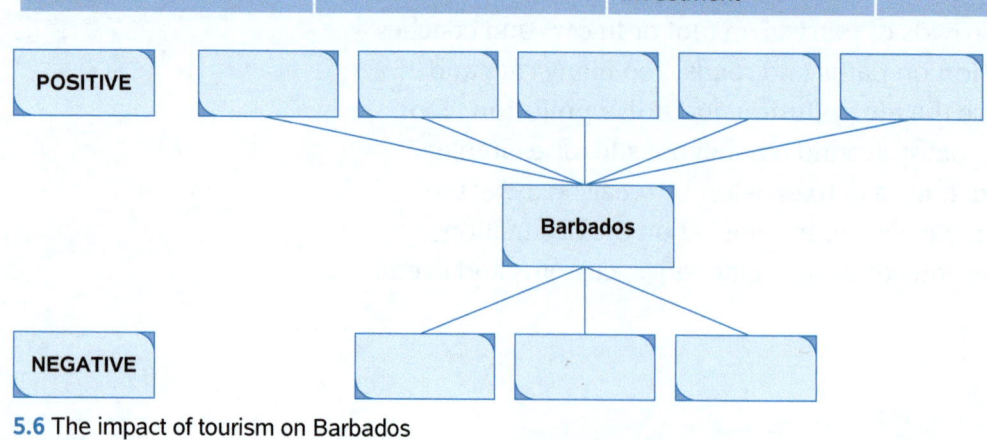

POSITIVE

Barbados

NEGATIVE

5.6 The impact of tourism on Barbados

## 5.8 Sustainable tourism

**Sustainable tourism** tries to reduce the negative impact of tourists so attractions can be enjoyed by tourists in the future. Sustainable tourism requires careful **management** of the destinations. This means controlling how the area is used. **Ecotourism** is a form of sustainable tourism. Ecotourists may aim to help the local communities by using local transport and hotels rather than international chains. They may also choose their transportation carefully to reduce air pollution. Many ecotourism holidays support conservation in certain areas.

> **KEY WORD**
>
> **Sustainable** an activity that can be maintained without destroying the chance of it being continued in the future.

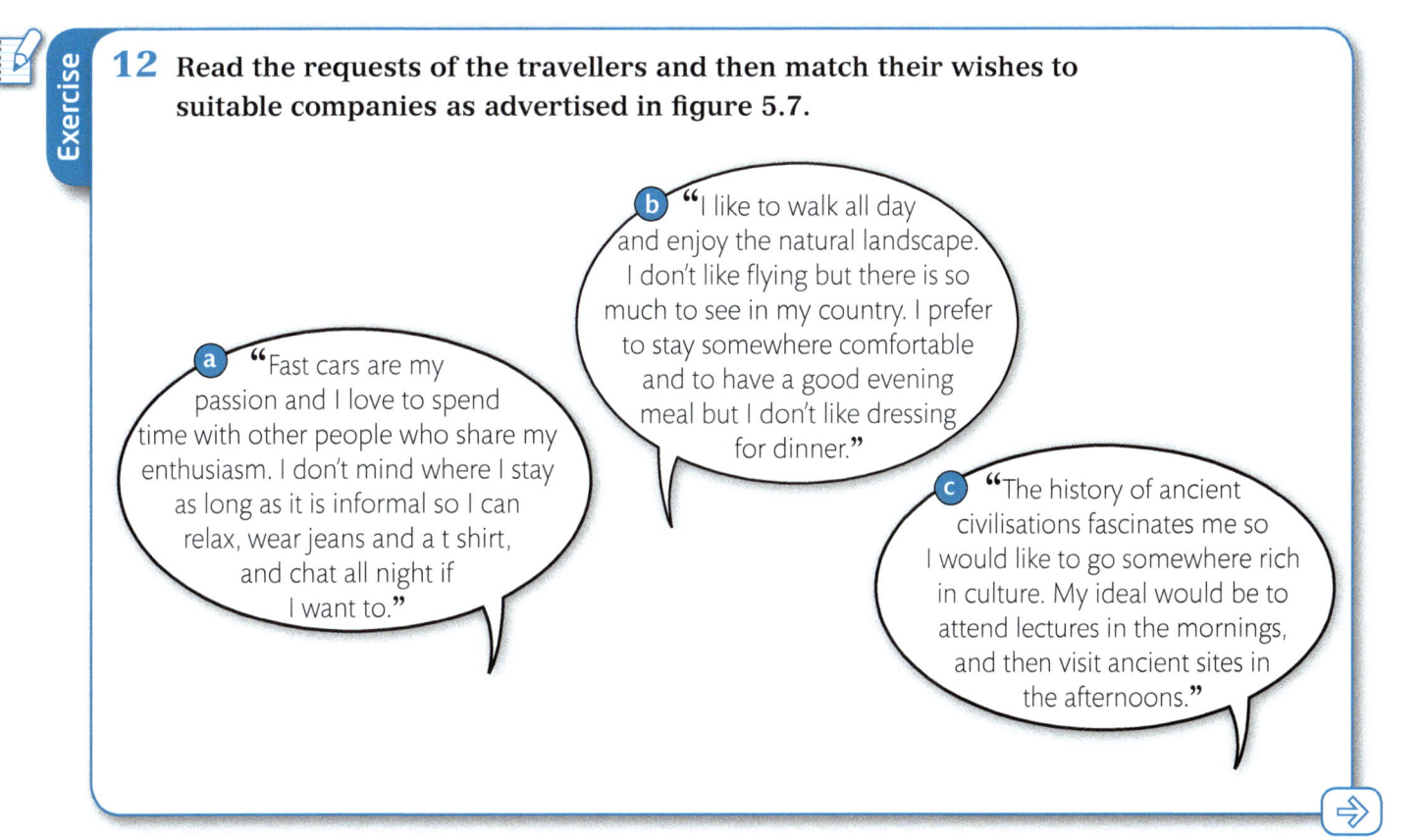

## 5.9 National Parks

**National Parks** are found all over the world. They are areas of the countryside where the natural landscape is being protected and carefully managed. Money from tourists visiting National Parks is often used to help conservation. Yellowstone National Park, USA was the world's first National Park and it is one of the largest. It is an area of wilderness and no people are allowed to live in the area. The Peak District was the UK's first National Park in 1951. It is much smaller than Yellowstone but the Park also includes many small towns, villages and farms. People live and work in this National Park. Part of The Great Barrier Reef in Australia is a marine National Park.

**Exercise**

**12** Read the requests of the travellers and then match their wishes to suitable companies as advertised in figure 5.7.

**a** "Fast cars are my passion and I love to spend time with other people who share my enthusiasm. I don't mind where I stay as long as it is informal so I can relax, wear jeans and a t shirt, and chat all night if I want to."

**b** "I like to walk all day and enjoy the natural landscape. I don't like flying but there is so much to see in my country. I prefer to stay somewhere comfortable and to have a good evening meal but I don't like dressing for dinner."

**c** "The history of ancient civilisations fascinates me so I would like to go somewhere rich in culture. My ideal would be to attend lectures in the mornings, and then visit ancient sites in the afternoons."

# 5 Leisure and tourism

**d** "I only have a few days but would love to go somewhere different and enjoy some shopping – retail therapy will do me good and give me some energy for the next lot of work. I love exotic food and luxury hotels."

**e** "I would like to retrace the footsteps of the great discoverers. I would prefer to travel as they did, not by plane, and to stay in accommodation which is typical of the places we pass through. I would like join an organised tour as it could be dangerous on my own."

**f** "I have already done bungee jumping, paragliding and sky diving in New Zealand and Australia, so my next challenge is to go white water rafting. Seeing wildlife would be a real bonus."

**g** "I want to spend a long weekend relaxing, away from it all. No car, no computer, no pressure. I want to walk everywhere and to cook what I want to eat from locally grown produce."

**h** "In my two week holiday I want to experience some of the natural wonders of the world although I am very aware that tourism can destroy them. The best solution for me would be to find a holiday which uses local accommodation, food, transport and tour guides so that neither the environment nor the local way of life are threatened."

**i** "We like to take our own car when we go on holiday. We have two young children so we like to be somewhere near water so that we can swim and sunbathe. We like to drive to places of interest once or twice during the holiday, but the most important thing is to have quality time as a family."

**Costa Rica** invites young people to come and live the life of a villager for 3 months. You will eat and sleep with a family and help with conservation in a nature reserve. Find out more at:
www.Costa-Rica-Experience.com

Dream setting in the **ITALIAN LAKES**. Self-catering, well-equipped villa on beautiful Lake Garda just 5 minutes walk from Desenzano with its grand piazza and lakeside ice cream bars and pizza restaurants. Easy day drives to Venice, Verona and Milan. Perfect for children and adults.
www.villas-in-italy.eu

Shop until you drop in Hong Kong, Tokyo, New York or London! Your chosen destination for 3-5 nights offers endless opportunities to sightsee, window shop, and of course, to buy in famous stores, malls and street markets. Shops, gourmet restaurants and chic bars are on the doorstep of your luxury hotel.
www.City-sHopping.com

Get away from the buzz of your working life in a Welsh farm cottage situated in the Brecon Beacons. Walk along the River Usk, climb to the top of Pen y Fan, or enjoy a stroll through the unspoilt countryside. Local produce is available from the farm, which you can cook on a wood burning stove.
www.Welsh-hideaway-cottages.co.uk

Cross Asia from west to east or east to west just like the traders of the past. Travel by train and camel caravan to the ancient cities of the Silk Route.
www.Oriental-escapes.com

Share your love of racing cars with other like-minded fans at the Le Mans 24 hour racetrack. Meet the teams and smell the tension during the race on our 4 star campsite right on the circuit.
www.lemans-caraholics.com

See, sample and save when you holiday in our environmentally friendly lodge in Port Douglas, Australia. Basic accommodation in timber huts and menus based on local produce. Trips, escorted by local guides include scuba diving at the Great Barrier Reef, a visit to an opal mine and a safari in a wildlife park with koalas, crocodiles, kangaroos and possums.
www.Oz eco-holidays.au

Enjoy a relaxing evening with good food and wine beside a blazing log fire after a day climbing the peaks of the Lake District. The Black Sheep Pub, Bowness has comfortable rooms and offers bed and breakfast, and dinner by arrangement to its guests.
www.Black-Sheep.co.uk

A holiday with a difference in Zambia. Test your nerve in a kayak or on a raft shooting the rapids of the Zambesi River. You can also experience the thrill of big game watching on safari. After your adventures you can relax in our luxurious holiday village.
www.zambia-adventure.com

Explore the Eastern Mediterranean in luxury on our cruise ship 'Cleopatra'. You will learn about Ancient **Greece, Byzantium and Egypt** in talks given by our on-board historian, and will then visit the ancient sites. Every morning you will awake to a new place and a new experience. Truly a voyage to remember!
www.cleopatra-cruises.com

5.7 Holiday advertisements

**Exercise 13** Match the terms below with the correct definitions and copy into your notebook.

1 The free time when someone is not working.
2 Tourism where people try to limit their impact on the local people and natural environment.
3 Travel more than 5 hours flying time from home.
4 A holiday booked through an agent which includes accommodation, travel, food and activities.
5 Holidays within the home country.

a Eco-tourism
b Package holiday
c Leisure time
d Domestic tourism
e Long haul

## 5 • Leisure and tourism

**14** Copy and complete the crossword below using the clues below.

**Across:**
1. Tourism limiting the impacts on people and the environment.
3. Tourism only at certain times of the year.
8. Transport, accommodation, food and activities all arranged and included in one price.
9. Somewhere attracting large numbers of tourists.
10. Time when someone is not working.
11. Waste dropped on the ground by people.
13. Management of resources for use in the future.
14. Type of holiday involving exciting and extreme experiences.

**Down:**
2. Roads, airports, electricity, water etc.
4. Transnational companies taking money out of a country.
5. Type of industry providing a service.
6. Tourism within the home country.
7. A person travelling away from home for at least one night.
12. A city or town area.

## Talking points

Why is tourism the major industry for many countries?

What are the dangers of relying on tourism for one's income

a) as an individual and
b) as a country?

What are the advantages and disadvantages of being a tourist destination?

Why have adventure tourism and eco-tourism become more popular in recent years?

### Extension

**Internet Search: Find out about…**

Tourist destinations

Tourist attractions

Revenue from tourism in your country of birth

Think about the questions from the start of the chapter. Can you answer these now?

- Who is a tourist?
- Where are the most popular tourist destinations?
- Why is tourism growing?
- What is seasonal employment?
- When were National Parks created?

# 6 Energy and water resources

**In this chapter you will answer...**
- What are fossil fuels?
- Who uses fuelwood?
- Where are hydroelectric power stations?
- Why is there an energy crisis?
- When are there water shortages?

## KEY WORDS

Sources of energy are **renewable** or **non-renewable**. People today need more and more energy and water for their daily lives

Where the demand for energy and water is greater than the supply we face an **energy crisis** and water **shortages**

## 6.1 Sources of energy

People need energy for cooking, heat, light, transport, work and entertainment. **Non-renewable** sources of energy will eventually run out. They are being used faster than they can form. This means they are **finite**. **Renewable** sources of energy will never run out or stop. This means they are **infinite**.

## 6.2 Non-renewable energy sources

Coal, oil and natural gas are **fossil fuels**. Fossil fuels take millions of years to form. They have been formed by the pressure of rocks on layers of dead plants and animals.

Fossil fuels are removed from the ground by **mining**. This is a **primary industry**. They can be expensive to mine if they are very deep underground. People are using the earth's fossil fuels faster than they can be made. This means that the supplies will eventually run out.

## KEY WORDS

**Renewable** a source of energy that will never run out or stop

**Non-renewable** a source of energy that will eventually run out

**Fossil fuel** fuels formed by the pressure of rocks on layers of dead plants and animals over millions of years

**Greenhouse gas** a gas which absorbs the heat radiated from the earth's surface

**Global warming** the increase in the average temperature of the earth's atmosphere

**Resource** a supply of a material that can be used by people for example coal, water, gold

**Fuel** something that is burned to provide energy

### Exercise

1. Match the words below with their meanings then copy the completed definition into your notebook.

   1 finite           a to exhaust
   2 renewable        b soak up
   3 fuel             c non-renewable
   4 to run out       d heat
   5 thermal          e to produce
   6 absorb           f infinite
   7 to generate      g energy source

## 6.3 Locating a thermal power station

Fossil fuels are burned in thermal **power stations** to produce heat for electricity. Water is heated to form steam. The steam turns **turbines** to produce electricity. Thermal power stations are located near sources of water, as water is needed to produce steam.

Fossil fuels contain **carbon**. When the fuel is burned in a **thermal** power station to provide energy, **carbon dioxide** gas is produced. This is a **greenhouse gas**. Burning fossil fuels also produces $SO_2$ (sulphur dioxide) gases. The power stations have tall chimneys to put these gases higher into the **atmosphere**. This is to reduce air pollution to the area surrounding the power station. Thermal power stations are usually on the **rural-urban fringe**. They are on the edge of large urban areas. This reduces air pollution in the urban area. There are also enough people nearby to work in the power station. Thermal power stations need good communications. Coal is **imported** by road or rail; oil and gas are imported by pipelines.

### KEY WORDS

**Thermal** producing heat

**Turbine** a machine with blades that are turned round by steam, water or air to produce electricity

**Atmosphere** the gases which surround the Earth

## 6.4 Fuelwood

**Fuelwood** is wood from trees. The wood is burned to produce heat for cooking and keeping warm. In many poorer countries fuelwood is the most important source of energy. This may be because there are no fossil fuels available or they are too expensive to mine. The area may not be suitable for renewable energy sources. Even fuelwood is running out in some places. Where populations have rapidly increased more and more trees have been cut down for fuel. The trees do not grow back fast enough, which means people have to walk further and further to find fuelwood. Cutting down the trees also means the ground is easily eroded by wind and rain.

## 6.5 Greenhouse gases

When fuelwood and fossil fuels are burned **carbon dioxide** gas is produced. This is a **greenhouse gas**. Carbon dioxide gas is like glass in a greenhouse. The air inside a greenhouse is warmer than the air outside. This gas absorbs the heat **radiated** from the earth's surface. This causes the **atmosphere** to get warmer.

**Global warming** is the increase in the average temperature of the earth's atmosphere. This is caused by the increase in the amount of greenhouse gases.

## 6 · Energy and water resources

> **Exercise 2** Copy and complete the paragraph below by giving the passive of the verb in the brackets.
>
> When fossil fuels are *burned*, heat and carbon dioxide _are produced_ (to produce). The heat _____ (to use) to turn water into steam. Turbines _____ (to turn) by the steam and electricity _____ (to generate).
>
> The radiation from the earth _____ (to absorb) by carbon dioxide gas. The atmosphere _____ (to heat) and the earth becomes warmer.
>
> Fossil fuels _____ (to extract) faster than they form so they are running out.

### 6.6 Renewable energy sources

**Renewable** energy sources will never run out. They are infinite. **Geothermal** energy (geo = earth; thermal = heat) comes from heat beneath the surface of the earth. The heat is from **magma**. This is rock which is so hot (1000°C) it has melted. Water is piped down into the magma. It is heated to steam. The steam is used to heat buildings or create electricity. Geothermal power can only be used in a few places on earth in places such as Iceland. The earth's crust has to be thin so pipes can reach the magma.

**Wind** power uses wind to turn **windmills**. These generate electricity. When the wind is strong a lot of electricity can be produced. Wind is stronger on high land or at sea. However, the wind does not always blow. Therefore this energy source does not always work.

**Solar** power is energy from the **sun**. Houses and industries use **solar panels** to trap the heat and light from the sun. This source of energy works best during the daytime and in very sunny places. **Biogas** is given off when plants rot. This gas can be trapped and burned to produce electricity

**Hydroelectricity** is created by falling water (hydro = water). A **dam** is a wall built across a river. The dam holds back the river water. This forms a lake called a **reservoir** behind the dam. Water falls down through pipes in the dam onto **turbines**. These turn to create electricity.

> **KEY WORD**
>
> **Dam** a wall built across a river to control the flow

Energy and water resources • 6

**3** Match the numbers on the diagram with the options from the box below. Copy your answers into your notebook.

**6.1** Sources of energy

| magma | **Wind power** | turbine |
| dam | steam | reservoir |
| **Geothermal power station** | windmill | **Hydroelectric power station** |

**4** Answer the clues below then find the words in the word search.

a _____ dioxide gas is produced when fuels are burned.
b These take millions of years to form and are non-renewable sources of energy.
c A black, solid fossil fuel.
d The renewable energy from heat beneath the earth's surface.
e A lake formed as a store of water for producing energy.
f Gas given off when vegetation rots.
g A source of energy that will never run out.
h Energy from the sun.
i These are turned by the wind.
j The molten rock beneath the earth's surface.
k Energy produced by falling water.
l A wall built across a river.

| G | T | Y | S | U | G | J | S | D | G | C | V | W |
| E | Q | A | O | F | J | C | A | R | B | O | N | A |
| O | E | P | L | O | I | O | R | R | W | V | X | E |
| T | Y | U | A | L | K | A | F | E | C | B | B | E |
| H | Y | D | R | O | E | L | E | C | T | R | I | C |
| E | D | T | A | E | K | I | W | H | T | E | O | M |
| R | E | S | E | R | V | O | I | R | Y | N | G | N |
| M | A | G | M | A | W | L | N | A | N | E | A | E |
| A | C | A | L | R | O | E | D | J | M | W | S | J |
| L | Z | V | P | Y | D | A | M | K | S | A | D | G |
| D | H | X | D | U | E | D | I | A | O | B | I | S |
| S | U | V | V | N | N | E | L | I | I | L | J | T |
| A | K | F | O | S | S | I | L | F | U | E | L | A |

77

## 6 • Energy and water resources

### 6.7 Locating a hydroelectric power station

Hydroelectric power is generated by water falling down through a **dam**. A dam is built across a large river to form a reservoir. The reservoir is a large lake which stores water. Hydroelectric power stations are built where there is a lot of water. They are often in **mountain** areas. **Large rivers**, or **melting snow** and **heavy rain** provide a lot of water to the rivers and reservoirs. Rivers in mountain areas flow through **steep sided valleys**. This makes it easier to build a dam. A reservoir floods an area of land in a valley. An area of **low population density** is ideal so few villages or farmlands are flooded.

> **Exercise**
>
> **5** Use ideas from the information above to give reasons why Figure 6.2 is an ideal site for a HEP station.
>
> 6.2 A Hydroelectric power (HEP) station

### 6.8 Nuclear power

Uranium and plutonium are the raw materials for **nuclear power**. Nuclear energy comes from splitting (**fission**) **atoms** of uranium or plutonium. This produces a very large amount of energy. No gas is produced so nuclear power does not cause global warming. The waste materials are very **radioactive**. Radioactivity can cause **cancer** in people. This waste has to be very carefully stored so that the radioactivity cannot escape.

**KEY WORDS**

**Nuclear** power created by splitting atoms

**Radioactivity** high energy particles given off by waste materials of nuclear power

### 6.9 Locating a nuclear power station

A nuclear power station has to be located on flat land. It must not be somewhere which experiences earthquakes. There needs to be a good water supply for cooling the reactor and a workforce nearby. Transport needs to be good so the raw materials can be imported and the waste material exported. It should be far enough from towns and cities so people are not worried about leaking radioactivity.

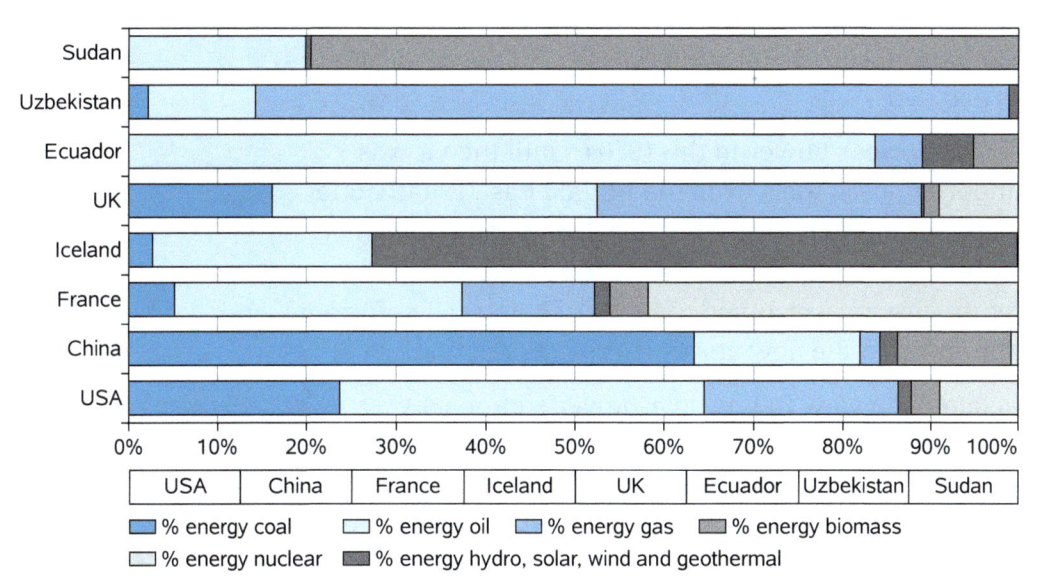

6.3 Sources of energy in selected countries

Legend:
- % energy coal
- % energy oil
- % energy gas
- % energy biomass
- % energy nuclear
- % energy hydro, solar, wind and geothermal

## Nuclear energy in France: No oil. No gas. No coal. No choice.

**6** Put the paragraphs below into order in your notebooks. The 'A' paragraph is in its correct place.

A The splitting of the atom in 1932 marked the beginning of the nuclear age. The energy released by the **fission** of small amounts of uranium offered a cheap alternative to the non-renewable sources. The greatest drawback to nuclear power, however, is the **radioactive** waste, which causes long term **contamination**.

B In April 1986 the devastating accident at Chernobyl, Ukraine highlighted the dangers of radioactivity. European governments and their populations began to question the idea of nuclear power as the answer to the increasing demand for electricity.

C In the first decade of the 21st century France is the second largest producer of nuclear energy, after the USA. France produces more electricity than the domestic market consumes so it exports electricity to its European neighbours. In the eyes of its inhabitants, and in the eyes of the world, French nuclear power policy is a success story.

D The question of what to do with the radioactive waste threatened to upset the situation. Initially, the plan was to bury the waste permanently on sites in France. The thought of contaminating French soil caused protests and a revised plan was accepted. The waste was stored so that parts of it could be recycled and further

**Note**
Hint: Highlight references to dates, time and places. Then look at the tenses used: the past perfect tense (had done) will be earlier in sequence than the simple past (did) or the present tense (does).

research could be undertaken. A full scale rejection of the nuclear programme was avoided.

E  France developed its nuclear power in the 1970s. Until then it was dependent on imported fossil fuels from the Middle East. It had none itself. Other governments had had to convince their populations that nuclear power was a safe and economical way to answer the demand for energy. However the French welcomed the idea of being self sufficient, and of leading the world in the new age of energy production.

F  By inviting local people to view the nuclear power stations, by emphasising the benefits to the community in terms of employment and commerce, by solving the problem of nuclear waste disposal in public opinion, and by exploiting the prospect of the cheapest electricity in Europe through the 1990s, successive French governments have kept the French people's vote for nuclear power. By the end of the 20th century France had 58 functioning nuclear power plants.

G  The French government did not react in the same way to the Chernobyl disaster. It published reports on the prevailing winds that had kept the radioactive emissions away from French soil. The huge investment in nuclear power meant that there was no going back to traditional sources of energy, and the French government had to ensure that French public opinion stayed positive towards nuclear energy.

**7  Comprehension questions:**

a  What are the non-renewable sources of energy?
b  What is the biggest problem with nuclear power?
c  Give 3 ways in which the French government made nuclear energy popular.
d  How did the accident at Chernobyl influence other countries?
e  How did France overcome worries about permanent contamination of French soil?
f  How many nuclear power stations did France have in 1999?
g  Apart from providing electricity for its own population, how does France benefit from its nuclear power policy?

**8  Which of the following statements are advantages (A) or disadvantages (D) of nuclear power? Copy and complete the table below in your notebook.**

| | |
|---|---|
| Nuclear power stations can produce more energy than thermal power stations | |
| Waste material is radioactive and very dangerous | |
| No gases are given off when energy is produced | |
| Storing the waste materials is very expensive | |
| It is a clean fuel | |
| A lot of attention is paid to safety and security. | |

## Exercise

**9** Study Figure 6.3 on page 79. Are the following statements true or false? Copy the correct statements in your notebook.

a Over 80% of Uzbekistan's energy is from oil.
b The USA depends more on coal than China.
c Sudan uses more fuelwood than the other countries.
d France gains over 40% of its energy from nuclear power.
e The UK uses more renewable sources of energy than Iceland.
f Sudan is very dependent on hydroelectricity for its energy.
g The UK gains a greater amount of its energy from natural gas than China.
h Oil is the main source of energy in Ecuador.
i China gains over 60% of its energy from burning coal.

## 6.10 Energy crisis

The world's population is growing rapidly. People now need more energy for their daily lives. Most of this energy comes from **fossil fuels**. However fossil fuels are non-renewable and will eventually run out. Renewable energy sources do not produce as much energy as fossil fuels and they are only available in certain places. If there are not enough sources of energy in the future then there could be an **energy crisis**.

## 6.11 Sources of water

People use water in their homes for drinking, washing, cleaning and cooking. These are **domestic** uses of water. Farmers use water for **irrigation** of crops and for feeding livestock. Industries use water as a **raw material** for cooling or for producing steam for energy. Water falls as rain, snow or hail. It is stored on the earth's surface in rivers (**channel stores**) and in lakes, reservoirs, sea and ice (**surface stores**). Fresh water is stored in the rocks as **groundwater stores**.

## 6.12 Water shortages

Supplies of water are not evenly distributed across the world. A **water surplus** is where there is more water than people need. A **water deficit** is where there is less water than people need. **Wells** bring the groundwater to the surface. In many places people are using up the groundwater stores faster than they are being refilled by rain. This means that groundwater becomes harder to find. A **drought** is a long period of time without rainfall. This means the groundwater stores may not fill up for years. The surface stores of water will also dry up. This can lead to **water shortages**. Where the water shortages last a long time the farmers are unable to grow crops, industries may not be able to run, and the health of people may suffer. A **water crisis** may develop in areas where there is not enough water to meet the needs of a population.

### KEY WORDS

**Channel store** water stored in rivers and streams

**Surface store** water stored on the earth's surface in lakes, oceans and ice

**Groundwater store** water stored in rocks beneath the earth's surface

**Well** a hole in the ground which reaches stores of groundwater

**Irrigation** adding water to crops

**Water surplus** when there is more water than people need

**Water deficit** when there is less water than people need

# 6 ● Energy and water resources

## 6.13 Competition for water

A **drainage basin** is the area drained by a river and its **tributaries**. Rivers carry water from high land (**upstream** sources) to the sea (**downstream**). Tributaries are smaller rivers which join a large river. Some rivers run through several countries. These are **transnational rivers**. If people upstream build dams across the river to form a reservoir then they can control their water supply. However they can also control the water supply to the areas downstream. This can cause major problems in countries with transnational rivers.

> **KEY WORDS**
>
> **Drainage basin** the area drained by a river and its tributaries
>
> **Transnational river** a river which runs through several different countries

### Whose water is it anyway?

The River Euphrates and the River Tigris are transnational rivers. They both have their sources in Turkey. They then flow downstream south east through Syria and Iraq to their delta on the Persian Gulf. The Rivers Tigris – Euphrates provide fresh water for farmers and cities. Today growing populations need more water for food production and electricity for domestic and industrial use. Drought in the region during the hot summer months makes the need more important.

The South eastern Anatolia Development Project in Turkey plans to use the waters of the Euphrates and Tigris to produce hydroelectric power and to irrigate the arid lands of Anatolia. 22 dams have been constructed on the two rivers and 19 hydroelectric power stations. These rivers will provide 22% of Turkey's electricity by 2020. However, Syria and Iraq rely on the flow of water in these rivers for their own agriculture, domestic use and power. These countries are concerned about Turkey's project.

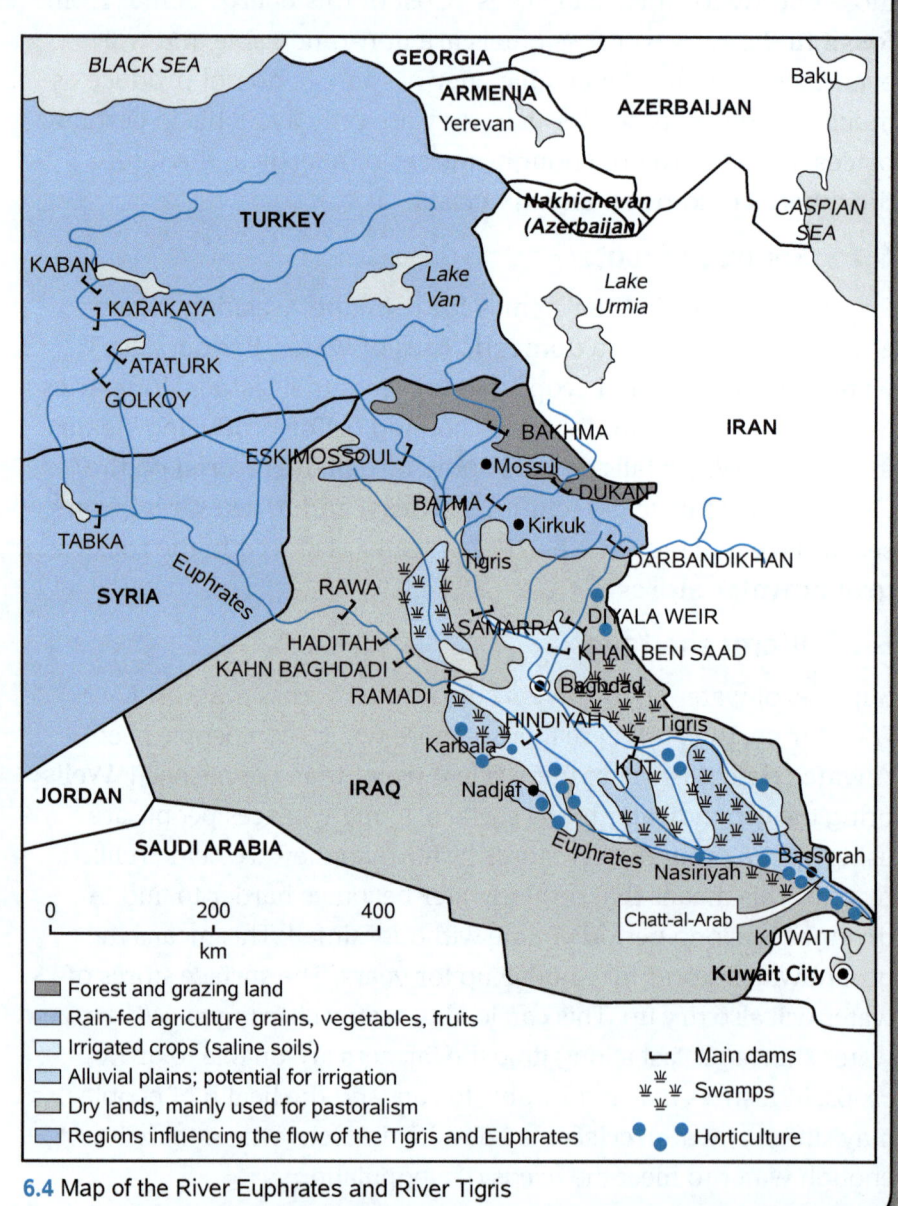

**6.4** Map of the River Euphrates and River Tigris

## Language

**Interrogatives: Who? Whom? Which? Whose?**

These interrogatives (question words) are used to ask questions about persons or things.

**Who?** is used to find out the person/people or subject of an action. It is always the subject of the verb in the sentence.

**Whom?** is used to find out about the person/ people that are the object of the verb. It can be used with a preposition – to whom, from whom, on whom etc.

**Which?** is used to identify something from two or more possible answers. It can be used as an interrogative adjective in front of a noun. It can also be used after a preposition.

**Whose?** is used to find out the possessor or owner of an idea or thing.

## Exercise

**10** Find the appropriate missing interrogative. When you have copied the completed sentences into your notebook, answer the questions using the information in this chapter.

a Through w____ countries does the Euphrates flow?

b On w____ must Syria rely for most of its water supply?

c W__ relies most on the Euphrates for irrigation?

d W__ of these rivers is prone to flooding?

e To w____ could Syria and Iraq appeal to resolve the situation?

f W____ of Turkey's regions suffers badly from lack of development, drought and unemployment?

g W_____ hydroelectricity comes mainly from the dams on the Euphrates and its tributaries?

### Extension

**11** Find the correct option from each column below and copy into your notebook.

| Source | Renewable/ non renewable | Non-polluting/ polluting | Reliable/ unreliable | Plentiful/ Scarce | Cheap/ expensive |
|---|---|---|---|---|---|
| fuelwood | | | | | |
| water | | | | | |
| wind | | | | | |
| biogas | | | | | |
| solar | | | | | |
| geothermal | | | | | |
| nuclear | | | | | |
| oil | | | | | |
| natural gas | | | | | |
| coal | | | | | |

## 6 • Energy and water resources

**Exercise**

Find the answers to the questions below and explain the reason for each choice in your notebooks.

**12** Which site would be best for a geothermal power station?
   a  in the mountains away from towns and villages
   b  on a plain in the open countryside
   c  on the rural-urban fringe

**13** Groundwater is:
   a  more accessible than water in rivers
   b  less accessible than water in rivers
   c  as accessible as water in lakes and reservoirs

**14** Global warming is a result of:
   a  too much carbon dioxide in the atmosphere
   b  too many hot summers
   c  too much solar energy

**15** A water crisis arises when:
   a  water is used to generate hydroelectric power
   b  irrigation reduces the water flow in rivers
   c  stores of water are not refilled by rainfall and melting snow

**16** Match the energy source in the box below to the correct description.
   a  A solid that was formed from decomposed and fossilised vegetation over millions of years.
   b  Atoms are split apart to generate heat but not producing any polluting gases.
   c  The power from falling water.
   d  Heat from magma beneath the earth's surface which is used to produce high powered steam.
   e  A gas given off when vegetation has decayed over millions of years.

| Nuclear power | Geothermal power | Natural Gas | Coal | Hydroelectric power |

# Energy and water resources 6

**17** Copy and complete the flow chart below with the appropriate stages in energy production using words from the grid below. (HINT: waste materials go in the circles).

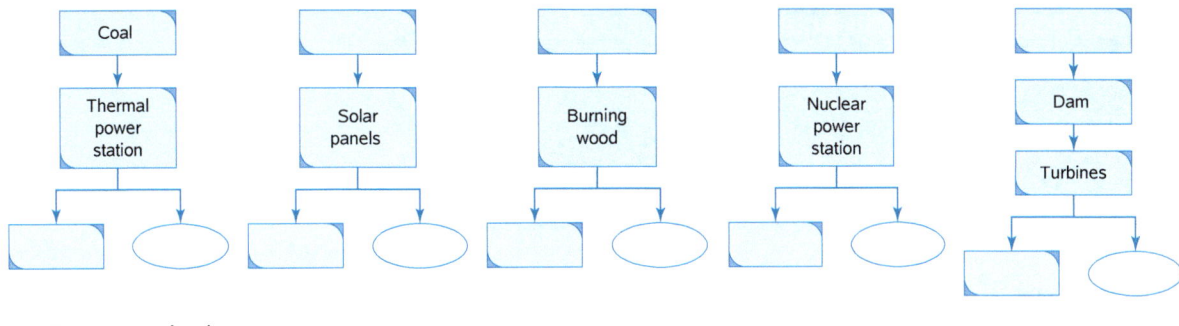

```
[    ]        [    ]        [    ]        [    ]        [    ]
  ↓             ↓             ↓             ↓             ↓
Thermal       Solar         Burning       Nuclear         Dam
power         panels         wood          power           ↓
station                                    station       Turbines
  ↓             ↓             ↓             ↓             ↓
[ ] ( )       [ ] ( )       [ ] ( )       [ ] ( )       [ ] ( )
```

**6.5** Energy production

| electricity | sun | radioactive waste | carbon dioxide |
| heat | carbon dioxide | fuelwood | uranium |
| heat | water | heat | heat |

## Talking points

Why is energy crucial for a country's development?

How can energy consumption be reduced
a) for a family and b) for a country?

Discuss the benefits of electric cars, trams and bicycles?

Do you think nuclear is the fuel of the future?

### Extension

Internet search: Find out about...

Nuclear energy
Renewable sources of energy
Fossil fuels

Think about these questions from the start of the chapter. Can you answer these now?

- What are fossil fuels?
- Who uses fuelwood?
- Where are hydroelectric power stations?
- Why is there an energy crisis?
- When are there water shortages?

# 7 Plate tectonics

**In this chapter you will answer...**
- What are tectonic plates?
- Where do plates move apart?
- Why do earthquakes occur?
- Who chooses to live on plate boundaries?

## 7.1 Structure of the earth

The centre of the earth is called the **core**. It is very, very hot (about 6000°C). The heat from the earth's core has melted a layer of rock around it. This layer of rock is the **mantle**. The **molten** rock is **magma**.

Magma is like a thick liquid that is heated by the core. The hottest magma rises away from the core towards the earth's surface. As it gets nearer the surface of the earth it cools and sinks back down towards the core. These patterns of movement are **convection currents**. The **crust** is the solid surface of the earth. The earth's crust is broken into several very large pieces called **tectonic plates**, which float on the magma in the mantle. The convection currents cause the plates to move around very slowly.

### KEY WORD
**Tectonic plates** are sections of the earth's crust. **Convection** currents cause them to move. Movement of the plates causes earthquakes and volcanic eruptions.

### KEY WORDS
**Crust** the solid surface of the earth

**Plate** a large section of the earth's crust

**Magma** molten rock beneath the crust

**Earthquake** shaking of the crust as a result of the sudden movement of plates

**Volcano** a mountain formed by magma being released at the earth's surface

**To melt** to change a solid to a liquid

**Molten** something that has been changed to a liquid

### Language

Basic word stems get more precise meanings when they take prefixes. Sometimes the new words are used more often than the original words. Learning the meaning of prefixes is a good way to increase your vocabulary and to work out the meaning of words you have not met before.

**Common prefixes:**
- **con-** – moving together to become one
- **di-** – moving apart into several pieces
- **e/ex-** – moving out of
- **sub-** – moving under
- **trans-** – moving across

Stem verbs:

| | |
|---|---|
| To verge – to move in a certain direction | to *con*verge – to move together<br>to *di*verge – to move apart |
| To merge – to unite | To *sub*merge – to go under the surface |
| To rupture – to burst | To *e*rupt – to burst out of |
| To duct – to lead/channel | To *sub*duct – to channel under |
| To form – to give shape to something | To *trans*form – to change from one form to another |

86

## 1 Complete the table below by filling in the missing words.

| verb | noun | adjective |
|---|---|---|
|  |  | convergent |
|  | divergence |  |
|  |  | eruptible/eruptive |
| subduct |  | ——— |
|  | transformation | transformable/transformative |

## 7.2 Types of crust

The crust is the solid surface of the earth. There are two types of crust. The **oceanic crust** is the surface of the earth under the sea and the **continental crust** which is the land that we stand on. Most of the Eurasian plate is continental crust. The Pacific plate is just oceanic crust. However a tectonic plate can have both oceanic and continental crust.

## 7.3 Plate margins

**Plate margins** are where two tectonic plates meet. Convection currents cause the plates to move around very slowly. **Convergent plate margins** are where convection currents are pushing two plates into each other. This means these plates are converging. **Divergent plate margins** are where two plates are being pulled away from each other. This means they are diverging. At some plate margins two plates are being moved alongside each other. These are **transform plate margins**.

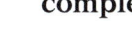

## 2 Match the correct definitions to the words below and copy the completed terms in your notebook.

1 plate　　　　　　　　a movement of hot magma within the mantle
2 crust　　　　　　　　b a large section of the earth's crust
3 magma　　　　　　　c the solid surface of the earth
4 convection current　　d movement away from each other
5 core　　　　　　　　e molten rock beneath the crust
6 divergent　　　　　　f the centre of the earth

## 7 • Plate tectonics

**Exercise 3** One word to the right of each highlighted word *does not* match. Copy the correct word groups in your notebook.

| a boundary | centre  | edge     | margin   |
|------------|---------|----------|----------|
| b diverge  | collide | separate | divide   |
| c depart   | diverge | disperse | converge |
| d crease   | crumple | smooth   | fold     |
| e section  | piece   | part     | whole    |

### 7.4 The distribution of earthquakes and volcanoes

Nearly all earthquakes and volcanoes occur on plate margins. Volcanoes occur where two plates converge (push together) or diverge (pull apart). Earthquakes happen when two plates converge, diverge or move alongside each other. The Pacific Rim of Fire is the edge of the Pacific plate. All around the Pacific Ocean there are volcanoes and earthquakes as the Pacific plate moves. A few volcanoes occur in the middle of plates. These places are called **hotspots**, such as Hawaii.

### 7.5 Divergent plate margins

Divergent plate margins are where two plates are being pulled away from each other. Convection currents in the mantle pull the two plates apart. A gap forms between the plates. Magma rises to the surface in this gap. A **volcanic eruption** occurs when the pressure is released at a weak point. A **mid-ocean ridge** is a line of hills and mountains under the sea. It forms when magma erupts on the seabed at a divergent plate margin. Iceland is an island on a divergent plate margin. The North American plate is being pulled away from the Eurasian plate. Iceland has been formed by volcanic eruptions over millions of years.

**Exercise 4** Work out the anagrams to correctly match them with the right number on the diagram.

a SCURT
b LEMNAT
c GAMMA
d ALCNOVO
e ENTONVICOC RECURNT

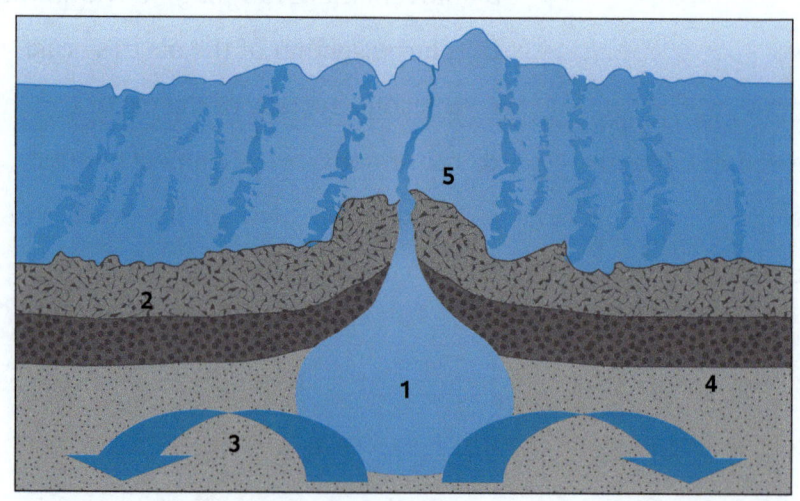

7.1 Divergent plate margin

## 7.6 Convergent plate margins and fold mountains

Convergent plate margins are where two plates are being pushed towards each other. Where the two plates hit each other the continental crust is crushed and folded. It forms lines of mountains called **fold mountains**. The Andes and the Himalayas are examples of fold mountains.

## 7.7 Convergent plate margins and subduction

When oceanic crust is pushed into continental crust the heavier oceanic crust is forced down into the mantle beneath the lighter continental crust. This is **subduction**. This movement of the plates causes earthquakes. The oceanic crust melts in the mantle to become magma. The pressure from subduction pushes magma up through lines of weakness in the continental crust. The magma erupts as violent volcanic eruptions. The Nazca plate is subducting beneath the South American plate. Countries such as Mexico, Peru and Chile experience earthquakes.

**Exercise**

5  Work out the anagrams below and correctly match them with the right number on the diagram.

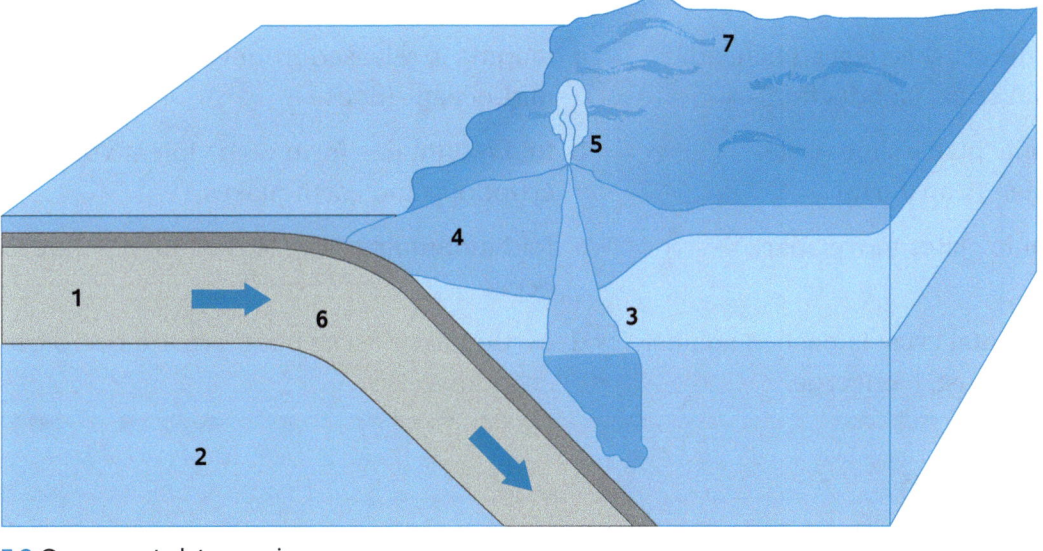

7.2 Convergent plate margin

a  ANICOEC TRUSC

b  TANELM

c  AGAMM

d  TONICALENNT RUSCT

e  OCONVAL

f  DIONSBUTUC

g  OFLD TOIMSNUAN

## 7 • Plate tectonics

### 7.8 Transform plate margins

Transform plate margins are where two plates are moving alongside each other. They move either in opposite directions or in the same direction at different speeds. **Friction** builds up between the two plates. They may move suddenly if the friction is overcome. This sudden movement of the plates causes an earthquake.

No magma rises to the earth's surface at transform plate margins, so no volcanoes are found here. The Pacific plate and the North American plate meet at a transform plate margin in California. This is the San Andreas fault. Los Angeles and San Francisco lie on this plate margin, and so these cities experience many earthquakes.

> **KEY WORD**
>
> **Friction** the resistance between two moving objects

**Language**

**Conditional sentences introduced by 'if'**
When a general or universal truth is being stated, use the *present tense* in the 'if' clause *and* the following clause:
For example 'If water is heated to 100°C, it boils'.

**Exercise**

**6** Choose the correct ending for the following conditional sentences which state general truths about plate tectonics. Copy the correctly matched statements into your notebook.

| | |
|---|---|
| 1 If oceanic crust is pushed beneath continental crust, (subduction) | a magma is released from volcanoes forming mid-ocean ridges. |
| 2 If tectonic plates slide past one another, (transform) | b fold mountains form with violent volcanic eruptions and earthquakes. |
| 3 If tectonic plates move apart, (diverge) | c fold mountains form and major earthquakes occur. |
| 4 If continental crust is pushed against continental crust, (converge) | d earthquakes occur but there are no volcanic eruptions. |

### 7.9 Volcanic eruptions

Volcanoes are found at convergent (subduction) and divergent plate margins. At these plate margins magma rises from the mantle through the crust to the earth's surface. When magma erupts from a volcano it becomes **lava**. **Shield volcanoes** are formed at divergent plate margins. The magma erupts as liquid lava and flows down the sides of the volcano forming gentle slopes. **Composite volcanoes** are at convergent plate margins where subduction occurs. The magma is put under high pressure so this causes violent and explosive volcanic eruptions. The eruptions produce solid lava, ash and hot gases. These form **pyroclastic flows**. A pyroclastic flow (pyro = fire; clastic = rock) moves at 100mph down the side of a volcano. The temperature could be over 1000°C.

# Plate tectonics  7

**Exercise 7** Give the correct comparative of the words in brackets and copy the completed statement into your notebook.

a Oceanic crust is (heavy) and (dense) than continental crust.
b Composite volcanoes are (steep) than shield volcanoes.
c Lava at divergent margins is (runny) than at subduction zones.
d Eruptions at convergent margins are (loud) and (explosive) than at divergent margins.
e Magma is under (high) pressure at convergent margins than at divergent.

**Exercise 8** Choose the correct statements from the options below and copy into your notebook.

a Plates move towards each other at divergent plate margins.
b At a subduction zone the oceanic crust sinks beneath the continental crust.
c Plates move towards each other at convergent plate margins.
d A volcano erupts when mantle in the magma rises through the earth's crust.
e At a subduction zone the continental crust sinks beneath the oceanic crust.
f A volcano erupts when magma from the mantle rises through the earth's crust.

## 7.10 Earthquakes

Plates are moved very, very slowly by convection currents. At both convergent and transform plate boundaries friction builds up between the plates. The plates will move when the friction between them is overcome. This sudden movement of the plates against each other causes an earthquake. The sudden movement of the plates produces **seismic waves** which can be felt on the surface as **tremors**. The seismic waves start at the **focus**. This is the point within the crust where the two plates suddenly move. This is the origin of the earthquake. The **epicentre** of the earthquake is the point on the earth's surface directly above the focus. This is where the earthquake is felt most and most damage is done. An earthquake can last from a few seconds to a few minutes.

## 7 ● Plate tectonics

**Language**

**Conditional sentences introduced by 'if'.**
When an action in the future is dependent on a certain condition, use the *present* tense in the 'if' clause followed by the *future*:
For example 'If global warming continues, sea levels will rise'.

**Exercise**

**9** Choose the correct ending for the following conditional sentences and copy the correctly matched statement into your notebook.

1  If a pyroclastic flow occurs,

2  If warnings of volcanic activity are given,

3  If the epicentre of an earthquake is in a large city,

4  If an earthquake occurs in the middle of the night,

5  If the epicentre of an earthquake is in an area of low population density,

a  there will be very little damage and few deaths.

b  areas on the slopes of the volcano will be covered in hot ash.

c  most people will be asleep.

d  there will be a large amount of damage to buildings.

e  people will evacuate their homes.

### 7.11 Magnitude of earthquakes

The **magnitude** is the strength of an earthquake. It is measured on the **Richter Scale**. The scale measures from 0 to 10. The strongest earthquake ever recorded was 9.5 on the Richter scale. It was near Chile in 1960.

**Exercise**

**10** Study the table below and match the magnitude to the description for each category. Copy your answers into your notebook.

| Description of the effects | Richter Magnitude |
| --- | --- |
| Tremors hardly felt | 7.0 – 7.9 |
| Tremors just noticeable and recorded | 6.1 – 6.9 |
| At most slight damage to well constructed buildings. Windows rattle, plaster cracks, bricks fall. Over a small area poorly constructed buildings can suffer serious damage. | Less than 3.5 |
| Can cause destruction in areas up to 100 km from the epicentre. Chimneys fall, houses move, walls crack. | 8 or greater |
| Major earthquake causing destruction over larger areas. Bridges twist, buildings collapse | 5.5 – 6.0 |
| Great earthquake causing devastation in areas several hundred kilometres across. Most buildings collapse or are seriously damaged, objects are thrown in the air, earth's surface moves | 3.5 – 5.4 |

## Life on the line – L'Aquila and Sichuan

The Eurasian and African plates meet along a line which runs through North Africa and crosses the Mediterranean near southern Italy and Greece. The town of L'Aquila lies in central Italy north east of Rome. It is situated on a hillside in the valley of the river Aterno in the Apennine mountains. Part of the town lies in an ancient lake bed.

In the early morning of the 6th of April 2009 a powerful earthquake struck the region. The epicentre of the earthquake was L'Aquila. The **magnitude** measured 6.3 on the Richter scale. Aftershocks continued to shake the region for several days, hindering attempts to find survivors. Government funds were **pledged** for the rebuilding of modern and ancient buildings.

298 people died, 1,500 were injured and 66,000 were made homeless. Tent camps, seaside hotels and even cars formed **temporary** accommodation and provided some shelter from the low night temperatures. Volunteers from all over Italy and abroad rushed to the scene to help find survivors, to tend the injured and to bring food and water. The town was closed for several weeks because buildings were in danger of collapse. Eventually reconstruction started and the town returned to its normal way of life. Once the initial emotions of grief and relief subsided however, a tide of anger developed because of the **shoddy** construction of many of the modern buildings. Many felt that their loved ones would not have been victims of the disaster if building guidelines for earthquake zones had been followed.

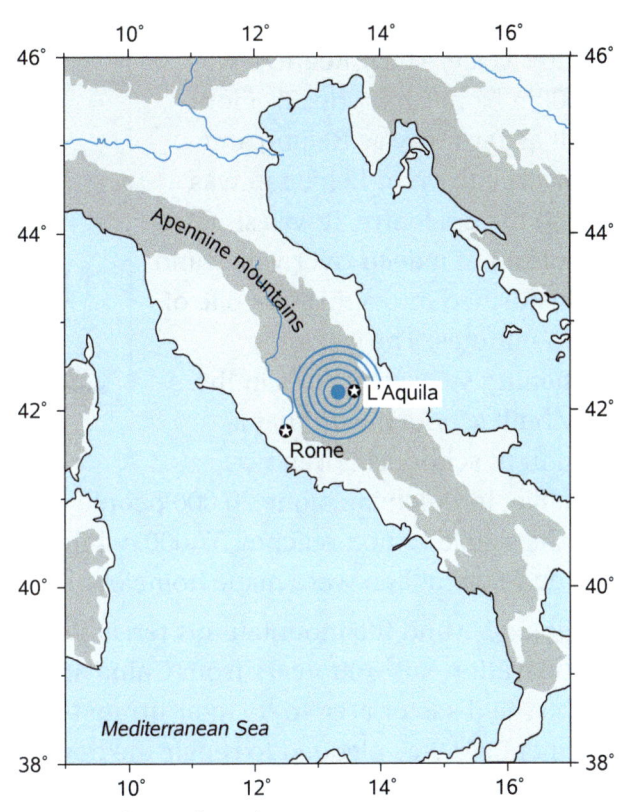

**7.3** Map of L'Aquila region

**7.4** Earthquake damage in L'Aquila, Italy

Sichuan Province lies in south west China. It is mountainous to the west, with deep river valleys to the east. A fault line runs north east through the Longmen Shan mountains from the Himalayas. Earthquakes occur frequently along this fault because of the **collision** of the Indo-Australian Plate and the Eurasian plate.

## 7 Plate tectonics

On May 20th 2008 Sichuan suffered a colossal earthquake measuring 8.0 on the Richter scale. The **epicentre** was about 90km from Chengdu. Tremors were felt as far away as Beijing and Bangkok. The town of Beichuan was nearest to the epicentre. It was situated at the bottom of a deep river valley and was transformed into a massive pile of rubble in minutes. The lack of strengthening steel structures in the recently built school meant that a generation of school children was buried alive. In Beichuan alone 20,000 people died. The **death toll** for the whole region reached 87,000, while 375,000 were injured and five million were made homeless.

**7.5** Map of area affected by the Sichuan earthquake

The remoteness and the mountainous terrain delayed the rescue operation but volunteers from China and abroad rushed to the disaster area to do their **utmost** to help. Government aid was pledged to repair the devastated region and to improve the infrastructure, and wooden huts were put up to house the **homeless**. Yet fears for the living increased as engineers inspected the many waterways in the region. Further aftershocks could **breach** dams, causing floods and mudslides to engulf the settlements downstream. The tremors could trigger more **landslides** which might bury whole communities beneath them. As for the town of Beichuan, the devastation was too great, and the location too dangerous for a new town to rise from the ruins. The mayor of the town **dedicated** the site as a **permanent** memorial to those who perished.

**11** Comparing and contrasting. Find the answers to the questions below and write them in your notebook.

   a What do the two regions have in common?
   b Which region is more remote?
   c Which region's death toll was the greater?
   d Which earthquake was the stronger?
   e What was the response of the Italian and Chinese governments?
   f How could the impact of the earthquakes have been reduced in both regions?

## Plate tectonics 7

### Language

**How to express comparisons (showing similarities) and contrasts (showing differences)**

| Comparisons | Contrasts |
|---|---|
| Both ____ and ____ | Unlike ____, |
| Like[ + noun], | While ____, |
| Not only ____ but also ____ | Whereas ____, |

The following sentences which show similarities and differences in the two regions hit by earthquakes;

**Similarities:**
**Both** L'Aquila **and** Beichuan lie on fault lines.
**Like** L'Aquila, Beichuan lies on a fault line.
**Not only** L'Aquila **but also** Beichuan lie on fault lines.

**Differences:**
**Unlike** L'Aquila, Beichuan lies at the bottom of a valley.
**Whereas** L'Aquila is perched on a hillside, Beichuan lies at the bottom of a valley.
**While** L'Aquila is perched on a hillside, Beichuan lies at the bottom of a valley.

### Exercise

**12** In the following sentences insert an appropriate term from the examples above and copy into your notebook.

a _____ Beichuan has been abandoned, L'Aquila is being rebuilt.
b _____ the survivors of L'Aquila, the survivors from Beichuan had to move to temporary accommodation.
c _____ the inhabitants of L'Aquila _____ the inhabitants of Beichuan felt angry about the shoddy construction of many modern buildings.
d Volunteers _____ from Italy and China _____ from abroad rushed to help rescue people from the ruins of the devastated towns.
e _____ the damaged dams threatened the lives of the inhabitants of Sichuan after the earthquake, the dangerous state of the buildings was the major threat in L'Aquila.

### Language

**Verbs which express harm**
Verbs which express harm to **people**: hurt; harm; injure; wound; mutilate
Verbs which express harm to **things**: break; damage; destroy; smash; devastate; demolish; wreck

## 7 • Plate tectonics

**Exercise**

**13** Complete the following sentences with a suitable verb from the examples on the previous page. Copy the completed sentences into your notebook.

a The earthquake _____ ancient monuments and modern buildings.
b Falling walls _____ people as they slept.
c Tremors _____ dams.
d To make the area safe again, construction workers _____ unstable buildings.
e The collapse of the school at 2.30pm killed or _____ all the teachers and pupils inside.

**Extension**

**14** Compare the descriptions of the 2008 and 2009 earthquakes in L'Aquila and Sichuan according to their magnitude. Write three sentences comparing and contrasting the strength and damage in each place.

### 7.12 Tsunami

A **tsunami** is a wave in the ocean which is formed by an earthquake beneath the seabed. The sudden movement of the plates may cause the water to move and form waves. These waves become larger as they get closer to land. Tsunamis can cause a large amount of damage in coastal areas. Tsunami warnings can be sent to places at risk. This means people can **evacuate** to higher and safer land.

**KEY WORD**

**Evacuate** to move people from a dangerous place to somewhere safe

### 7.13 Earthquake prediction and preparation

Most earthquakes occur on plate margins. Therefore it is possible to say where earthquakes may happen. However, an earthquake cannot be predicted. This means it is not possible to say when an earthquake will occur. Some of the world's largest cities such as Tokyo and Los Angeles are on plate margins. Some buildings have been constructed to be **earthquake proof**. This means they should not fall over during an earthquake. **Earthquake drills** train people in what to do when an earthquake happens. By practising the drill regularly the people will be prepared.

**Language**

**Conditional sentences introduced by 'if'**

When a particular condition is quite unlikely to happen, use the *simple past* in the 'if' clause followed by 'would' + verb:

For example, 'If people stopped eating meat, many pastoral farmers would lose their livelihood'.

## Exercise

**15** Choose the correct ending for the following conditional sentences, and copy the completed sentences into your notebook.

1 If London lay on a transform plate margin,

2 If people were warned of an earthquake,

3 If an earthquake under the sea bed caused a tsunami,

4 If buildings were reinforced with steel and rubber,

a they would be able to move to a safer place.

b coastal regions would be in danger.

c they would sway but should not collapse.

d it would experience earthquakes.

## Language

**Conditional sentences introduced by 'if'.**
When it is impossible for an action to happen because the particular condition did not occur, use the past perfect in the 'if' clause, followed by 'would have' + the past participle of the verb. For example, 'If France had had many natural energy resources, it would not have turned to nuclear energy'.

## Exercise

**16** Choose the correct ending for the conditional sentences below and copy the completed sentences into your notebook.

1 If Beichuan had not been situated in such a dangerous location,

2 If L'Aquila's monuments had been reinforced,

3 If people had been warned,

4 If the dams had not been damaged,

a they would have withstood the earthquake better.

b the town would have been rebuilt.

c there would not have been a danger of flooding.

d they would have left the danger zone.

### 7.14 Volcano prediction and preparation

Most volcanoes occur on plate margins. It is often possible to know when a volcano is about to erupt. This means people living close to the volcano can be given a warning. **Early warning systems** allow people to **evacuate** the danger area. People may be warned a few days before the eruption or just a few hours. This means fewer people are killed or injured in volcanic eruptions than in earthquakes.

# 7 Plate tectonics

**Exercise**

**17** Look at the following list of ways in which areas could plan for volcanoes or earthquakes. Divide them into those which are best for earthquake planning and those best for volcanic eruptions (some may suit both). Make a list of each in your notebook.

- **a** Do not build in river valleys running down the mountain as they are the likely paths of pyroclastic flows
- **b** Put wide open spaces in towns and cities where the public can meet where they would be safe from falling buildings and debris
- **c** Restrict the height of buildings as tall buildings are most likely to collapse
- **d** Put in land use zoning. Build urban areas a good distance from the mountain and agriculture or forest closer to it
- **e** Dig deep foundations for buildings so they are less likely to fall over
- **f** Reinforce the building structure with steel frames and rubber counterweights so allowing them to sway without falling over
- **g** Set up early warning sirens in the area so people know when they should evacuate
- **h** Earthquake drills in schools and at workplaces so people know what to do
- **i** Identify and inform people of safe evacuation routes

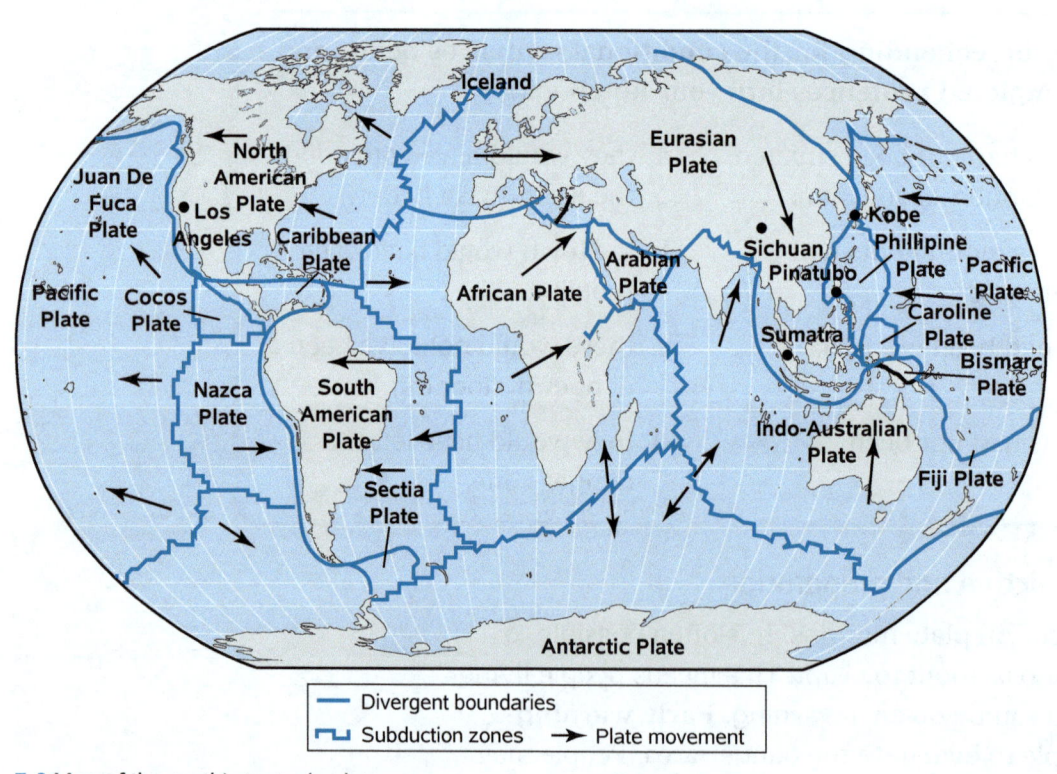

7.6 Map of the earth's tectonic plates

# Plate tectonics • 7

**18** Using information from Figure 7.6 on the previous page, copy the table below in your notebook and fill in the missing data.

| Location: | Plate boundary: | Types of crust: oceanic/oceanic continental/continental oceanic/continental | Subduction: yes/no | Potential Hazard: volcano/earthquake/tsunami |
|---|---|---|---|---|
| Kobe | convergent | | | |
| Sichuan | transform | | | |
| Iceland | divergent | | | |
| Los Angeles | transform | | | |
| Sumatra | convergent | | | |
| Pinatubo | convergent | | | |

**19** Look at the list below of reasons why people live on plate margins. Put them into a table with reasons based on fact and reasons based on personal feelings.

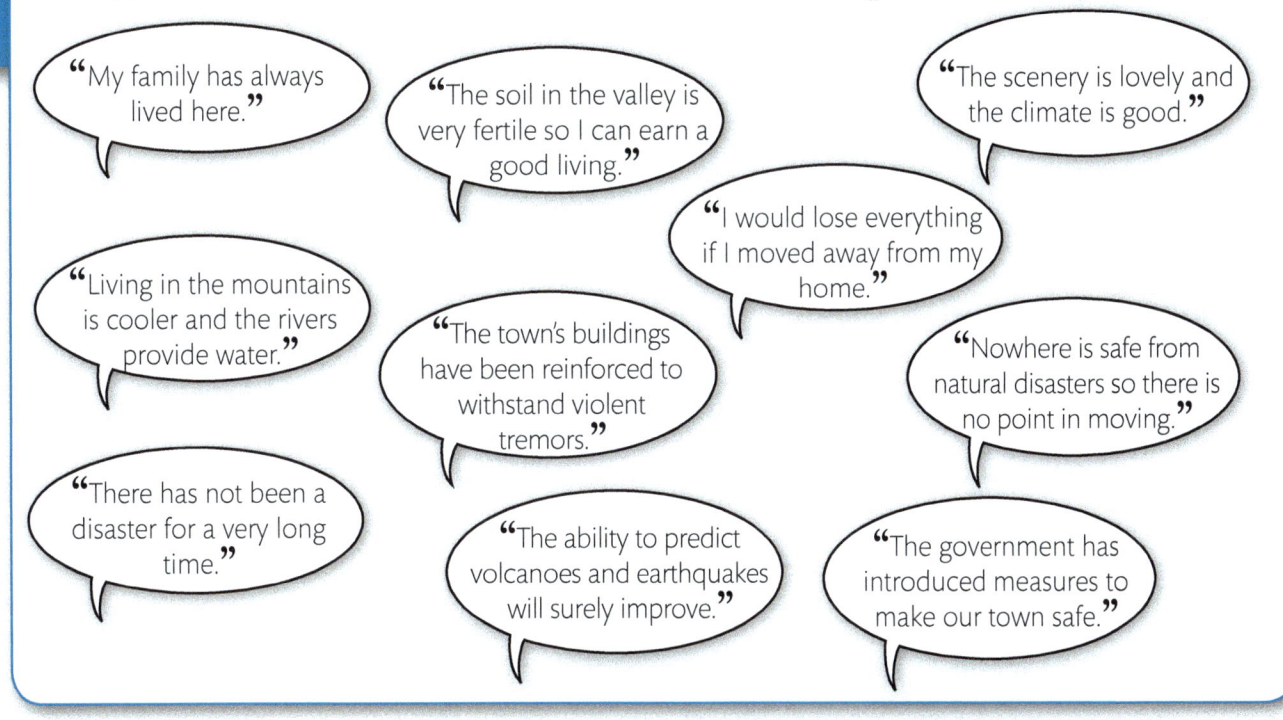

"My family has always lived here."

"The soil in the valley is very fertile so I can earn a good living."

"The scenery is lovely and the climate is good."

"I would lose everything if I moved away from my home."

"Living in the mountains is cooler and the rivers provide water."

"The town's buildings have been reinforced to withstand violent tremors."

"Nowhere is safe from natural disasters so there is no point in moving."

"There has not been a disaster for a very long time."

"The ability to predict volcanoes and earthquakes will surely improve."

"The government has introduced measures to make our town safe."

**20** Copy the diagrams showing the movement of plates, then label them using the options in the box below. Two of the movements have the same label.

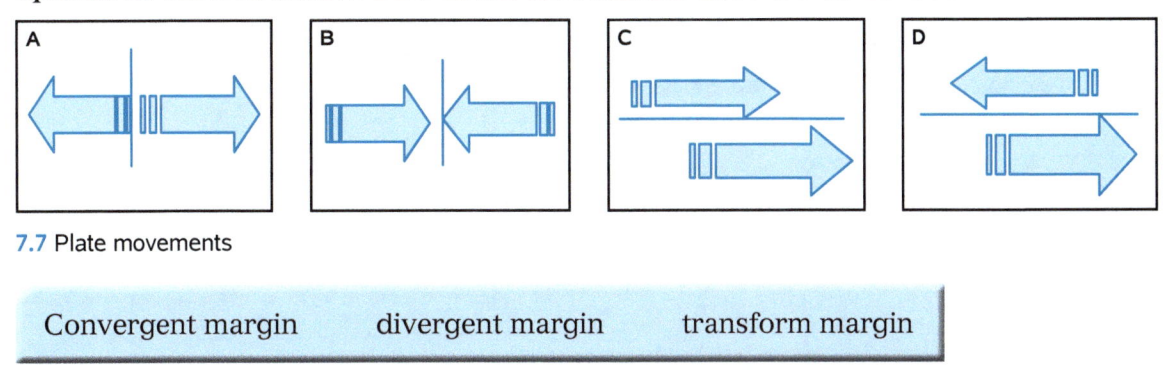

A    B    C    D

7.7 Plate movements

Convergent margin    divergent margin    transform margin

## 7 • Plate tectonics

**Exercise**

**21** Choose the correct answers from the options below and copy into your notebook.

a Composite volcanoes have:
  i steep sides
  ii slope gently
  iii form at divergent plate margins

b Fold mountains are caused by:
  i plates sliding past one another
  ii plates colliding
  iii plates moving apart

c A mid-ocean ridge is caused by:
  i plates colliding
  ii plates moving apart
  iii plates sliding past one another

d A subduction zone is where:
  i continental crust is forced beneath oceanic crust
  ii oceanic crust is forced beneath continental crust
  iii continental crust collides with continental crust

### Talking points

Why is it easier to predict volcanoes than earthquakes?
Where are volcanoes most likely to occur?
Should settlements in known earthquake zones be banned?
Would you prefer to live in an earthquake zone or beside a volcano? Why?

### Extension

**Internet search: Find out about...**
Seismic activity in your country of birth
The Pacific Ring of fire
Earthquake management in your country of birth
Active volcanoes

Think about the questions from the start of the chapter. Can you answer these now?

- What are tectonic plates?
- Where do plates move apart?
- Why do earthquakes occur?
- Who chooses to live on plate boundaries?

# 8 Weathering

**In this chapter you will answer...**
- What is the difference between weathering and erosion?
- When does freeze-thaw weathering happen?
- Which rocks are weathered by carbonation?
- Where does exfoliation occur?
- Why is chemical weathering faster in the tropics?

**KEY WORD**

**Weathering** is the disintegration and decomposition of rocks in situ. Changing temperature, rainfall and rock type have an important influence on the type of weathering occurring

## 8.1 Weathering

**Weathering** breaks rocks into smaller pieces. It is the effect of rainfall and temperature on rocks. Weathering occurs **in situ**. This means the rocks stay in the same place and are not moved. This is different from **erosion**. Erosion is when rocks are moved around or hit by something moving so that they break into smaller pieces.

**KEY WORDS**

**In situ** staying in the same place

**Disintegration** breaking into smaller pieces

**Decomposition** changing the chemicals which make up a rock

## 8.2 Types of weathering

Rocks can be weathered in three ways:

- **Physical (or mechanical) weathering** causes rocks to **disintegrate**. This means the rocks fall apart into smaller pieces.
- **Chemical weathering** causes rocks to **decompose**. This means the minerals that make up the rock are changed by a chemical reaction.
- **Biological weathering** is when plants cause rocks to break up.

8.1 Weathering in situ compared to erosion by moving agents

**Exercise**

1  Using the information above, copy and complete the following table in your notebook.

| Noun | Verb |
| --- | --- |
| disintegration |  |
|  | to compose |
| decomposition |  |
| integration |  |
|  | to erode |
| exfoliation |  |
|  | to fluctuate |

101

## 8 Weathering

**Exercise**

**2** Copy and complete the following sentences using words from the box below.

a As the water freezes it _____ and this makes the _____ wider.
b This freezing and _____ makes the cracks in the rock wider and the rock becomes _____.
c When temperatures _____ above and below 0°C then _____-thaw weathering may occur.
d The ice _____ the crack even more.
e When the _____ drops below 0°C _____ in cracks in the rock will freeze.
f Eventually the _____ falls apart.
g During the next _____ the water in the crack _____ when the temperature _____ below 0°C.
h When the temperature rises again the ice _____ and water fills the cracks.

| fluctuate | temperature | melts | water | thawing |
| widens | freeze | expands | drops | rock |
| crack | weaker | freezes | night | |

**3** Put the sentences above in the correct order to describe the process of freeze-thaw weathering. (Hint: start with c and finish with f)

### 8.3 Physical weathering

**Physical weathering** causes rocks to **disintegrate in situ**. This means the rocks break up. They form smaller pieces of rock with sharp edges. Physical weathering happens when there are changes in temperature over a short period of time. The temperature needs to be **fluctuating**. Two types of physical weathering are **freeze-thaw weathering** and **exfoliation**.

### 8.4 Freeze-thaw weathering

**Freezing** is when water becomes ice. This happens at a temperature of 0°C. Water expands when it becomes ice, taking up more space. **Thawing** is when ice turns to water. This happens when the temperature rises above 0°C. **Freeze-thaw weathering** occurs when the temperature keeps fluctuating above and below 0°C. When the temperature drops below 0°C water in a crack in a rock will freeze. The ice thaws during the day when the temperatures rise. The water freezes when the temperature drops again at night and the ice widens the crack even more. This is freeze-thaw weathering.

### 8.5 Exfoliation

**Exfoliation** is when pieces of the outer layer of rock breaks away. Exfoliation happens in places where there is a very big difference in temperature between the night and day. This is most common in deserts. During the day in deserts the temperature may rise to over 40°C. At night the temperature may drop to below 5°C. During the day the heat causes the outer layers of the rocks to expand. At night the cold temperature causes the outer layers of the rocks to get smaller and they contract. This makes it weaker until it breaks up.

### 8.6 Chemical weathering

The **composition** of a rock is the chemicals or minerals that it is made from. Chemical weathering causes rocks to **decompose**. This means the composition of the rocks is changed, because chemical reactions have occurred. Chemical weathering usually needs water from rainfall, and warm temperatures. **Carbonation** and **oxidation** are types of chemical weathering.

### 8.7 Carbonation

**Carbonation** is the chemical weathering of **chalk** and **limestone** rocks by rainfall.

# Weathering 8

Chalk and limestone are made of **calcium carbonate**. When rain falls on chalk and limestone a chemical reaction occurs.

The air contains gases such as **water vapour** and **carbon dioxide**. Water vapour reacts with carbon dioxide to form **carbonic acid**. All rainfall contains carbonic acid. This reacts with the calcium carbonate. The mineral changes and becomes **soluble** in water. This means the rock **dissolves** in rainwater and is washed away. Carbonation is when chalk and limestone are dissolved in rainwater.

> **KEY WORD**
> **Chemical reaction** the response of one chemical to the addition of another chemical

## 8.8 Oxidation

**Oxidation** is a chemical reaction between some minerals in rocks and the **oxygen** in the air. Oxidation changes iron minerals in rocks from a light grey colour to a brown-red colour. This is called **rusting**. The change in colour shows the change in the composition of the rock. This chemical reaction causes the rock to break up.

**Exercise**

4  Cause and effect. Match the starter sentences with their endings. Copy the completed sentences into your notebook.

| a Chalk and limestone dissolve in rainwater............... | ............... because water expands when it freezes. |
|---|---|
| b Oxidation turns iron minerals a brown-red colour............... | ............... because there is a big difference between night and daytime temperatures. |
| c The cracks in rocks get wider............... | ............... because chemical weathering has occurred. |
| d Exfoliation occurs in deserts............... | ............... because rainwater contains a weak carbonic acid. |
| e The mineral composition of rocks may change............... | ............... because the minerals react with oxygen in the air. |

## 8.9 Biological weathering

**Biological weathering** is when plants cause rocks to break up. The **roots** of plants cause rocks to disintegrate. Plant roots grow down through soil and rocks to find water and minerals. The roots can grow through cracks in rocks to find **groundwater**. As the roots grow the cracks are made wider and eventually the rock breaks up. Dead plants can cause chemical weathering. The plants produce acids when they rot. These acids may cause a chemical reaction in the rocks.

## 8.10 Climate and rate of weathering

**Climate** is the average rainfall and temperature of a place over a long period of time.

The **rate** of weathering is the speed of weathering. Heat causes chemical reactions to occur faster. Most chemical weathering needs

> **KEY WORDS**
> **Climate** the average rainfall and temperature of a place over a long period of time
> **Mineral composition** the different minerals (chemicals) which make up a rock
> **Sedimentary rock** rocks formed by layers of sediment under water
> **Igneous rock** rock formed by magma or lava cooling

rainfall. Chemical weathering occurs fastest where it is warm and there is a lot of rainfall. This means chemical weathering will occur quickly in warm, wet places such as rainforests in the **tropics**. In cool, wet places chemical weathering will occur slowly, for instance in Britain and New Zealand.

Physical weathering occurs fastest in places where temperatures rapidly fluctuate over a

## 8 • Weathering

short time. Rainfall is not always necessary. Freeze-thaw weathering occurs most rapidly where temperatures fluctuate just above and below 0°C over a short time. Rainwater is needed. Exfoliation happens most rapidly where there are large changes in temperature between night and day. It does not need rainfall.

> **Exercise**
>
> **5** Are the following statements true or false? Copy the correct statements into your notebook.
> a Chemical weathering occurs fastest where temperatures rapidly fluctuate.
> b Chemical weathering occurs fastest in warm, wet places.
> c Chemical weathering does not happen where it is cold and wet.
> d Tropical areas such as the rainforest will experience the most chemical weathering.
> e Limited physical weathering occurs in tropical areas where there is little change in temperature.
> f Physical weathering occurs quickly in deserts.
> g Rainfall is needed for weathering to occur.

### 8.11 Rock type and mineral composition

Certain rock types are made up of different minerals. This is the **mineral composition** of the rock. Certain rock types are more affected by certain types of weathering. Limestone is composed of calcium carbonate. This means that it can be weathered by carbonation. However granite is not affected by carbonation as it does not contain calcium carbonate. Rocks containing iron minerals will be weathered by oxidation.

### 8.12 Rock type and lines of weakness

**Lines of weakness** are cracks in rocks which are attacked by weathering. Water and air can enter these cracks and break down the rock by physical or chemical weathering. A rock with lots of lines of weakness will be more easily weathered. Chalk and limestone are **sedimentary** rocks. They are formed in layers. Each layer is separated by a **bedding plane**. These are horizontal lines of weakness in the rock. There are also vertical lines of weakness called **joints**. Rain water flows through limestone through the joints and bedding planes. The rock is weathered by carbonation. Limestone **caves** are formed by carbonation. Granite is an **igneous** rock. It is formed when **magma** slowly cools as it rises towards the surface of the earth. As it cools horizontal bedding planes and vertical joints form. These are lines of weakness in the rock. Granite is weathered to form **tors**.

> **Language**
>
> **Verbs in formal and informal English**
>
> In English there is often more than one way to express the action of a verb. **Phrasal verbs** are used frequently in informal (everyday) conversations, while one word verbs tend to be used in formal or technical language.
>
> Informal = the match was **put off** until the following Saturday because the pitch was flooded.
>
> Formal = The match was **postponed**.... (prefix post- = after)
>
> [Hint: the one word verbs often have prefixes that make their meaning more precise so it is helpful to know the meanings of the prefixes.]
>
> Prefixes: com- = bringing or putting together
> de- = undoes the action of the stem verb
> dis- = moving away (opposite meaning to the stem verb)
> ex- = moving out of/away

# Weathering  8

**6** Copy the table below into your notebook and match the phrasal verb with the correct verb in the following table.

| Phrasal verb | One word verb |
| --- | --- |
| To work together | To destabilise |
| To break up | To exfoliate |
| To change the make up | To dissolve |
| To make up | To combine |
| To make unstable | To expand |
| To lose a layer | To decompose |
| To absorb into liquid | To disintegrate |
| To spread out | To compose |

**7** Copy the sentences below into your notebook and put the appropriate verbs from the table above into the correct form.
 a Freeze-thaw weathering _____ the cracks as water becomes ice.
 b The calcium carbonate in limestone is _____ by the carbonic acid in rainwater.
 c When a plant dies it _____ producing chemical reactions in the surrounding rock.
 d Granite rocks _____ in climates which fluctuate rapidly above and below 0°C.
 e Physical, chemical and biological weathering often _____ to weaken sedimentary rock.
 f Sedimentary rock is _____ of layers of sediment, while igneous rock is _____ of cooled magma from the earth's mantle.
 g Rocks _____ when they have been weakened through physical weathering.

**8** Look at the following photos and match them to the descriptions below.

 a Enchanted Rock in Texas is a granite dome. Cracks in the granite have allowed rainwater to enter and weaken the rock. Vegetation has also contributed to the weathering. The outer layer of granite has been separated from the lower layers.

## 8 • Weathering

Fluctuating temperatures have caused the joints in the surface layer to widen. In places the top layer of rock has broken away and disintegrated along the vertical joint lines.

**b** The Rock of Gibraltar towers over the western end of the Mediterranean. It is composed of limestone. To the west and south there are more gentle slopes but to the north and east the rock face rises sheer to 426m above sea level. Rainfall has seeped down through the joints and bedding planes in the limestone. Weathering has formed over 100 caves in the rock. In the caves stalactites and stalagmites have formed.

**c** Uluru is a massive mound in the desert of Central Australia. It is formed of sandstone. It is 8km round and rises 348m above sea level. The rock has been weathered so iron minerals in the sandstone cause the rock to appear red. The high daytime temperatures can reach over 40°C and contrast with the low temperatures at night which can drop to below 0°C. This rapid change accelerates physical weathering.

**9** Copy and complete the table below using the previous information.

| Location | Rock type | Appearance | Weathering processes? |
|---|---|---|---|
|  | Granite | Sheets of rock breaking up on the surface |  |
|  | Sandstone | Red isolated mound |  |
|  | Limestone | Sheer rock faces; caves |  |

**10** Which of the flow diagrams below illustrates physical weathering, chemical weathering and biological weathering?

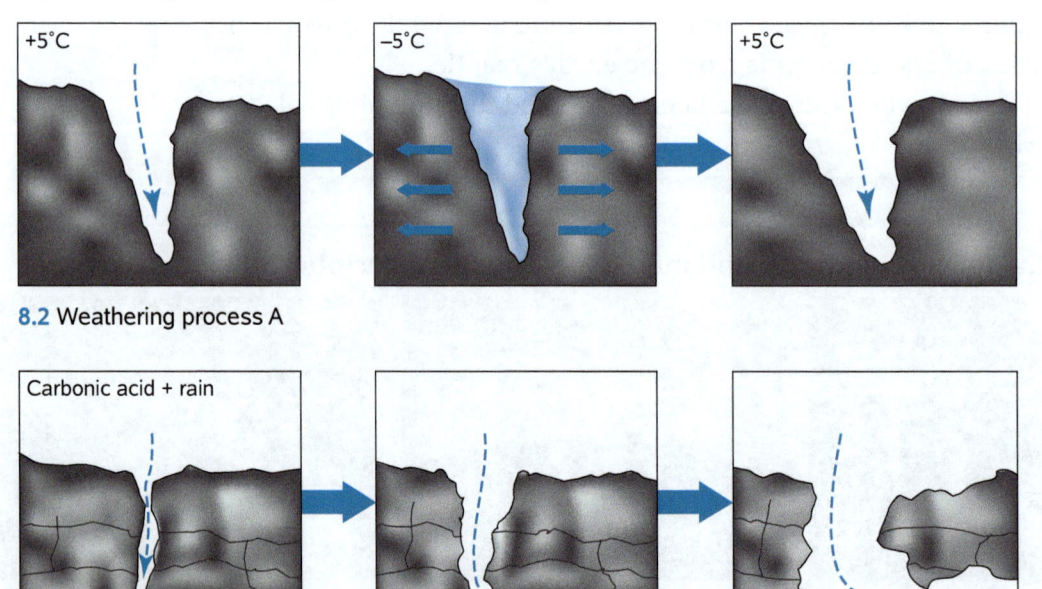

8.2 Weathering process A

8.3 Weathering process B

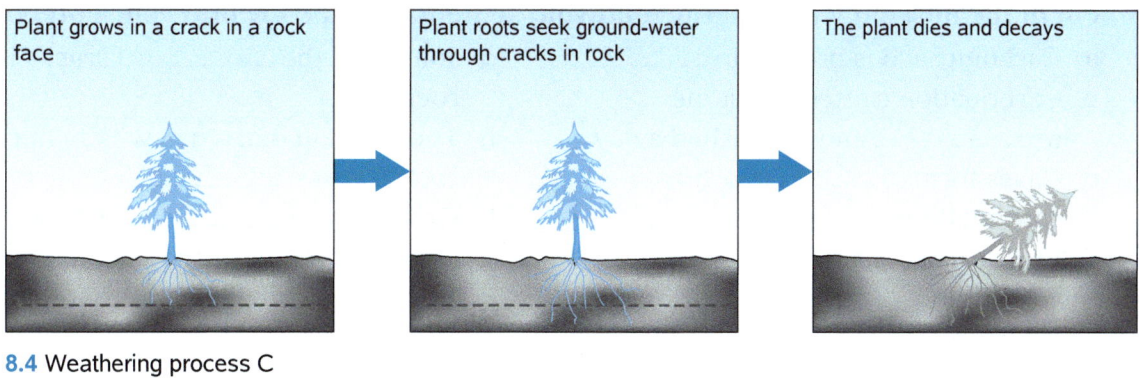

8.4 Weathering process C

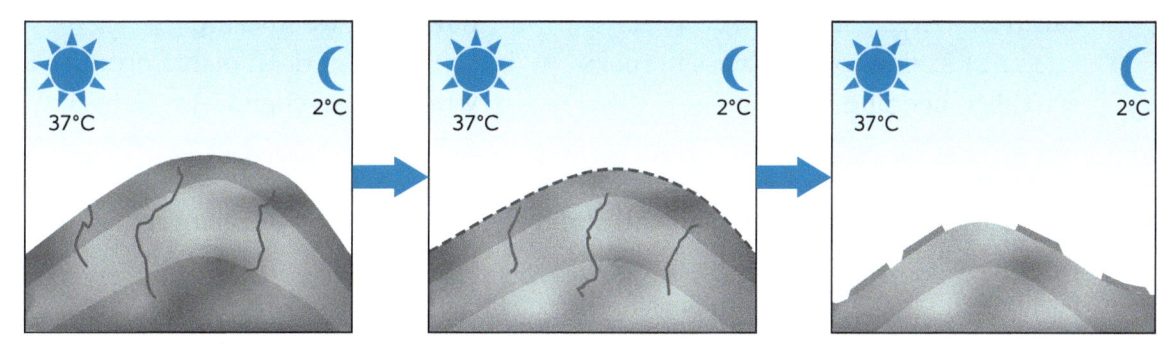

8.5 Weathering process D

**11** Study figure 8.2 and answer the questions below in your notebook.
  a  Where is the rainwater going?
  b  What happens when temperatures fall below 0°C?
  c  Why has the crack widened?
  d  What effect will this have on the rock?
  e  Which process does this flow chart illustrate?

**12** Study figure 8.3 and answer the questions below in your notebook.
  a  What kind of weathering is this?
  b  How does this kind of weathering affect the rock?
  c  Which climates speed up this kind of weathering?

**13** Study figure 8.4 and answer the questions below in your notebook.
  a  What happens to the crack as the roots get bigger?
  b  What kind of weathering is this?
  c  When the plant dies the roots decay and chemicals are produced. What kind of weathering does this process cause?

**14** Study figure 8.5 and answer the questions below in your notebook.
  a  Are the changes in temperature gradual or rapid?
  b  In which regions do these fluctuating temperatures often occur?
  c  Where are the points of weakness in the rock?
  d  What is this weathering process called?
  e  Which types of rock are affected by this process?

## 8 ● Weathering

**Exercise**

**15** Fill in the missing words in the following sentences and copy into your notebook.
   a  Carbonic acid is present in _____.
   b  Carbonation causes limestone to _____ and be washed away.
   c  Caves form in _____ by carbonation.
   d  Freeze-thaw is a type of _____ weathering.
   e  When the top layer of rock becomes detached from lower layers it is called _____.
   f  _____ lines of weakness in rocks are called bedding planes.
   g  Joints are the _____ cracks in rocks.
   h  The reaction of oxygen with minerals in rocks causes _____.
   i  Granite is an _____ rock which is not weathered by carbonation.
   j  Plant roots grow down through cracks in rocks to find _____. _____, thus widening the cracks and causing biological weathering.
   k  _____ dead plants produce acids which cause chemical weathering.

**Exercise**

**16** Choose the correct options form the statements below. Copy the correct sentences in your notebook.
   a  Weathering is different from erosion because it occurs *now and again/between moving objects/in situ*.
   b  Freeze-thaw weathering needs *fluctuating/constant/low* temperatures.
   c  Exfoliation is a process similar to peeling *a banana/an onion/an orange*.
   d  Plants cause *only biological/only physical/both biological and chemical* weathering.
   e  Physical weathering affects *only sedimentary/sedimentary and igneous/only igneous* rock types.
   f  Oxidation is a chemical weathering process which makes rocks appear *red/black/white*.

### Talking points

Explain the role of a) rainfall and b) temperature fluctuation in the weathering process.

Why is granite a more popular surface for kitchen work surfaces than limestone?

How do plants contribute to the weathering process?

### Extension

**Internet search: Find out about…**
Weathering
Desert rock formations
Exfoliation

Think about the questions from the start of the chapter. Can you answer these now?
◉ What is the difference between weathering and erosion?
◉ When does freeze-thaw weathering happen?
◉ Which rocks are weathered by carbonation?
◉ Where does exfoliation occur?
◉ Why is chemical weathering faster in the tropics?

# 9 Rivers

**In this chapter you will answer...**
- What is the difference between corrasion and corrosion?
- Where do oxbow lakes form?
- When does a river deposit its load?
- Why do rivers flood?

## 9.1 Drainage basins

River channels carry water to the sea. A **drainage basin** is the area drained by a river and its **tributaries**. A **tributary** is a smaller river which joins a bigger river. A **confluence** is where two rivers meet. Water reaches rivers from rainfall and from water flowing over land and through soil and rocks. All the rainwater that falls on a drainage basin is carried to the sea by the tributaries and main channel of one river. The **source** is where a river starts. A river flows downhill to the **mouth**. The **mouth** is where a river meets the sea. The **discharge** is the amount of water in a river at a certain place and at a certain time. Tributaries add more and more water to the main river channel so the discharge increases further downstream, nearer the mouth.

### KEY WORD
**Rivers** and their **tributaries** flow through drainage basins. They carry water from high land to the sea. Rivers create landforms by erosion and deposition

## 9.2 Long profile

The **gradient** is how steep an area of land is. The **long profile** shows the change in gradient of the land a river flows through. Rivers usually start on high land and flow downhill to the sea. In the **upper course**, rivers flow down steep gradients to reach lower land. The **lower course** is more gentle as the river is closer to **sea-level**. When the river reaches sea level the channel flows over flat land.

### KEY WORDS
**Tributary** a smaller river which joins a bigger river

**River erosion** when the moving water wears away the river bed and banks

**River load** the material carried by a river

**Deposition** when the river puts down the load it is carrying

**Flood** when there is too much water for the channel to carry so it spreads over surrounding land

## 9.3 Cross sections

A **cross-section** shows the shape of a river channel. The **river bed** is the bottom of the channel. The **river banks** are the sides of the channel. When the water reaches the top of the banks the river is **bankfull**. A **flood** is when the water flows over the top of the banks and onto surrounding land. Water flows fastest in the middle of the river channel. **Friction** slows down water near the bed and banks.

## 9 Rivers

**Exercise 1** Match the adjectives with their opposites and copy into your notebook.

1 narrow
2 shallow
3 fast
4 full
5 large
6 rough
7 gentle

a slow
b small
c smooth
d wide
e empty
f steep
g deep

**Exercise 2** Match the labels below to the letters on the diagrams and write your answers in your notebook.

| | |
|---|---|
| Narrow, shallow channel | Cross Section of a river near the source |
| Long Profile | Steep gradient of upper course |
| Flat land at sea level | Gentle gradient of lower course |
| Rough river bed with large rocks | River banks |

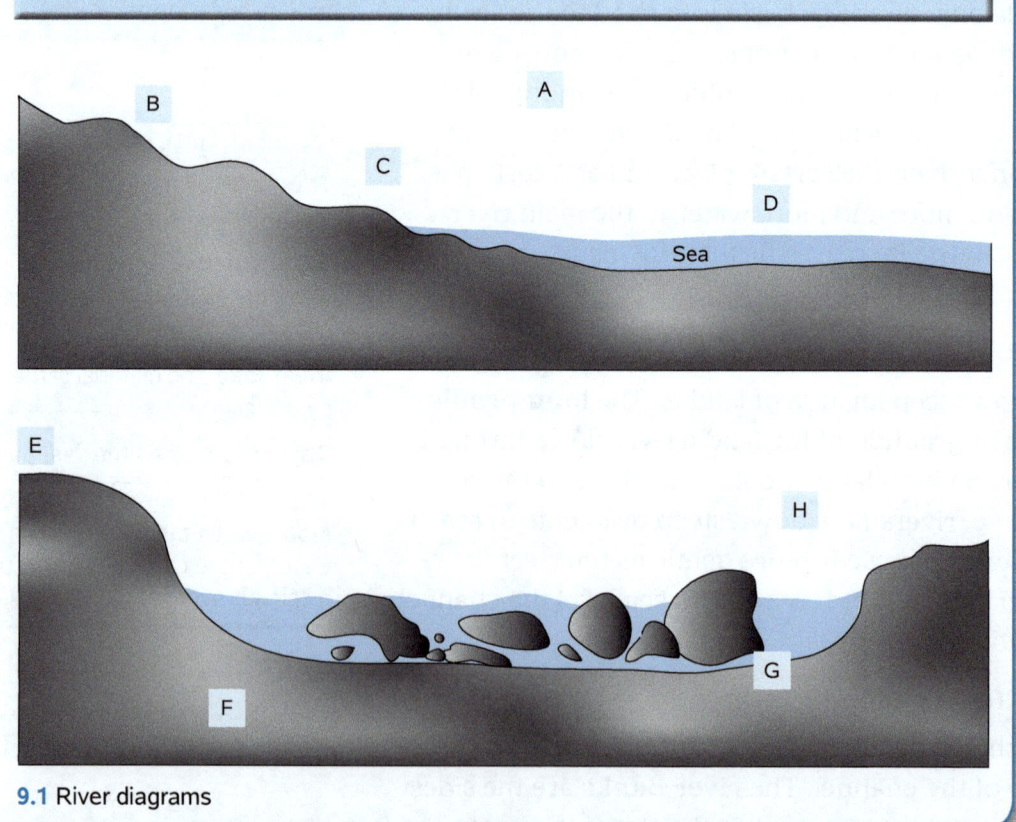

9.1 River diagrams

### 9.4 The source

The **source** of a river is where it begins. It is usually in high land areas. There is not much water in the river channel at the source. This means that the discharge is low. Therefore the river channel is narrow and shallow. There are usually lots of large rocks. This makes the river bed rough and so the river does not have

110

much power. As tributaries add water to the river the discharge increases and the river channel gets deeper and wider. In the upper course the river flows through **v-shaped valleys**.

**3** Fill in the blanks in the sentences below using appropriate adjectives from Exercise 1 and copy into your notebook.

a The river channel in the upper course is _____ and _____.
b There are _____ rocks and boulders in the upper course channels.
c The rivers in the lower course flow over _____ gradients.
d The _____ water is found in the middle of the river channel.
e Rocks and boulders make the channel _____ so the water does not flow so quickly.

**4** Use comparative forms of the adjectives from the table in Exercise 1 to fill in the blanks in the sentences below.

a The river channels in the lower course are _____ and _____ than those in the upper course.
b The water flow is _____ near the river bed and banks than in the middle of the channel because of friction.
c The river channels in the lower course are _____ than in the upper course because there are fewer large rocks.
d Rivers in the upper course flow over _____ land than in the lower course.
e Tributaries are _____ than the main river.

## 9.5 River erosion

- **River erosion** is when moving water wears away the river bed and banks. Rivers carry the eroded material away. A river erodes the land in four ways:
- **Hydraulic action** is the power of water hitting cracks in the bed and banks. The water pulls away pieces of soil and rocks.
- **Corrasion** is when the rocks carried in the river hit the river bed and banks. These rocks wear the land away.
- **Corrosion** is when the river water dissolves rock in the bed and banks. Rivers erode chalk and limestone by corrosion.
- **Attrition** is when pieces of rock in the river hit each other as they are carried along. This makes the rocks smaller and smoother.
- Most erosion occurs when there is a high discharge. This means there is a large amount of water in the river. Most erosion occurs when the river is flowing quickly. This is when the water has a high **velocity**.

## 9 • Rivers

**5** Match the words with their definitions. Copy the completed terms into your notebook.

1 discharge
2 mouth
3 corrasion
4 drainage basin
5 attrition
6 river bed
7 corrosion

a The area drained by a river and its tributaries
b Rocks in the river hitting the river bed and banks so wearing them away
c The bottom of the river
d The amount of water in a river at a certain place and a certain time
e The river water dissolves rock
f Where the river meets the sea
g Rocks hit each other so become smaller and smoother

### 9.6 Landforms of river erosion: waterfalls

**Waterfalls** form where a river flowing over **hard rock** meets **softer rock**. The water more easily erodes the soft rock. The falling water creates a **plunge pool** at the bottom of the waterfall. This is a deep hollow. The plunge pool is formed by hydraulic action by the falling water and by corrasion by rocks in the water. When the waterfall erodes into the softer rock it undercuts the hard rock. This creates an **overhang** of hard rock. Eventually **gravity** causes this overhang to collapse. The rock falls into the plunge pool and increases corrasion. When the overhang collapses the water begins eroding the soft rock again. This means that the waterfall retreats upstream. Very slowly the waterfall gets closer to the source of the river.

**6** Copy and complete the following paragraph using words from the box below.

When a river flowing over _____ rock meets softer rock a _____ may form.
The water _____ the soft rock down. This leaves a cliff of hard rock. The _____ falls over this cliff. The falling water erodes a _____ pool by _____ action and _____.
The waterfall erodes the soft rock behind it to _____ the hard rock. This leaves an overhang of hard rock. _____ causes this overhang to collapse. The rock falls into the _____ _____ and increases _____. This makes the pool _____ and deeper.

| plunge | hard | corrasion | river |
| erodes | Gravity | waterfall | corrasion |
| undercut | hydraulic | larger | plunge pool |

### 9.7 Landforms of river erosion: pot holes

**Pot holes** are formed by corrasion. Stones carried in the river may get stuck on rock in the river bed or banks. The flowing water causes the stones to move round and round on the rock. Over time a small hollow is carved out. This is a pot hole.

## 9.8 Transporting river load

The river **load** is the material such as rocks, soil and vegetation, carried by a river. **Bedload** is the heaviest material such as boulders and large stones. Bedload is transported by **traction**. This means it is rolled along the river bed. Smaller stones and sand are moved by **saltation**. This is when they are bounced along the river bed. They are too heavy to be carried in the water. Sand and silt are carried in **suspension**. This means they are carried in the water without touching the river bed. A river with a lot of material in suspension looks cloudy and brown or grey. Material carried in **solution** is dissolved in the water. It cannot be seen. Some river load such as pieces of vegetation just **float** on the surface of the water.

## 9.9 Change in river load

**Upstream**, nearer the source, more load is carried by traction. This is because the river has not yet eroded the material. The load in a river becomes smaller and smoother further **downstream**. This is because it has been eroded by attrition as it is transported by the river. Nearer the mouth more load is carried by suspension. This is because attrition has made the load much smaller.

**Exercise**

**7** Match the diagrams below to the following descriptions.

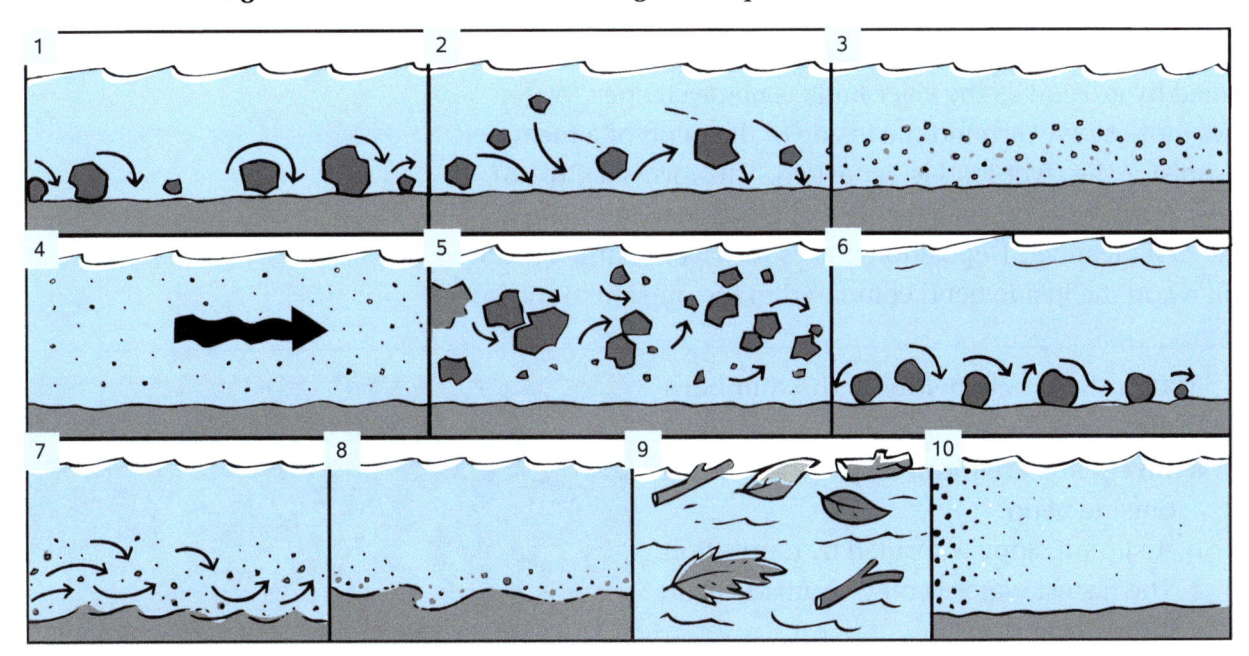

9.2 Processes of river transport and erosion

a **Attrition**: rocks and stones hit against one another and gradually get smaller and smoother.
b **Corrasion**: the river banks and bed are worn away when stones and rocks hit against them.
c **Corrosion**: the chemicals in the water erode the banks and the river bed.
d **Deposition**: the river puts down silt when it overflows its banks or when it meanders.
e **Floating**: leaves and twigs are carried along on the surface.
f **Hydraulic action**: the force of the water wears way the banks and the bed.
g **Saltation**: the flow of water bounces rocks and stones along the river bed.
h **Solution**: Fine material is dissolved in the water and cannot be seen.
i **Suspension**: the river carries small particles in its water, not touching the banks and river bed and making the water look cloudy.
j **Traction**: the river rolls rocks and boulders along its bed.

## 9.10 Deposition

**Deposition** is when the river puts down the load it is carrying. A river deposits its load when it slows down. A river slows down and deposits its load when:

- it meets the sea
- it goes round a bend
- it floods onto surrounding land.

## 9.11 Meanders

The **lower course** is where the river gets closer to sea level. The discharge is higher because tributaries have added more water to the main channel. As the river gets closer to sea level it cannot erode downwards into the rock. Therefore the river begins to erode sideways. This forms **meanders** and **ox-bow lakes**. **Meanders** are large bends in the river. Meanders form where the river flows across flat land near sea level. In a meander water flows faster around the outside of the bend. This fast water erodes the river bed and bank. A **river cliff** is formed by erosion as the river bank is made steeper. Water flows more slowly around the inside of the bend of a meander. This means the river load is deposited. This forms a **slip-off slope**. A slip-off slope is a gently sloping beach on the inside bend of a meander. Deposition makes the river channel more shallow on the inside bend compared to the outside of the bend.

> **8** Match the labels below to the numbers in Figure 9.3.
> a River cliffs are formed by erosion of the outside bend.
> b A slip-off slope is formed by deposition.
> c The fastest water is on the outside bend of the meander.
> d The slowest water is on the inside bend of the meander.

9.3 Photo of a meander

## 9.12 Oxbow lakes

An **oxbow lake** is an old meander bend which has been cut off from the river channel. Erosion on the outside bends of two meanders continues until they become closer and closer together. The **meander neck** is the area of land between the two meanders. Erosion makes this neck narrower and narrower.

Eventually the river erodes through the neck. Now the river flows through a straight channel instead of around the meander. The river deposits its load along its banks. This deposition blocks off the meander. The old meander now becomes a lake. This is an oxbow lake.

**9** Are the following statements true or false? Copy the correct statements into your notebook.
  a The river flows fastest around the inside bend of a meander.
  b Erosion occurs on the outside of a meander bend and deposition occurs on the inside of the bend.
  c A slip-off slope is formed by erosion on the inside of the meander.
  d A river cliff is formed by erosion on the outside bend of the meander.
  e An oxbow lake is formed when a meander is cut off from the main river channel.
  f The river bed is more shallow on the outside bend of a meander than the inside bend.

**10** Find the synonyms for the following from the box below and copy in your notebook. A synonym is a word with a similar meaning.
  a basin    b course    c to deposit    d to erode    e flood
  f lake     g meander   h velocity      i vulnerable to   j waterfall

| bend | bowl | cascade | channel | to wear away |
| inundation | prone to | to put down | rate of flow | pool |

**11** Use one of the above terms to complete the sentences, making sure it is in its correct grammatical form (look at singular/plural usage and verb agreements). Copy the completed sentences into your notebook.
  a When a river bursts its banks it _____ the surrounding land.
  b The area drained by a river and its tributaries is called a drainage _____.
  c A _____ forms where a river bed changes from hard rock to soft rock.
  d A river often widens and forms _____ when it reaches flat land near sea level.
  e In time oxbow _____ form when the river _____ the narrow neck of land.
  f Water moves most rapidly in the middle of a river _____.

## 9.13 Floodplains

A **floodplain** is the flat land on each side of a river channel. It is formed by the river flooding. A river floods when there is too much water to stay in the river channel. When a river floods the water spreads out across the land surrounding the channel. This water slows down and deposits its load. The larger material is deposited first alongside the river channel. This forms banks called **levees**. The smaller material is called **silt**. This is deposited to form the flat land of the floodplain.

## 9.14 Deltas

A **delta** forms where a river meets the sea. The water slows down and the river deposits its load. This is mainly silt. The main river channel may split into smaller channels called **distributaries**. The channels cut through the delta to the sea.

## 9 • Rivers

### 9.15 Use of floodplains and deltas

Silt is very fertile. This means it is very good for growing crops. Therefore floodplains and deltas are very often used for agriculture. Floodplains are very flat. This makes them ideal for building on. Houses, factories and farms may all be built on floodplains. Millions of people across the world live on floodplains. However, floodplains always experience flooding, therefore people living on them and using them are always at risk.

> **Language**
>
> **Despite and although**
>
> Despite + noun, although + clause (subject verb) are used to bring two ideas which would normally be in opposition into one sentence.
>
> For example, *The weather was bad. Tourists kept arriving* = *Despite the bad weather, tourists kept arriving* or *Although the weather was bad, tourists kept arriving.*
>
> **12** Use the appropriate word from the box below to fill in the gaps in the sentences below. Copy the completed sentences in your notebook.
>
> | despite | although | however | on the other hand |
> |---|---|---|---|
>
> a _____ the threat of flooding, millions of people live on floodplains.
>
> b _____ crops may be destroyed by flooding, arable farming uses the fertile soil of floodplains.
>
> c Large factories, warehouses and power stations are built on flat floodplains _____ the risk of flooding.
>
> d Flooding deposits fertile silt which is used for growing crops _____ the flooding also destroys many farms and homes.
>
> e Crops may be damaged by flooding _____ animals can move so they make good use of the fertile pastures.

### Comprehension

**Delta dwelling**

Bangladesh has the largest delta in the world. The country is at the **confluence** of the Ganges, the Brahmaputra and the Meghna rivers. The delta stretches for nearly 300km along the coast and covers 105,000km². The capital Dhaka lies on the delta and has a population of over 12 million.

Most of Bangladesh lies less than 12m above sea level. Some areas of the lower delta are at sea level. Bangladesh has a wet tropical climate and experiences the monsoon and cyclones. In addition melting snow in the Himalayas increases the discharge flowing into Bangladesh.

The Ganges-Brahmaputra widens as it reaches the coast. The river velocity slows down and the river load is deposited. Distributaries cross the delta making a network of channels. Monsoon rains, cyclones and high tides cause flooding of

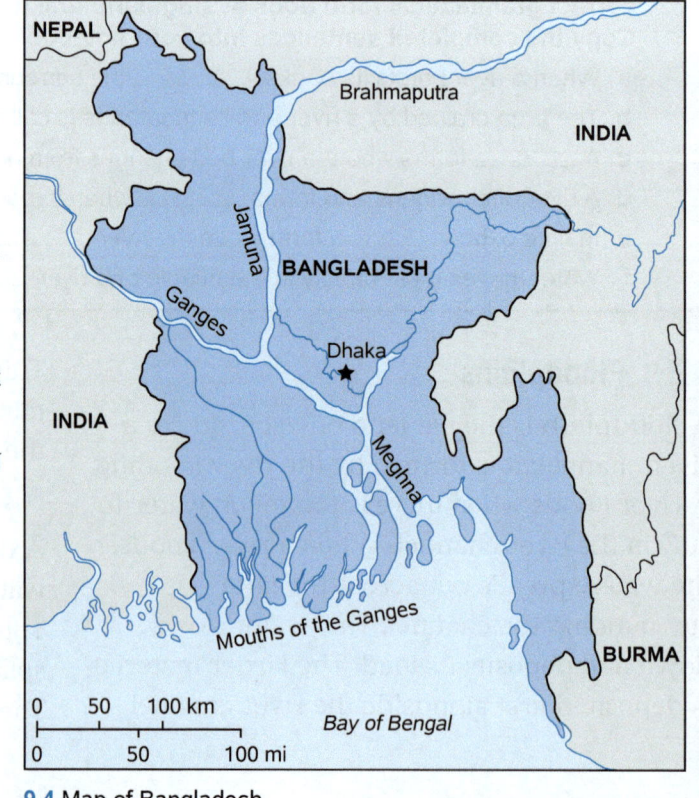

9.4 Map of Bangladesh

this land. Dwellings, crops and livestock are soon **inundated**. The Ganges – Brahmaputra Delta is called the Green Delta because of the fertility of the soil. Over 140 million people live on the delta, making their livelihood from agriculture, mostly on small subsistence farms. They settle on land which is barely above the water level. The regular flooding brings new nutrients to the soil, and the paddy fields of the delta are very productive. The many waterways provide fish for the population of the delta. In a good year there can be three harvests of rice. When natural disasters strike, however, the people of the Green Delta face famine, homelessness, disease, **destitution** and death.

**9.5** Daily life on the Ganges River

In 1998 heavy monsoon rains combined with increased melt water from the Himalayas and high tides in the Bay of Bengal to flood over two thirds of the country. Over 1,000 people died and 30 million were left homeless as the floods continued from July to September. The rural poor were worst affected but parts of Dhaka were also under water for a long time, making normal life impossible. Crops were destroyed, livestock drowned, water was contaminated, and disease was widespread because of the lack of sanitation. No work, no produce, no shelter and no income meant extreme hardship for everyone. Aid workers arrived, bringing food, medicines and money.

People living on the delta have learned to live in their environment and to exploit the fertile soil, plentiful water supplies and fish. However such benefits come at a cost. The natural dangers of monsoons, cyclones and storm surges are enough to worry about but human activity has made things worse. **Subsidence** caused by the extraction of groundwater has made more land vulnerable to flooding. Upstream the diversion of river water to irrigate crops has reduced the amount of silt carried downstream. This has allowed land to disappear. The contamination of the rivers by industry poisons fish and people. The spreading urbanisation around Dhaka and deforestation in the mountains shorten the **lag times** after downpours. This increases the rate of discharge and erosion. Climate change caused by global warming will make the situation worse. Increased snow melt in the Himalayas and rising sea levels in the Bay of Bengal could increase the flood damage. If the sea levels were to rise by one metre it is estimated that 50% of Bangladesh would be under water. In such an overpopulated region the consequences would be disastrous.

## 9 • Rivers

**13** Read the following statements and decide who said what from the choices in the box below. Copy your answers into your notebook.

a "When the waters rise I can do nothing but watch all my hard work being destroyed. If the rice crop fails we will have nothing to eat."

b "It is not the depth of the flood that is the greatest cause of death but the contamination which spreads diseases such as cholera and typhoid."

c "I can't go to school when the floods come, and my mother won't even let me go out to fetch food because of the snakes."

d "Global warming can no longer be ignored as natural disasters such as the 1998 floods in Bangladesh are occurring more and more frequently."

e "The waters stretch as far as I can see, and the bodies of dead animals float past the aid station as we give food and water to the hungry people."

f "Our country needs and deserves international aid to help us survive the effects of deforestation."

| emergency aid worker | international ecologist | school child in Dhaka |
| subsistence farmer | member of medical team | Bangladeshi politician |

### Reported speech

To report what someone has said or done in the past you need to change **verbs** and **pronouns**.

Verbs change in the following ways:

a from the present simple/continuous to the past simple/continuous: is = was; do = did; can = could
b present perfect to the past perfect: has been = had been; has done = had done
c from the future to the conditional: will = would; will be = would be.

Pronouns change from first and second persons:

I; we; you; = he/she/it/they

Me; us; you = him/her/it/them

For example, = He said "I am ill". = He said that he was ill.
They said "We will go to the city." = They said that **they would** go to the city
My friend said "I haven't seen that film." = My friend (**He/she**) said that **he/she hadn't** seen that film.

**14** Put the statements in Exercise 13 into reported speech.

a The schoolchild said that _____.
b The subsistence farmer said that _____.
c The international ecologist _____.
d The Bangladeshi politician _____.
e The member of the medical team _____.
f The emergency aid worker _____.

## Language

### Reporting verbs

It is possible to avoid repeating the verb to say in reported speech by using 'reporting verbs'. These add meaning: often the emotion or opinion of the speaker can be expressed.

Make the same verb and pronoun changes as you did in the reported speech exercise.

**NB:** Past simple in the direct speech can stay the same or can be changed to the past perfect tense. The past perfect tense makes it clear that the statement refers to an action that was over when the speaker gave the information.

He said, "My animals drowned in the floods".

He stated that his animals *drowned/had drowned* in the floods.

**15** Which of these reporting verbs would you use to report the statements a to f? Rewrite the sentences using the reporting verbs and copy into your notebook.

**To predict** to say what you think will happen in the future

**To fear** to say what you hope won't happen

**To complain** to say what has upset or annoyed you

**To announce** to say something important publicly to a large number of people

**To assert** to say something that you believe strongly

**To state** to give formally a factual piece of information

a The nurse said, "There will be more deaths if aid does not arrive."

*The nurse predicted that there would be more deaths if aid did not arrive.*

b The meteorologist said, "Monsoon rains in the rainy season have caused unusually heavy flooding in the delta."

c The farmer said, "My family is starving because no one warned us of the flood."

d The politician said, "We can take measures to lessen the flood damage."

e The ecologist said, "If the world ignores the reality of global warming the flooding will get worse."

f The student said, "I have no chance of passing my exams if I can't attend school."

**KEY WORD**

**Meteorologist** someone who predicts the weather

## Exercise

**16** Look at the suggestions for coping with the delta environment and sort them into the categories given in the box below.

| International measures | Emergency measures | Preventive measures |
| --- | --- | --- |

a Early warning systems to alert population to future flood

b Construction of flood shelters on concrete pillars for the delta dwellers

c Construction of dams to control the water flow in the delta

d Crop storage in shelters above the water level

e Education about the importance of clean water and the avoidance of disease

f Agreements with neighbouring countries to protect the natural flow of transnational rivers

g The provision of food, drinking water and medicines

h Control of chemical waste from factories

i Controls on irrigation and extraction of groundwater

j Construction of levees to stop rivers overflowing their banks

k Support for policies to reduce global warming

## 9 • Rivers

**17** Match the descriptions in the box below with the correct river landforms. Copy the completed terms in your notebook.

1. It is a large, deep area of water into which a waterfall pours water.
2. A steep rise in the river bank on the outside bend of a meander.
3. The area of low-lying, flat land near the coast with a large number of small rivers flowing into the sea.
4. There is not much water in the channel here and there are many large rocks on the river bed.
5. A curved, shallow pool of water which lies on flat land beside a meandering river.
6. A bowl carved out of a large rock which forms part of the river bank.
7. Two rivers meet at this point causing the discharge and the power of the river to increase.

a river at its source
b plunge pool
c pot hole
d confluence
e river cliff
f oxbow lake
g delta

**18** Match the letters on Figure 9.6 with the options below.

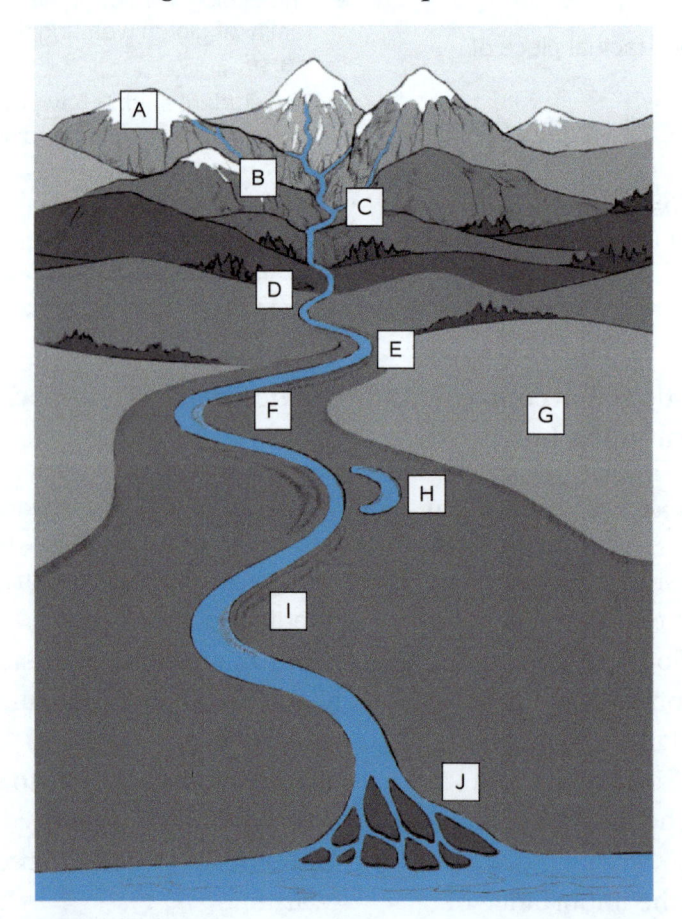

9.6 A river's course

| Waterfall | Tributary | Source | Meander | Delta |
| Flood plain | Levee | Oxbow lake | Plunge pool | Slip-off slope |

## Talking points

How is global warming affecting the world's rivers?
What problems can arise when rivers cross international boundaries?
Should people be allowed to live on flood plains?
How can living conditions be improved for people living in flood zones?

### Extension

**Internet search: Find out about…**
Floods
River management
Life on the River Delta

Think about the questions from the chapter.
Can you answer these now?

- What is the difference between corrasion and corrosion?
- Where do oxbow lakes form?
- When does a river deposit its load?
- Why do rivers flood?

# 10 Marine processes

**In this chapter you will answer...**
- What causes waves?
- When are cliffs eroded?
- Why do spits develop?
- Where do sand dunes form?

## 10.1 Coasts

- **Marine** processes are carried out by the sea. The **coast** is where the land meets the sea.
- **Cliffs** are steep walls of rock. They form a sudden end to the land where it meets the sea.
- **Beaches** are gentle slopes of sand or **shingle** into the sea. Shingle is lots of small stones. These stones are also called pebbles.
- **Coastal sand dunes** are hills of dry sand found at the coast. They are often covered in long grass.
- **Marshes** are very flat areas of plants which are sometimes covered in sea water. They often form at river mouths.

## 10.2 Tides

**Tides** are the rise and fall of the sea against the coast. Tides are caused by the moon. High tide is when the sea has risen and covered land at the coast such as beaches and marshes. Low tide is when the sea has fallen so the land at the coast is shown. There are two high tides and two low tides during 24 hours.

## 10.3 Waves

**Waves** are the movement of surface water. Waves are caused by the **wind**. Wind is moving air. When wind blows over water it picks up the water surface to form waves. When the wind is strong the waves are bigger. Waves form at the surface of the sea. The sea becomes shallow where it meets the coast. This causes the waves **to break**. When a wave breaks on a beach the water flows up the beach. This is the **swash**. Gravity causes the water to flow back down the beach to the sea. This is the **backwash**. There are two main types of waves: destructive and constructive. **Destructive waves** form where there are strong winds. These waves are more powerful. They have lots of energy. Destructive waves have a high **wave height** and short **wave length**.

This means these waves put a lot of pressure on the coast. Destructive waves cause **erosion**. They have a strong backwash which pulls material away from the coast.

---

**KEY WORD**

**Coasts** are where the land meets the sea. **Waves** cause erosion and deposition on coastlines and they move material along the coast. Waves create landforms on the coast.

**KEY WORDS**

**Spit** a long, thin, flat beach which extends out into the sea

**Cliff** a steep wall of rock

**Beach** gentle slope of sand or shingle into the sea

**Longshore drift** movement of sand or shingle along a beach by the waves

**Coral reef** a ridge of calcium carbonate rock and living coral

**Wave height** the distance between the peak and the trough of a wave

**Wave length** the distance between two peaks

Constructive waves form when there are gentle winds. These waves are not very powerful. They have a strong swash which pushes material onto the coast and deposits it. Constructive waves have a low wave height and a long wave length.

**1** Match the labels in the box below with the numbers on the diagrams.

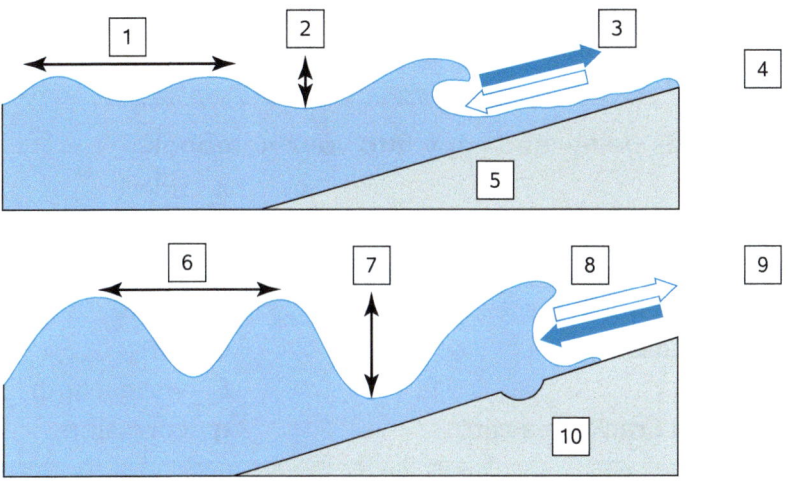

**10.1** Diagrams of waves

| Short wave length | Strong swash | High wave height |
| Destructive waves | Low wave height | Weak swash |
| Long wave length | Weak backwash | Strong backwash |
| Constructive waves | | |

**2** Are the following statements true or false? Copy the correct statements into your notebook.
  a  The wind causes tides to form.
  b  The swash of a wave runs up the beach and the backwash flows back down the beach.
  c  Constructive waves have higher energy than destructive waves.
  d  Destructive waves have a low wave height and short wave length.
  e  Waves are formed by wind blowing over the water.
  f  The stronger the wind, the bigger and more destructive the waves.
  g  Waves erode the coast.
  h  Waves deposit material on the coast.

## 10.4 Marine erosion

- **Marine erosion** is the breaking up of the coast by waves. The waves carry away the eroded material. Waves erode the coast in four ways: hydraulic action, corrasion, corrosion, attrition.
- **Hydraulic action** is the pressure of breaking waves on cracks in cliffs. This causes the cracks to become larger and the rock becomes weaker.

## 10 • Marine processes

- **Corrasion** is when waves throw pieces of rock at cliffs. The rocks hit the cliffs. They make parts of the cliff weaker and break pieces off.
- **Corrosion** is when cliffs made of rock such as limestone and chalk are dissolved in seawater.
- **Attrition** occurs on beaches. The swash of waves moves sand and shingle up the beach and the backwash pulls it back down. This movement causes the stones to hit against each other. This slowly makes them smaller and smoother.

**Exercise**

**3** Match the definitions with the words below and copy into your notebook.
1 Steep walls of rock at the coast
2 The movement of surface water caused by the wind
3 The movement of the sea against the coast caused by the moon
4 Waves throw stones at the cliffs and break pieces off
5 The distance between two wave peaks
6 Where the land meets the sea
7 The pressure of breaking waves on cracks in a cliff

a tides
b hydraulic action
c waves
d coast
e cliff
f wave length
g corrasion

### 10.5 Landforms of marine erosion: bays and headlands

**Bays** and **headlands** are formed on coasts with areas of hard and soft rock. Waves easily erode the soft rock. The soft rock is eroded to form a **bay**. This is a dent in the coast line. Hard rock is more resistant to erosion. Hard rock forms **headlands** on either side of a bay. The headland sticks out into the sea because it is eroded much slower.

**Exercise**

**4** Which of the words from the options below are the odd ones out? Copy the correct words into your notebook.
a hard, resistant, weak, strong
b dent, lump, hollow, cavity
c strong, weak, fragile, frail
d stones, sand, shingle, pebbles
e powerful, strong, gentle, dominant

### 10.6 Landforms of marine erosion: cliff erosion

A **cliff** is a wall of rock. It forms a sudden end to the land where it meets the sea. Erosion by the sea at the bottom of a cliff makes it steeper. Waves erode the bottom of a cliff. Wave erosion makes cracks larger and wider to form a **wave-cut notch** at the bottom of the cliff. This makes the cliff unstable. Eventually gravity causes the cliff to collapse. A **wave-cut platform** is a flat area of solid rock at the bottom of a cliff. It is usually covered by the sea at high tide. A wave-cut platform shows where the cliff used to be. It is evidence of **cliff retreat**.

## 10.7 Landforms of marine erosion: headland erosion

A headland sticks out into the sea. Waves break on both sides of a headland. Hydraulic action may form **wave-cut notches** at the base of a cliff. Erosion of these cracks over a long period of time may form a **cave**. This is a deep hollow in the base of the cliff. An **arch** is formed when waves erode right through caves in a narrow headland. Marine erosion processes make an arch bigger and weaker. Eventually gravity causes the arch to collapse. This leaves an area of headland separated from the main land. This is a **stack**. The headland is now shorter than before.

10.2 Examples of headland erosion

**Exercise**

5  Study the four photographs above. Match the words below with the corresponding points on each photograph.

   Arch          Cliff          Headland

6  Complete the following paragraph using the simple past tense of the verbs in brackets. Copy the completed paragraph into your notebook.

   The waves _____ (to erode) the headland by hydraulic action and corrasion. Waves _____ (to make) cracks in the cliff larger and wider to form wave-cut notches. Over time caves _____ (to form) in the base of the cliff. Eventually waves _____ (to break) through areas of weakness in the narrow headland to form two arches. One arch _____ (to collapse) leaving a stump.

# 10 ● Marine processes

**7** Put the following sentences into the passive form.

  a Hydraulic action will make cracks in the arch larger.
  b Gravity will cause the arch to collapse.
  c Corrasion made the headland weaker.
  d Corrasion and hydraulic action eroded this headland.
  e Breaking waves have eroded the stack to form a stump.

## 10.8 Longshore drift

**Longshore drift** is the movement of sand and shingle along a beach by the waves. Waves are controlled by the wind. If the wind is blowing directly onto the coast the swash moves straight up the beach. It pushes shingle and sand up the beach. If the wind is blowing waves onto the coast at an angle the swash flows up the beach at an angle. It therefore moves the shingle up at an angle. The backwash pulls shingle and sand back down the beach. The backwash always flows straight back down the beach due to gravity. When the waves break on the beach at an angle the swash and backwash carry shingle and sand along the beach in a **zigzag** movement.

## 10.9 Landforms of marine deposition: beaches

**Beaches** are gentle slopes of shingle and sand eroded from cliffs or coral reefs. The sand and shingle may have fallen from cliffs near the beach or been deposited onshore by waves. Beaches at the bottom of a cliff can slow down the erosion of the cliffs. This is because the waves break on the beach rather than directly on the cliff. The swash and backwash of waves erode shingle by **attrition**. The largest stones are found at the top of the beach, furthest from the sea. This part of the beach may only be reached by waves at high tide. The smallest material is found lower down the beach. This is where the waves cause most attrition as the beach is covered during the day by the tide going in and out. Therefore the stones are made smaller and smoother.

## 10.10 Landforms of marine deposition: spits and bars

**Spits** are beaches that stick out into a river mouth or bay. Waves move shingle and sand along a beach by longshore drift. Where a beach ends at a river mouth the material is deposited. Over time this deposition builds up a new part to the beach. Longshore drift adds more material to the beach so it continues to grow out into the river mouth. The movement of the river usually stops a spit growing right across the mouth. However if the river is not very powerful the spit may grow right across to form a **bar**. A bar across a bay may also be formed by waves pushing sand and shingle onshore. A **lagoon** is a lake which is formed where a bar separates an area of water from the sea.

> **8** Are the following statements true or false? Copy the correct sentences into your notebook.
>
> a Longshore drift moves beach material down the beach.
> b Beach material is moved along a beach by longshore drift.
> c Longshore drift only occurs if the wind is blowing waves directly onto the beach.
> d The swash moves sand and shingle up the beach in the direction the wind is blowing.
> e Spits grow across bays or river mouths.
> f River currents help the spits grow across the river mouth.
> g Spits are formed by longshore drift and deposition of beach material.
> h Shingle and sand on a beach are eroded by corrosion.

## 10.11 Coastal sand-dunes

**Coastal sand dunes** are hills of sand created by the wind. Sand dunes are formed by strong winds blowing dry sand from the beach onshore. Sand dunes form behind a sandy beach where there is a big difference between high and low tide. This means the sand on the beach dries out. They form above the level of high tide. This means that the sand remains dry and is not covered in sea water. Sand is moved by the wind by **saltation**. Saltation is when grains of sand bounce along the ground. The moving sand builds up behind plants or pieces of wood on the beach. Plants such as **marram grass** grow on sand dunes. The roots of the grass are very long to reach water. The roots and leaves also hold the sand together. This helps the sand dune to grow bigger.

## 10.12 Salt marshes

**Salt marshes** are flat areas of plants and mud that are covered by sea water at high tide. Salt marshes form at a river mouth or behind a spit. This is where a river slows down and deposits its load. The plants that grow on a salt marsh have adapted to survive in salty sea water.

## 10.13 Coral reefs

**Coral** lives in shallow, warm water. The **minimum** temperature of the water for coral is 18°C. The **optimum** temperature for the growth of coral is between 25–29°C. Coral grows in shallow seas because it needs sunlight for **photosynthesis**. Photosynthesis is how plant cells make food. The **maximum** depth for coral is 90m. Coral needs clear, clean water to grow in.

**KEY WORDS**

**Minimum** the lowest amount of something

**Maximum** the highest amount of something

**Optimum** the ideal amount or level

## 10 • Marine processes

Coral makes calcium carbonate and this forms reefs. **Coral reefs** are ridges of calcium carbonate rock and living coral. There are three types of coral reef:

- **Fringing reefs** grow on the edge of a tropical island or coast. The reef is separated from the land by a shallow channel of water.
- **Barrier reefs** also grow on the edge of a tropical island or coast. However a deep channel of water separates the reef from land.
- An **atoll** is a circle of coral reef which formed around a volcanic island. The atoll began as a fringing reef around a volcano in a tropical sea. Over time the volcano became extinct and sank back into the sea. However the coral reef continued to grow.
- A **lagoon** in the centre of the atoll shows where the volcano crater used to be.

### Exercise

**9** Complete the following sentences using the appropriate words from the box below. Copy the completed sentence into your notebook.

a The _____ temperature for coral growth is 18°C. This is the _____ temperature it can grow in.

b For coral to grow the temperature must be _____ 18°C.

c The _____ temperature for coral growth is between 25–29°C. This is the _____ temperature.

d The _____ depth for coral growth is 90m. This is the _____ depth it can grow in.

e For coral to grow the sea must be _____ 90m deep.

| at the most | minimum | ideal | lowest |
| greatest | at least | maximum | optimum |

### Comprehension

**Where sea meets land…**
**….Sands on the move**

The Atlantic Ocean pounds France's western coastline. The strong winds and waves have moved sand from off shore onto the beaches and piled it up into dunes. The Great Dune of Pyla, lying just south of the Bay of Arcachon is one of many massive dunes along this coast, and is the largest dune in Europe. It consists of fine sand and can reach a height of over 107m. It is 2500m long and 500m wide. Vegetation helps to stabilise the dune, as plant roots grow down through the sand in search of water. The vegetation protects it from the **ravages** of the wind. Tourism is an important source of income for the region. The Great Dune attracts many visitors who make the ascent to enjoy the amazing views of the Atlantic Ocean, the Bay of Arcachon, the pine forests of the Landes and on a clear day the distant Pyrenees. Hang–gliders enjoy launching themselves into the strong winds from its slopes and the beaches of the coast are always popular with holiday makers.

However damage to the vegetation on the dune, erosion caused by people climbing the dune and rising sea levels threaten not only the coastline but also the regions inland. The dune is always changing. Strong winds blow sand off the crest of the dune, burying whatever lies in its shadow. Roads, villas and trees are swallowed up by the sand mass. The dune is moving east at a rate of 3–4m per annum. As it does so the sea erodes the beach at its base. Fortifications from World War II have already disappeared from view beneath the waves.

## Where sea meets land…
## …..Rainforests of the sea

Coral reefs only tolerate temperatures above 18°C. When the temperature of the water rises, **coral bleaching** and eventually death of the coral occur. Australia's Great Barrier Reef stretches for more than 2300km along the Queensland coast. It is composed of 200 reefs and 540 inshore islands. The reefs protect the islands from the waves of the Pacific Ocean. The Great Barrier Reef is protected as a World Heritage Site and is regarded as one of the seven natural wonders of the world. The diversity of the underwater world of the Great Barrier Reef with its sharks, whales, manta rays, turtles and many other species attracts divers from all over the world. The white coral beaches of the many islands are the perfect holiday setting. Tourism is a major industry of the region but brings with it dangers for the **ecology** of the Reef. At sea, **over-fishing**, damage from trawling the sea bottom and anchors being dropped on to the delicate coral in addition to oil spills and litter from boats, disrupt the habitat. On land waste water from farms enters the sea and increases the acidity of the water. Climate change and rising sea levels upset the fine ecological balance of the reef environment and threaten its wildlife.

The Maldives are in the Indian Ocean 671km south west of Sri Lanka. It has an area of sea and islands of 90,000 km². It consists of 26 **atolls** and 1192 small islands. Only 200 of them are inhabited. However its popularity as a dream tourist destination swells the population of 300,000

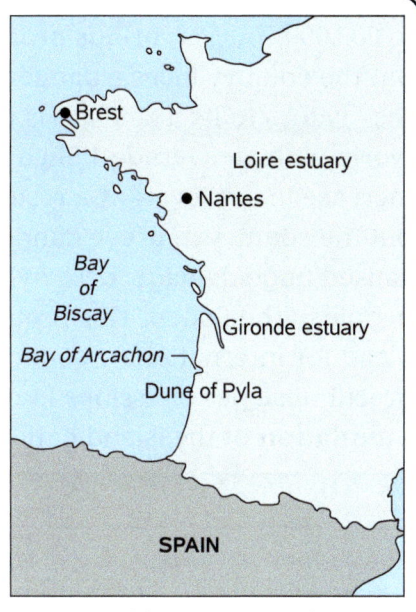

**10.3** Map of the west coast of France

**10.4** The Great Dune of Pyla

## 10 • Marine processes

to 900,000. Tourism brings problems as well as prosperity but the country faces a danger beyond the activities of the visitors to its islands. It is the lowest country in the world with an average 1.5m above sea level. Any increase in sea levels as a result of global warming will put the country in grave danger. The 2004 **tsunami** caused huge damage, destroying villages and killing 108 people in the floods. This prompted the government to plead for international cooperation in reducing greenhouse gas emissions in order to avoid the total **inundation** of the island nation.

### Language

**How to form the superlative of adjectives**

Adjectives of one syllable add -st (if they end in an 'e') or -est if they end in a consonant):
*warm – warmest; fierce – fiercest; large – largest*

If the adjective ends in a vowel and 'd', 'g' or 't' the end consonant doubles: *hot – hottest; big – biggest; wet – wettest;* **but** *cold – coldest; long – longest; short – shortest.*

If the adjective ends in 'y', it changes to 'i' and adds -est:
*sunny – sunniest; rainy – rainiest; noisy – noisiest; dusty – dustiest.*

Irregular superlatives: *good – best; bad – worst; far – farthest/furthest.*

Adjectives of more than one syllable do not change but use 'most' in front.

If the adjective stands in front of a noun, or if the noun is understood but not repeated, 'the' is used: *the most dangerous aspect; the most fragile environment; of all the continents the Antarctic is the most mysterious and the iciest.*

### Exercise

**10** Complete the following sentences using the superlative form of the adjectives in the box below (not all are needed). Copy the completed statements into your notebook.

a The Great Dune of Pyla is the _____ in Europe.
b The Maldives form the _____ country in the world.
c The _____ temperature that coral can tolerate is 18° C.
d The Great Barrier Reef is the _____ in the world.
e On a beach the _____ material is found nearest the sea.
f The cracks in the base of a cliff are the _____ point.

| bad | cold | constructive | dangerous | destructive | gentle |
| small | strong | good | high | hot | large |
| low | powerful | steep | weak | | |

Marine processes • 10

**11** Find two verbs with similar meanings from the box below for each of the following phrasal verbs. Copy your answers into your notebook.
- a to move into
- b to put down
- c to break up
- d to build up
- e to drag away

| to accumulate | to displace | to remove | to collapse |
| to drop | to spread | to crumble | to encroach |
| to deposit | to grow | | |

## Language

### Word order for adverbs

**The position of the adverb or adverbial phrase in a sentence can change the emphasis**

a To highlight the importance of the information it expresses put the adverb or adverbial phrase at the beginning of the sentence:

*Suddenly the cliff collapsed. Rapidly the sea encroached on the low-lying land. Little by little the waves eroded the base of the cliff.*

b Adverbs can also come between the subject and the verb if less emphasis is required:

*The cliff suddenly collapsed. The sea rapidly encroached on the low-lying land. The waves gradually eroded the base of the cliff.*

**NB:** Do not put adverbial phrases between the subject and the verb

c Adverbs and adverbial phrases can be put after the verb if no special emphasis is needed.

*The cliff collapsed suddenly. The waves encroached rapidly on the low-lying land. The waves eroded the base of the cliff little by little.*

d If the verb consists of more than one word (a compound verb) the adverb is placed after the auxiliary (has/had/will be/is/was/were) or modal (can/may might/should). Adverbial phrases either start the sentence or come after the whole verb.

*Islands could suddenly be inundated if sea levels rise. Without any warning islands could be inundated if sea levels rise. Islands could be inundated without any warning if sea levels rise.*

## Exercise

**12** Match the adverb which describes the speed of processes to the corresponding adverbial phrase. Copy your answers into your notebook.

1 slowly
2 rapidly
3 constantly
4 suddenly
5 gradually

a little by little
b all the time
c in a short space of time
d over a long period
e without any warning

**13** In your notebook, add an adverb or an adverbial phrase to the following statements.
- a The wildlife of coral reefs is endangered by tourism, over-fishing and water pollution.
- b Extinct volcanoes have sunk beneath the sea leaving lagoons surrounded by coral reefs.
- c The crest of a dune can collapse, burying everything in its shadow.
- d Longshore drift moves material along the beach and builds spits and bars across river mouths.
- e The Maldives could sink beneath the sea if global warming is not halted.

131

## 10 • Marine processes

**Extension**

### The case of the vanishing rock. Can you solve the mystery?

As cliffs crumble and the sea encroaches on the coast, huge amounts of rock seem to vanish.

**14** Using the knowledge of marine processes that you have gained from the chapter, complete the following account by giving the correct term for the processes described. What is this process called? Where does the rock end up?

- The base of the cliffs is pounded by waves causing the rock to crack.
- Sea water enters the cracks and dissolves minerals in the rock.
- Waves drag the pieces of rock down the beach and into the sea.
- The rocks bump against one another on the beach and get smaller and smoother.
- Winds push waves up the beach and the waves carry the small smooth rocks or pebbles with them.
- Gradually the pebbles and shingle which are getting smaller and smaller are moved along the beach.
- The waves leave the shingle and sand on the beach at high tide.
- The wind picks up sand and bounces it up the beach beyond the high tide line.

**15** The following questions and answers have been muddled up. Match the question to the answer and copy into your notebook.

Questions:
a What happens if a river's mouth is blocked?
b What happens to the base of a cliff if waves can reach it?
c What happens to the coastline if a beach disappears?
d What kind of rock would you expect to find between two headlands?
e When do atolls form?
f When does coral die?
g Which waves deposit beach material?
h Which waves remove beach material?
i Why can plants survive in salt marshes?
j Why do headlands get shorter?
k Why do sand dunes move?

Answers:
1 Constructive.
2 Destructive.
3 When an extinct volcano with fringing coral reefs is covered by the sea.
4 In temperatures below 18° or above 30 °C, or when it is not covered by water.
5 It becomes weaker and parts of it crumble and fall.
6 Lagoons and inshore lakes form
7 Land erosion and flooding.
8 Sand is piled up by the wind until gravity and the force of the wind cause the crest to topple over. The wind continues to pile up sand from the base, so the dune grows again.
9 Softer rock: it is more easily eroded by marine processes.
10 They have adapted over time to taking up salty water.
11 They are eroded by waves, then caves form, then arches and finally the arches collapse.

## Marine processes 10

### Talking points

What are the arguments against building coastal defences?

How will rising sea levels affect low lying countries?

What measures can be taken to protect these countries?

### Extension

Internet search: Find out about…
Sand dunes
Atolls
Coral
Coastal erosion

Think about the questions from the start of the chapter. Can you answer these now?

- What causes waves?
- When are cliffs eroded?
- Why do spits develop?
- Where do sand dunes form?

# 11 Weather and climate

**In this chapter you will answer...**
- What is the difference between weather and climate?
- When do cumulonimbus clouds form?
- Why are rainforests so wet?
- Where are deserts found?

## 11.1 Weather and climate

The **atmosphere** is the air that we breathe. The **weather** describes the characteristics of the atmosphere for one place for a short time, such as one hour, one day or one week. The weather describes the temperature, rainfall, **humidity**, wind and cloud cover for that place.

The **climate** is the average weather, such as temperature and rainfall, for a place. The average is worked out from weather records over a long period, for example, 30 years.

## 11.2 Weather stations

A **weather station** uses different instruments to measure the weather. It records the weather conditions every hour for a particular place. The information is used to make weather forecasts. A **rain gauge** is used to measure how much rain falls in a period of time. The rain is measured in millimetres (mm). A **maximum-minimum thermometer** measures the temperature. It shows the highest and lowest temperatures recorded. A **hygrometer** measures humidity. Humidity is measured as the percentage (%) of the total water vapour the air could hold at that temperature. Warm air holds more water vapour than cold air. A hygrometer is a **wet-dry bulb thermometer**. The difference in temperature between the wet thermometer and the dry thermometer is used to work out the humidity.

A **barometer** measures **air pressure**. Low pressure usually means wind and rain; high pressure usually means clear skies and little wind. An **anemometer** measures the speed and strength of the wind. A **wind vane** is used to show the direction the wind is blowing from. A **Stevenson screen** is a shelter for thermometers and hygrometers. It is a white wooden box with sides which allow air to flow through. It is white so that the sunlight is reflected away. The thermometers record the temperature in the shade rather than direct sunlight. The box is placed 1.2 meters above the ground. This means the ground surface does not affect the measurements.

> **KEY WORD**
>
> **Weather** is the characteristics of the atmosphere for one place for a short time. It can be measured and predicted. **Climate** is the average weather for a place over a long time.

> **KEY WORDS**
>
> **Latitude** the distance from the equator in degrees
>
> **Tropical** the area between the Tropic of Cancer and the Tropic of Capricorn
>
> **Humidity** the amount of water vapour in the air
>
> **Water vapour** water as a gas

## Weather and climate • 11

**Exercise**

**1** Match the words below with their correct definitions and copy them into your notebook.

1 hygrometer
2 weather
3 barometer
4 humidity
5 climate
6 anemometer

a The amount of water vapour in the air
b An instrument used to measure the speed of the wind
c An instrument used to measure the humidity of the air
d The characteristics of the atmosphere for a particular place
e An instrument used to measure air pressure
f The average weather for a place over a long time

### 11.3 Weather data

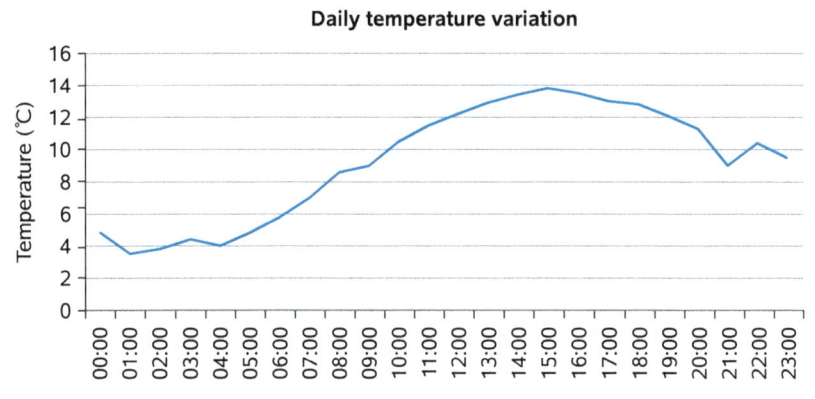

11.1 Daily temperature change

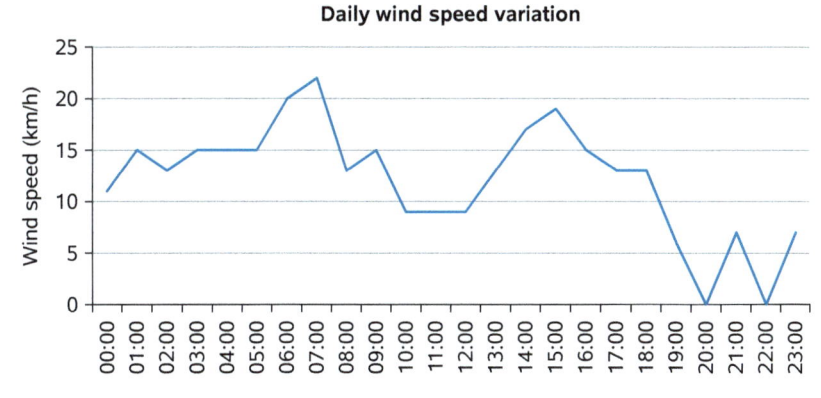

11.2 Daily wind speed change

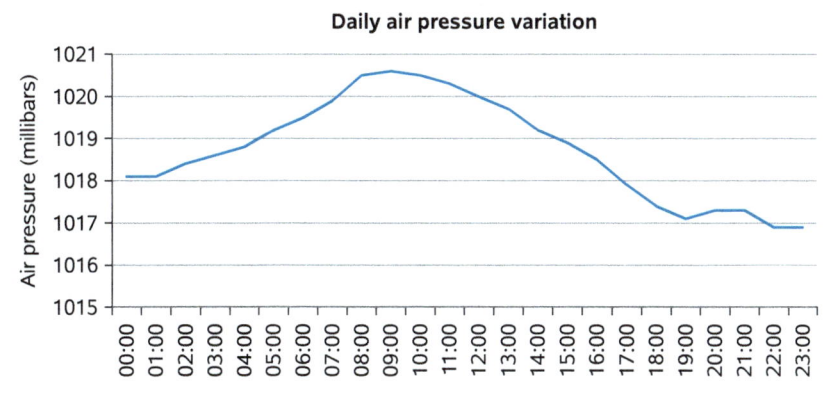

11.3 Daily air pressure change

135

## 11 Weather and climate

**2** Figures 11.1, 11.2 and 11.3 show weather data recorded for a day in April in Vancouver, Canada. Which graph shows data recorded using:
  a  an anemometer?
  b  a maximum-minimum thermometer?
  c  a barometer?

**3** Which of the following statements are true or false? Copy the correct statements into your notebook.
  a  The maximum temperature recorded was 15°C.
  b  The minimum temperature recorded for the day was 3.5°C.
  c  The highest temperature was recorded at 3pm and the lowest temperature at 1am.
  d  The maximum wind speed on this day was over 25km/h.
  e  The highest wind speed occured when temperature was lowest.
  f  The wind speed decreased from 3pm until 8pm and then it rose again.
  g  Air pressure peaked at 11am and then it decreased through the day.
  h  Wind speed shows the greatest variation through the day.

### 11.4 Clouds

Water vapour (gas) in the air **condenses** to form drops of water. **Condensation** is when a gas becomes a liquid. Clouds are made of tiny drops of water or ice crystals. **Cirrus** clouds are very high in the atmosphere. They are made of tiny ice crystals. Cirrus clouds are wispy. **Cumulus** clouds are fluffy clouds. They are individual clouds with flat bases. They occur with sunshine and blue sky. **Stratus** clouds are low, grey clouds that almost totally cover the sky. They often bring light rain. **Cumulonimbus** clouds are storm clouds. They are very tall clouds. They often bring heavy rain and strong winds.

11.4 Cirrus clouds

**4** Pick four adjectives from the table below that best describe:
  a  cirrus clouds
  b  cumulus clouds

| wispy | fluffy | individual | feathery |
| --- | --- | --- | --- |
| heaped | thin | high | puffy |

The amount of cloud in the sky is measured in **oktas**. 8 oktas means that the sky is totally covered in cloud. It is completely grey. 0 oktas means there are no clouds in the sky and it is completely blue.

11.5 Cumulus clouds

## 11.5 Tropical storms

**Tropical storms** begin where the sea is warm, usually over 27°C. This is usually between the Tropic of Cancer and the Tropic of Capricorn. Tropical storms start as the warm sea heats the air. The warm air rises and cools. Water vapour condenses to form cumulonimbus clouds. Rising air means **low air pressure**. Low pressure causes strong winds to develop. In the northern hemisphere the storms spiral in an anti-clockwise direction. They take up more moisture and increase in strength and area as they move across the warm waters of the Tropics. When the winds blow at more than 118 kilometers per hour (km/h) the storm is called a **cyclone** (in the Pacific Ocean), a **hurricane** (in the Atlantic Ocean) or a **typhoon** (in the Indian Ocean).

### The terror of Typhoon Ketsana

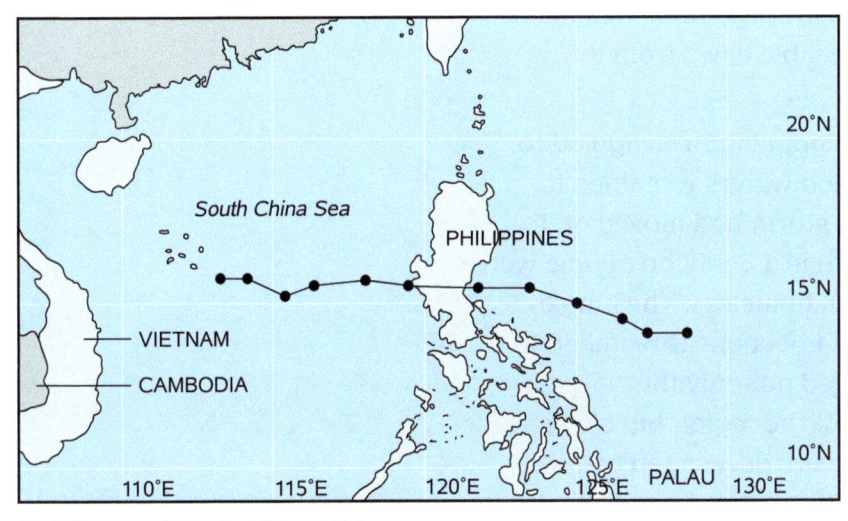

11.6 Course of Tropical Storm Ketsana

Typhoon Ketsana began to form on September 23rd 2009. A low pressure area developed 860 kilometers (km) North West of Palau in the Pacific Ocean. By September 25th it was classified as a tropical depression. As the winds became stronger it became a tropical storm. Later that day it struck the island of Luzon in the Philippines as a severe tropical storm with a diameter of over 400km. It then moved west across the South China Sea and making landfall in Vietnam and Cambodia as a typhoon.

Although the winds reached speeds of over 100km/h when the storm crossed the Philippines they did not cause the most damage. Ketsana brought torrential rain which lasted for hours. It was the heaviest rainfall for the Philippines capital, Manila, for 40 years. On 26th September 40 centimeters (cm) of rain fell in just 12 hours. The President of the Philippines soon declared a state of disaster for the country.

## 11 Weather and climate

Official buildings were turned into makeshift accommodation, and appeals were made for international aid to provide food, medicine and necessities.

86 people lost their lives in Manila in the first few hours. The death toll then grew to over 250 as rivers burst their banks and flood waters engulfed the countryside to depths of more than 6m. Whole villages were submerged in mud. Normal life was suspended as power and telephone lines were broken. Poor drainage systems meant that the waters did not subside in some areas, and families remained stranded on roof tops without food or water for days while the rain continued to fall. Roads turned into raging torrents sweeping everything away – neither vehicles, nor electricity pylons, nor even houses could withstand the force of the floods. For relatives living abroad, their anxiety for their loved ones was made even more acute by the lack of reliable news from the stricken country.

In the aftermath of the storm the population struggled to return to normality. The filthy flood waters remained in towns and villages long after the storm had moved on to the mainland. The lives of more than 1.8 million people were disrupted and 370,000 were made homeless. The human ordeal continued as diseases and infections threatened to claim more lives. Ketsana damaged not only the infrastructure and the economy of the region but also its agriculture: rice and corn fields were devastated by the waters, ruining the prospects of a good harvest. The unique storm and its consequences will live long in the national memory.

**5 Using the information above, answer the following questions in your notebook.**

a In which direction did Typhoon Ketsana move from September 23rd–29th?

b Using the information in the text put the stages of development of a typhoon in ascending order (weak to strong): typhoon; tropical depression; severe tropical storm; low pressure area; tropical storm.

c Did high winds or heavy rainfall have the most serious effects on the Philippines?

d Why did the President declare a state of calamity?

e How did the country's infrastructure cope with the disaster?

f What dangers threatened the inhabitants of the Philippines in the aftermath of the typhoon?

# Weather and climate 11

**6** Who said what? Choose the speaker for each of the following quotations from the box below.

a "Our country is in a state of disaster but we will recover."

b "We were too weak to swim and my wife started to panic but my dear neighbour pulled us out of the water to safety on his rooftop."

c "There were pictures from eye witnesses on the Internet of the terrible impact of Ketsana so why did none of the emergency services reach us for days?"

d "I cannot get any news about my parents and all flights to Manila from Hong Kong have been cancelled. I don't know what to do."

e "My team is working day and night in a temporary clinic. We are doing our best but the queues just get longer."

f "I have lost my home and my business beneath the layer of stinking mud and the water is not draining away."

g "My rice crop has been ruined so my family faces poverty and hunger."

h "My parents were at work when water started streaming into the house so I carried my little brother upstairs to the roof. We stayed there until the water level dropped and waited for my parents but they didn't come back."

| | | | |
|---|---|---|---|
| A Filipino hospital worker in Hong Kong | An old couple | Business man | Medical aid worker |
| President | | Rice farmer | Villager | Young schoolgirl |

**7** Which word in the box below best describes the feelings of each of the speakers?

| | | | |
|---|---|---|---|
| angry | sad | exhausted | grateful |
| anxious | critical | optimistic (thinking things will turn out well) | pessimistic (thinking things will turn out badly) |

139

## 11 ● Weather and climate

### Language

**Reported speech – Questions**

The same changes of tense and pronouns apply in reported questions but the word order changes to: question word – subject – verb – object – adverbs/phrases. The auxiliary **do/did** disappears and the simple past or past perfect is used instead. The future **will** becomes **would**. [**that** is not needed]

For example, *"How do typhoons develop?"* = *He asked how typhoons developed.*

*"Where did Ketsana make landfall?"* = *He asked where Ketsana had made landfall.*

*"What will the homeless do in the rainy season?"* = *He asked what the homeless would do in the rainy season.*

If there is no question word in the direct question, use **if** or **whether** to introduce the question in reported speech.

For example, *Did you see the pictures on the Internet?* = *He asked if/whether she had seen the pictures on the Internet.*

Verbs which introduce questions: ask; enquire; wonder

**8** Put the following direct questions into reported speech and write your answers in your notebook.

  a  A survivor asked," Why didn't the water drain away?"
  b  "How much rain fell in 24 hours?"
  c  "Why did we have no help?"
  d  "What is the worst consequence of Typhoon Ketsana?"
  e  "Will the country recover?"

**9** Put the quotations in the 'who said what' exercise into reported speech. Try to use reporting verbs: to declare; to complain; to regret: to explain; to describe how; to question.

### Exercise

**10** Which is the odd one out? Find the odd word from each list below. Copy each correct word group into your notebook.

  a  raging, streaming, torrential, trickling, wild
  b  isolated, stranded, abandoned, rescued
  c  resist, succumb, survive, withstand
  d  cyclone, hurricane, tsunami, typhoon
  e  cancel, continue, halt, suspend
  f  emerge, engulf, inundate, submerge
  g  combat, fight, struggle, surrender
  h  catastrophe, calamity, luck, disaster

### 11.6 Extreme weather: drought

A **drought** is a long period of time with no or below average rainfall. When rain falls it **infiltrates** the ground. **Infiltration** is when water runs from the surface of the ground into the soil. Water is stored in the soil or rocks (groundwater). Plants take up this water through their roots. In a drought plants may die as their roots cannot reach water in the ground.

## Weather and climate 11

**Exercise**

**11** Sort the adjectives in the box below into those which describe dry conditions and those which describe wet conditions. Copy and complete the table below into your notebooks.

| Dry conditions | Wet conditions |
|---|---|
|  |  |

| | | | | |
|---|---|---|---|---|
| arid | saturated | scorched | sodden | soggy |
| wet | parched | moist | dry | desiccated |
| soaked | humid | damp | dehydrated | drenched |

**11.7** Extreme drought conditions

**Exercise**

Using figure 11.7, choose the correct statement from the options below and copy into your notebook.

**12** In the foreground there is:
   a  a woman dragging her cow
   b  stunted trees and parched earth
   c  paddy fields

**13** In the middle ground there are:
   a  cattle
   b  dried up paddy fields
   c  clouds in the sky

**14** In the background there are:
   a  hazy mountains
   b  herds of cattle
   c  farmers harvesting rice

**15** Above the horizon the sky is:
   a  cloudy
   b  cloudless
   c  stormy

**16** Below the horizon the land looks:
   a  lush
   b  fertile
   c  barren

**17** From the photo the rice harvest looks:
   a  ruined
   b  ripe
   c  promising

**18** The cow looks:
   a  well fed
   b  strong
   c  emaciated (very thin and starving)

**KEY WORDS**

**foreground**  at the front
**background**  at the back

141

# 11 • Weather and climate

## Climate

The **climate** is the average weather for a place. The average temperature and average rainfall is worked out from measurements over a period of 30 years.

## 11.7 Climate graphs

A climate graph shows the average temperature and average rainfall for each month of the year. It can show how patterns change over the year. The **annual range** in temperature is the difference between the highest average temperature and the lowest during the year. **Seasonal distribution** describes the difference in temperature and rainfall in the seasons – winter, summer, spring and autumn.

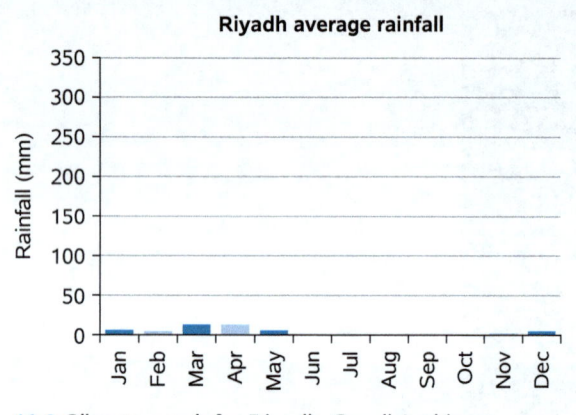

**11.8** Climate graph for Riyadh, Saudi Arabia

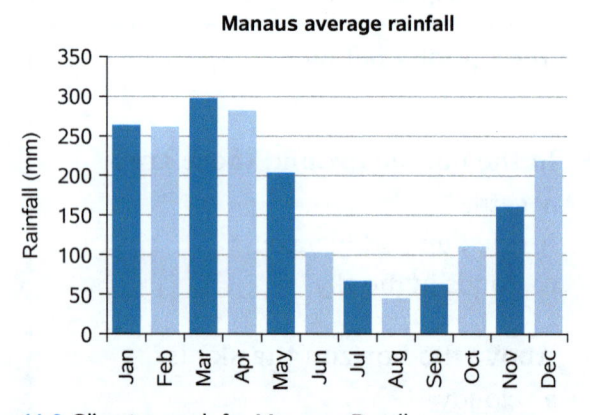

**11.9** Climate graph for Manaus, Brazil

**Exercise**

**19** Using the graphs above and the options in the box below, decide which types of graphs are:
   a the graphs showing average rainfall for Riyadh and Manaus?
   b the graphs showing average temperature for Riyadh and Manaus?

scattergraph    line graph    bar graph    pie chart    pictogram

142

# Weather and climate • 11

**20** Using the graphs, find out in which place is:
  a the minimum temperature 26°C?
  b the July temperature 35°C?
  c there the lowest annual range in temperature?
  d the maximum average monthly rainfall 30mm?
  e the minimum average monthly rainfall 45mm?
  f has the greatest seasonal change in temperature?

**21** Using the graphs and the options in the box below, pick the words that would best describe the climate of:
  a Riyadh, Saudi Arabia    b Manaus, Brazil

| desert | cold | seasonal | rainforest | warm |
| dry | wet | hot | humid | arid |

**22** Copy and complete the paragraphs below by filling in the blanks with the comparatives or superlatives of the words in brackets.
In Riyadh, Saudi Arabia, the _____ (cold) month is February with a temperature of 14°C. The _____ (hot) month is July with a temperature of 35°C. This is a much _____ (great) seasonal distribution compared to Manaus. In Manaus the _____ (warm) months are September and October. However the temperature is only 2°C _____ (hot) than the _____ (cold) month where the temperature is 25°C. This means Manaus has a much _____ (small) annual range in temperature than Riyadh.
Riyadh is much _____ (dry) than Manaus. The _____ (wet) months in Riyadh are March and April. However these months are still _____ (dry) than the _____ (dry) month in Manaus.

## Influences on climate

### 11.8 Latitude

**Latitude** is a measurement of distance from the equator. The latitude is measured in degrees. Lines of latitude join places of equal distance from the equator. The **equator** is the horizontal line dividing the earth into the **northern hemisphere** and the **southern hemisphere**. A hemisphere is half of the globe. The equator is 0° latitude. The Tropic of Cancer is 23.5° north of the equator. The Tropic of Capricorn is 23.5° south of the equator. The North Pole is 90° north and the South Pole is 90° south of the equator. The earth moves around the sun. The strength and intensity of the sun is influenced by latitude. The sun heats the earth most between the tropics. Further north or south of the tropics the heat from the sun is less intense. This means that climates are warmer nearer the equator and at lower latitudes.

## 11 Weather and climate

> **Exercise 23** Riyadh is latitude 25° north and Manaus is latitude 3° south. Find out if the following statements are true or false and copy the correct statements into your notebook.
> a Both Riyadh and Manaus are north of the equator.
> b Riyadh is north of the tropic of Cancer.
> c Manaus is nearer the equator than Riyadh. It has an equatorial climate.
> d Riyadh is within the tropics.

### 11.9 Pressure systems

**Low pressure** is usually found at the equator and around latitude 45° north and south. Warm air rises. Rising air leads to low air pressure. Rising air cools and water vapour condenses to form clouds and bring rain. These regions have a wet or damp climate. **High pressure** is usually found around 30° north and south of the equator, and at the poles. Sinking air leads to high air pressure. Air gets warmer as it sinks to the earth's surface. This leads to clear skies and dry weather. These regions have a dry climate. These are deserts.

### 11.10 Wind

**Wind** is moving air. Air moves from areas of high pressure to areas of low pressure. Winds may blow warm air into cold areas and cold air into warm areas. The **trade winds** blow warm air from the tropics towards the equator.

### 11.11 Distance from the sea

The sea heats up slower than the land surface. It also takes longer to cool down. Places close to the sea have **maritime climates**. This means that the sea stops them from becoming either very cold or very hot. They have a **mild** climate. Places a long way from the sea have **continental climates**. Their climates changes during the year from a very cold winter to a very warm summer. Riyadh has a continental climate. There is a large seasonal range in temperature. Riyadh is in the middle of the Arabian Peninsula

### 11.12 Ocean currents

**Ocean currents** are the movement of water in the sea. Ocean currents move warm and cold water around the oceans. Warm water heats the air above it. This leads to warm, damp climates. Cold water leads to cooler, dry climates. Warm ocean currents move north and south on the west sides of the oceans. This means that the east coasts of continents often have warm, damp climates. The west sides of continents are usually drier. Deserts are often on the west coast of continents such as the Atacama in South America and the Namib in Africa. This is where cold ocean currents bring dry climates.

### 11.13 Altitude

**Altitude** is the height of land above sea level. The temperature of the air decreases as the height increases. Temperature decreases by about 6°C with every 1000m increase in altitude. This means that on average a town at an altitude of 1500m will be 6°C colder than a town at 500m.

### 11.14 Tropical rainforest and desert climates

**Tropical rainforests** are found along the equator and between latitudes 25° north and south of the equator. Hot deserts are found around latitudes 30° north and south of the equator.

## Exercise

**24** Copy and complete the paragraphs below by deleting the incorrect options.

Rainforests have a *cool/warm, wet/arid* climate. The average temperature is around *6–10°C/25–28°C*. The temperature has a *low/high* annual range of about *3°C/20°C*. Rainfall is *high/low* all through the year. The *monthly average/annual* total is over 2000mm.

Rainforests grow along the equator where the direct sun *cools/heats* the air. The air *rises/sinks* and cools. The water vapour *condenses/evaporates* to form clouds and *heavy/no rain*.

Hot deserts are found around *altitude/latitudes* 15°–30° north and south of the *Tropic of Capricorn/equator*. This is where *low/high* pressure leads to *cloudy/clear, dry/damp* climates.

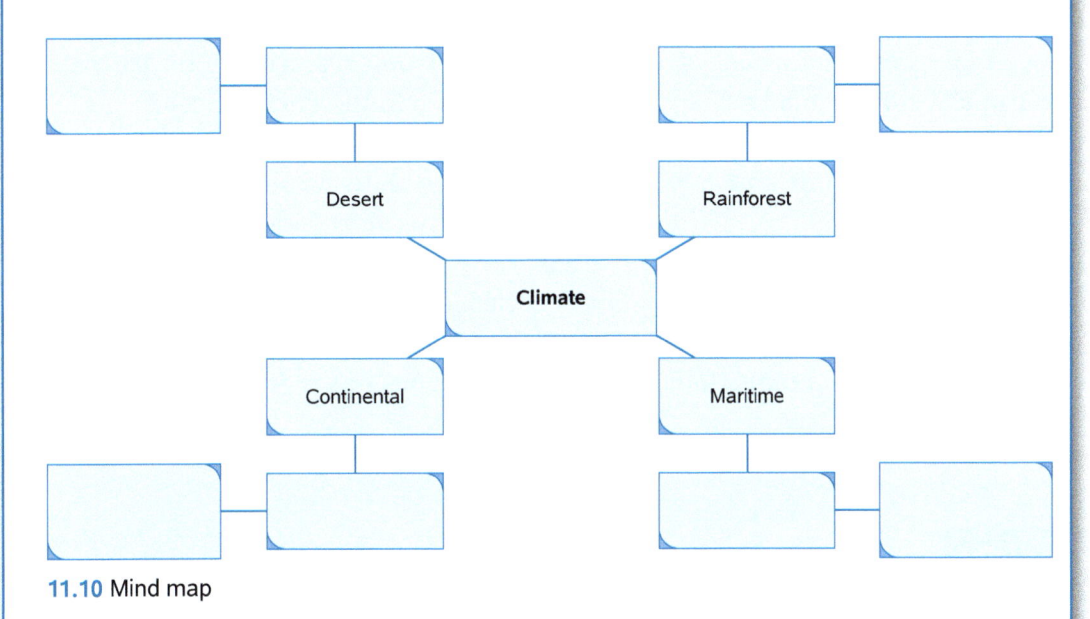

**11.10** Mind map

**25** Copy the mind map above into your notebook and put the following climate characteristics in the appropriate small boxes.

| hot | warm | dry | wet |
| hot summer | warm summer | cold winter | mild winter |

**26** In the larger boxes group the influences on each type of climate.

| cold ocean currents | low pressure | near the sea | low latitude | 30° latitude |
| warm ocean currents | high pressure | far from the sea | low altitude | |

## 11 • Weather and climate

**Extension**

**27** Match the following questions to their answers below and copy the completed statements into your notebook.

**Questions**
- a Where would you expect to find the coldest climates?
- b Around which latitudes are deserts found?
- c What happens when warm air rises? What does the sky look like?
- d What happens when cold air sinks? What does the sky look like?
- e What kind of weather would you expect when high pressure forms?
- f When is a tropical storm called a cyclone?
- g In which oceans do typhoons and hurricanes form?
- h Where are warm ocean currents found?
- i Why are tropical rainforests mostly found on the eastern side of continents?
- j Why is it colder in the mountains than on the coast?

**Answers**
1. Between 15° to 30° north and south of the Equator
2. Because the warm ocean currents heat the air. Water vapour condenses as warm air rises, causing precipitation
3. Clear skies and dry weather
4. High pressure forms; the sky is clear
5. At high latitudes i.e. the North and South Poles
6. When tropical storm winds are over 118km/h in the Pacific Ocean
7. Low pressure forms; the sky is cloudy because water vapour condenses
8. On the western side of oceans
9. The higher the altitude, the cooler the air
10. Typhoons in the Indian Ocean; hurricanes in the Atlantic Ocean

### Talking points

What causes climate change?
What are the links between severe storms, flooding and drought?
How can people prepare for droughts and floods?

**Extension**

**Internet search: Find out about…**
Flooding in the country of your birth
Typhoons, hurricanes and cyclones
Climate change

Think about the questions from the start of the chapter. Can you answer these now?
- What is the difference between weather and climate?
- When do cumulonimbus clouds form?
- Why are rainforests so wet?
- Where are deserts found?

# 12 Ecosystems and resource management

**In this chapter you will answer...**
- Why do some trees have buttress roots?
- Who lives in hot deserts?
- Where is desertification happening?
- What is sustainable development?

**KEY WORD**

Plants and animals live in **ecosystems**. Large ecosystems are influenced by the climate and by people. People need to use ecosystems sustainably for them to survive.

## 12.1 Ecosystems

An **ecosystem** is where plants and animals live and connect with their environment. Plants and animals are **organisms**. The **inorganic environment** is the air, soil, water and sun. Ecosystems can be very big or very small. A rock pool is a very small ecosystem. **Biomes** are very large ecosystems that cover whole countries. Deserts and rainforests are biomes.

## 12.2 Food chains

Plants and animals are linked to each other and the inorganic environment by **food chains**. Plants are **producers**. They produce food using the energy of the sun. This is **photosynthesis**. Plants also take minerals and water from the soil through their roots. Animals are **consumers**. They consume plants or other animals to get the energy for life. **Herbivores** are animals that eat plants. **Carnivores** are animals that eat other animals. **Omnivores** are animals that eat both plants and animals.

**KEY WORDS**

**Ecosystem** where plants and animals live and connect with their inorganic environment

**Food chain** plants and animals are linked to each other by producing and eating food

**Rainforest** forests found around the equator with a warm, wet climate

**Desert** arid land found between latitudes 15°–30° north and south of the equator with a hot, dry climate

**Biodiversity** the number of different species found in an area

**Sustainable development** meeting the needs of the present without harming the needs of the future

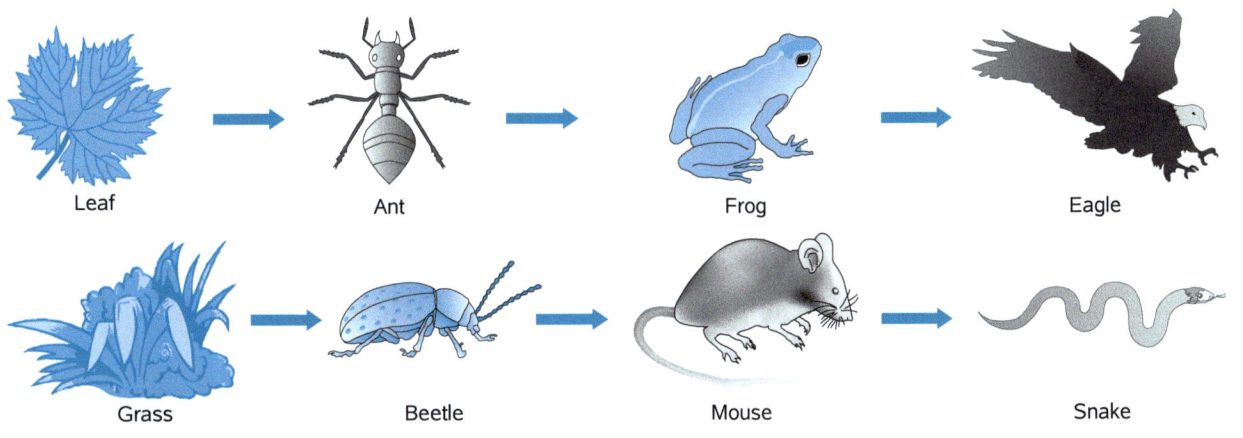

### Exercise

Leaf → Ant → Frog → Eagle

Grass → Beetle → Mouse → Snake

12.1 Food chains

1 Look at the food chains in figure 12.1. Copy and complete the table below by putting the animals and plants in the correct columns (some may go in more than one column).

| Producers | Herbivores | Carnivores | Consumers |
|---|---|---|---|
|  |  |  |  |

147

# 12 Ecosystems and resource management

## 12.3 Distribution of rainforest and desert ecosystems

**Rainforests** are found along the equator and between the Tropics. They are found between **latitudes** 24° north and 24° south. Rainforests are found on the continents of South America, Africa, Asia and Australasia. The Amazon in South America is the world's largest rainforest.

Hot **deserts** are found around latitudes between 15° and 30° north and south. They are found in North and South America, Africa, Asia and Australasia. The Sahara in Africa is the world's largest desert.

> **Exercise**
>
> 2 Are the following statements true or false? Copy the correct statements into your notebook.
>   a Rainforests are found around 0° latitude.
>   b Deserts are found north and south of the Tropics.
>   c Deserts are found at 20° altitude.
>   d A rock pool is an example of a biome.
>   e Countries are bigger than continents.
>   f Rainforests are found in the countries of Africa and Asia.
>   g Deserts are found on the continents of Africa and Asia.
>   h Eagles and snakes are carnivores.
>   i Plants are consumers.

## 12.4 Rainforest ecosystems: plants

Rainforests have a warm, wet climate. Average annual rainfall is over 2000mm each year. The average monthly temperature is around 27°C. Plants grow quickly in this climate. They form layers of different heights. Rainforest trees grow very tall as they compete with each other for the energy of the sun. They form a **canopy** layer. This layer stops sunlight from reaching the ground below. The tallest rainforest trees are called **emergents**. They stick out above the canopy layer. This means they get a lot of sunlight for photosynthesis. These tall trees are supported by **buttress roots**. The base of the tree is spread out wide to stop the tree falling over.

It is darker beneath the canopy layer. Smaller trees such as banana trees, form an **undercanopy**. These trees have very large leaves so they can use the small amount of light. A **shrub layer** of bushes and small plants can grow in spaces where large trees have fallen or near rivers.

Many rainforest plants have **drip-tips** on their leaves. These are pointed ends to the leaves. Drip-tips help rainwater run off the leaves. They stop the heavy rain

**12.2** Rainforest vegetation

from breaking the leaf. Nutrients reach the soil when plants die. However the soil of rainforests is quite infertile. This means there are not many nutrients in it. Rainforest plants grow quickly. Therefore the plants rapidly take up the nutrients through their roots and store them. They only return to the soil when the plants die.

> **Exercise**
>
> **3** Copy and complete the statements below in your notebook by matching the beginning and the end of each sentence.
>
> 1 Leaves have drip tips to…
> 2 Large leaves in the shrub layer…
> 3 Large trees have buttress roots to…
> 4 The canopy layer of trees…
> 5 The soil of the rainforest is…
>
> a …allow plants to make use of the small amount of sunlight
> b …reduces the amount of sunlight reaching the forest floor
> c …quite infertile as nutrients are stored in the vegetation
> d …support them as they grow so tall
> e …allow heavy rainwater to run off the leaves

## 12.5 Rainforest ecosystems: animals

Rainforests have a very large **biodiversity**. This means there are many different species (types) of plants and animals. Some rainforest birds and animals only live in the canopy layer and never touch the ground. Some birds and animals just live on the ground in the darkness.

> **Exercise**
>
> **4** Match the following definitions with the correct words in the table below and copy into your notebook.
>
> 1 canopy layer
> 2 biome
> 3 buttress roots
> 4 emergents
> 5 drip-tips
> 6 herbivores
> 7 biodiversity
>
> a an ecosystem found across continents
> b tallest trees which reach above the canopy for sunlight
> c animals that eat plants
> d the layer of tall trees which blocks out sunlight from the forest floor
> e roots which spread out at the base of a tall tree to support it
> f the number of different species
> g pointed ends to leaves to help rain run off

## 12.6 Use of rainforests by humans

Small groups of people have lived in rainforests for thousands of years. These are the **indigenous** people. They use the plants and animals for food, fuel for cooking, shelter and tools.

## 12 · Ecosystems and resource management

**Transnational companies** from industrialised countries now **exploit** the rainforests. They use the resources of the rainforests to make money. **Deforestation** is when trees are cut down and removed. Deforestation of rainforests is for **timber**, minerals, sources of energy and for land for agriculture. **Timber** is wood used for building, furniture making and paper making. Tropical **hardwoods** are particularly important. These are large trees which grow slowly, for instance mahogany, ebony, teak. Minerals mined in rainforests include gold, iron ore, aluminium ore and uranium. Oil and natural gas are mined in rainforest areas. Deforestation reduces the size of the rainforests. The resources allow both MEDCs and LEDCs to make money. However deforestation harms both the local environment and the local people.

> **Exercise**
>
> **5** Find the odd one out from the words below. Copy the correct word groups into your notebook.
>
> a bribery, corruption, fraud, honesty
> b indigenous, native, global, local
> c pessimistic, positive, hopeful, optimistic
> d exploit, conserve, manipulate, use
> e habitat, home, surroundings, overseas
> f natural, industrial, ecological, environmental
> g death, survival, extinction, disappearance
> h salvation, destruction, rescue, recovery
> i logs, wood, timber, leaves

### 12.7 Impact of deforestation

> **Exercise**
>
> **6** Copy and complete the gaps in the following sentences using words from the box below. Not all of the words are needed.
>
> a If the tropical rainforests are _____ greenhouse gas emissions will increase.
> b If they are not protected by law many species will become _____.
> c _____ companies cut down trees to supply the furniture trade.
> d The people who _____ the rainforest are often robbed of their land by unscrupulous developers.
> e The _____ environment will be at risk if the rainforests are not _____.
>
> | corrupt | honest | inhabit | conserved | destroyed | exploited |
> | global | local | extinct | logging | saved | indigenous |

### 12.8 Sustainable development

Sustainable development means to meet the needs of the present without harming the needs of the future. This means people can keep using rainforest products such as timber or minerals, but these resources must still be available for people to use in the future.

## Palm oil: salvation for the Indonesian rainforests or the agent of their final destruction?

1 Tropical rainforests cover over 60% of Indonesia, South-east Asia. They support the highest **biodiversity** in the world after Brazil. Industrialised countries have **exploited** these rainforests for rubber, **timber** and minerals to fuel their economic growth. This exploitation changed the traditional way of life of many of the **indigenous** population. It also led to serious concerns about the impact of **deforestation** on the local and global environment. Rainforests have been described as the 'lungs of the world' because they absorb carbon dioxide and give out oxygen (**photosynthesis**).

2 In the second half of the 20th century the solution to the **dilemma** of how to manage the global demand for energy whilst protecting the environment seemed to be at hand. The oil palm grows naturally in the undercanopy of the rainforests. The average yield from 100 kilograms (kg) of fruit is 20kg of oil. This can be used as industrial bio-fuel, as well as an ingredient in food and household products. It is cheap to grow oil palms without causing pollution. Oil palm plantations were seen as a superb example of **sustainable development**: the palms can live longer than 150 years and can be replanted so the energy source is **renewable**. As they grow they absorb $CO_2$, so they **offset** the $CO_2$ that is produced when bio-fuel is burnt. From 1994–2004 oil palm production increased by 400% in Indonesia. By 2007 the country was the top producer of palm oil in the world.

3 Unfortunately sustainable development has not proved to be the reality either for the native people of Indonesia or for the environment. Conservationists suspect that the creation of new plantations is to make money from the high profits from trade in **mahogany** and other tropical hard woods. Large areas of cleared land remain unplanted but deforestation by the palm oil companies continues. $CO_2$ is released into the atmosphere from the **slash and burn** methods of land clearance. The pollution of rivers and the **contamination** of the ground from the use of chemicals destroy the delicate balance of the environment.

4 They also question how environmentally friendly the oil palm plantations are. Unlike wild palms, cultivated palms are **felled** once they are 25 years old. This is because harvesting the fruit becomes too difficult if they grow higher than 10 metres. Soil in old palm oil plantations rapidly becomes poor in nutrients and cannot be used for other crops. The diversity of natural forests is never achieved – the only thing that grows in an oil palm plantation is oil palms! This is **monoculture**.

5 The destruction of the rainforest continues, and the disappearance of the natural **habitat** threatens the rich biodiversity of wildlife of Indonesia. Already the orangutan, the Sumatran tiger and the Asian elephant are in danger of **extinction**. As wild animals are forced to search for food near human settlements they are often killed as they threaten cattle and crops. Environmentalists fear that the situation has already gone too far for many of the **endangered** species to be saved.

6 The indigenous population is exploited too. They receive low wages for long hours. In addition, their land is sometimes taken without their agreement. They can do little about it because the traditional rights of ownership are not written down. Indigenous hunters complain that they cannot sustain their traditional way of life. They need money to buy food that the land

## 12 ● Ecosystems and resource management

and forest used to provide, so they turn to the palm oil companies for work.

7 Indonesia, its people and the biodiversity of its forests are at risk because of the **relentless** search for cheap energy. The palm oil industry was seen as sustainable development at first but now there are problems which must be faced if the future is to remain bright – for Indonesia and the world.

**7** Find the appropriate heading for each of the above paragraphs from the options below.

a The end of the line for certain species
b The geography of Indonesia
c The future for palm oil
d Palm oil as the answer to the problem
e The difference between theory and reality
f The reality of palm oil production
g The impact on the population of Indonesia

**8** Choose the correct answer to the following questions from the options below and copy into your notebook.

a Where is Indonesia located?
  A: south-west Asia
  B: south-east Asia
  C: north-east Asia
b What are its natural resources?
  A: wheat, iron, coal
  B: fish, potatoes, gold
  C: timber, rubber, minerals
c Why was palm oil seen to be the answer to global demands for energy?
  A: it is renewable and offsets $CO_2$
  B: it produces no $CO_2$
  C: it is non-renewable and offsets $CO_2$
d What are the uses of palm oil?
  A: rocket fuel
  B: soaps and margarine
  C: furniture polish
e What problems for the indigenous population have emerged?
  A: low wages and lost land
  B: awareness of global TV
  C: they can not speak the language
f What have been the effects on the biodiversity of the rainforests?
  A: biodiversity has increased
  B: biodiversity has decreased
  C: no effect on biodiversity

**9** What are the main arguments against palm oil production? Copy your answers into your notebook.

---

Idioms are colourful images which are used to express an idea. The meaning is not literal.
For example, *It is not my cup of tea = that is not to my taste.*

**10** Some idioms occur in the comprehension above. Match the idioms below to the meaning and copy into your notebook.

1 To close the stable door when the horse has bolted
2 To make hay while the sun shines
3 The end of the line

a A future where things will go well
b Acting promptly saves a lot of problems and extra work
c If too many people are involved little is achieved

4 Too many cooks spoil the broth
5 To turn a blind eye
6 To have all one's eggs in one basket
7 A rosy future
8 To be left high and dry

d Nothing else can be done
e Intentionally to ignore the real state of affairs
f To act too late to save the situation
g To be left helpless and without resources
h To depend on just one thing

**11** Which of the above idioms could be used in paragraphs 4, 5 and 7 of the Comprehension exercise?

### 12.9 Desert ecosystems

Hot deserts are found between latitudes 15°–30° north and south of the equator. They have an **arid** climate. They are very dry with only about 250mm rain each year. Some deserts may have no rain in some years. During the day the temperature may rise to over 45°C. At night it may be under 5°C. This is a large **diurnal** range in temperature. This means there is a big difference between night and day. Hot deserts are mostly sand and bare rock. There is very little vegetation (plants). Therefore there are very few animals. There is a low **biodiversity**. Desert plants are **xerophytic**. They can survive in the very dry climate. Many plants are **succulents**. This means they can store water in their leaves and stems. Their leaves and stems are **waxy** and have sharp **spines**. This reduces loss of water from the plants during the hot day. The spines also stop animals eating them.

Some plants are **ephemeral**. This means they only grow and flower when it rains. The seeds remain dormant (sleeping) in the soil until rain comes. The desert soil is very thin and dry. Some plants have very long roots that reach deep into the rock to reach groundwater. Some plants have roots that spread out near the soil surface. This means they can use the little amount of rain that falls. There are very few animals living in deserts. The food chains are very short. Many of the animals live underground and are **nocturnal**. This means they only go onto the ground surface at night when it is cooler.

12.3 A desert ecosystem

## 12 • Ecosystems and resource management

> **12** Use the photographs on previous page to fill in the gaps in the following paragraph. Copy the completed paragraph into your notebook.
>
> Deserts have _____ rock and sand with very little _____. The sky is usually _____ as _____ pressure causes air to sink to give clear, dry conditions. The lack of rainfall means vegetation is _____. Desert plants are _____ which means they can survive without rain for long periods. Plants have _____ to reduce loss of water in the hot sun and to stop animals eating them. _____ are plants which store water in their stems.

### 12.10 Use of deserts by humans

People have lived in deserts for thousands of years. In the past many of these people have been **nomads**. They moved around with herds of animals such as camels, cattle and goats. They followed the rain to find fresh plants for their animals. However many of the nomad tribes have now been forced to settle in towns and villages. Settlements have developed in deserts where there are natural resources such as oil, for example Riyadh in Saudi Arabia. Settlements have grown beside **oases** along trade routes such as Kashgar in China. An **oasis** is a natural spring where groundwater reaches the surface. Agriculture can take place along the shores of rivers, for example, The Nile in Egypt. Crops are given water by **irrigation**. Water is taken from the river to the fields through canals or pipes. Oil, iron ore, diamonds and uranium are all mined in deserts.

### 12.11 Desertification

In some places the desert is expanding. This is **desertification**. Land around some deserts has become more and more infertile. The soil is low in nutrients and there is not enough water to support plants, animals or people.

The **Sahel** is the area on the southern edge of the Sahara desert which is currently experiencing desertification.

Long periods of **drought** and **overgrazing** also lead to desertification. When too many animals feed on one area of land they eat all the vegetation. This means the wind can easily blow the soil away forming **dust-storms**. The animals also make the ground hard by trampling. This means rainwater runs over the land surface and carries the soil away. This is **soil erosion**.

Overpopulation is when there are too many people for the resources to support. There may not be enough energy supplies, water or fertile soil to grow crops. Trees provide wood for fuel and building. In some places the people have cut down all trees around the settlements. This means the soil is easily eroded. **Wells** have been dug to get **groundwater** for settlements. But as the settlements have grown the amount of groundwater has reduced. Desertification is also the result of **overcultivation**. This is when the nutrients have been removed from the soil by constant growing and harvesting of crops.

---

**Language**

Nouns which end in -ion or -ation often indicate a process

To exploit = exploitation

If the verb ends in -e this is dropped.

To devastate = devastation

Verbs which end in -ify change the 'y' to 'i' and add -cation.

To clarify = clarification

**13** Match the term to the definition in the box below. Copy your answers into your notebook.

1 desertification
2 irrigation
3 deforestation
4 conservation
5 exploitation
6 urbanisation

a Increasing the number of people living in towns and cities
b To remove trees from an area of land
c To protect and care for the natural environment or traditional life style
d Turning an area into desert
e To supply an area with water
f To use natural resources often belonging to others for one's own benefit

**14** Read the following descriptions and decide which of the above processes is occurring. (More than one process may occur at the same time)

a Land is cultivated year after year so all the nutrients are exhausted and it becomes infertile.
b Trees are felled to make space for new plantations of oil palms.
c Channels are dug to take water from lakes and rivers to fields of crops.
d The use of tropical hardwoods for furniture is banned (made illegal).
e International companies employ local workers to gather oil palm fruit for low wages.
f The constant movement of animals makes the ground so hard that rain water cannot penetrate.
g Logging and mining companies build roads through the forest to make the transport of logs and minerals easier.
h Long periods of drought dry the soil and turn it into dust which is blown away by the wind.
i MEDCs give money to compensate tropical nations on condition that they leave their forests standing.

## 12.12 Management of desertification

Planting trees is an important way of reducing desertification. **Shelter belts** are lines of trees which are planted to protect the soil from erosion by wind and rain. The roots of the trees help hold the soil in place. The trees reduce the speed of the wind.

### Language

**Modal verbs**

These are verbs which are used with another verb to indicate possibility, need, obligation, permission or probability. They are often used in persuasive speech or writing, such as appeals for aid or action. In their long form they are used with 'to + the infinitive'. They often have a short form which is used without 'to'. The short form is used more often than the long form.

To be able – can; *could
To be allowed to – may; *might
To have to – must
To be supposed to/ought to – shall; *should

For example, *MEDCs have to take action to save the planet*.
*MEDCs must take action to save the planet*.

The forms: **could/should/might** have a less strong, more conditional meaning than can/shall/may. They are also used in the past tense.

For example, *The orangutan might be saved from extinction*.

To make negative sentences put the 'not' between the shortened form and the infinitive.

For example, *We must not forget to protect the flora and fauna of the rainforests*.

In the negative form can + not = cannot

## 12 • Ecosystems and resource management

With passive constructions the word order is: part of the modal verb; (not); passive infinitive. For example, *The rainforests may/may not be saved*.

**15** In the following sentences about rainforests and deserts, choose the short form of the modal verb which fits best. Copy the correct sentence into your notebook.

   a Everyone *must/might* recognise the importance of the rainforests.
   b We *should/may* take global warming seriously.
   c When an area suffers many periods of drought it *may/must* become desert.
   d Cattle *must/can* cause desertification if they eat all the vegetation.
   e Logging and mining companies *might/should* not clear huge tracts of rainforest.
   f Trees *could/might* be planted in long belts to prevent soil erosion by the wind.
   g Farmers *should/might* not grow the same crops on the same land year after year.
   h In arid areas irrigation *could/must* improve the harvest.
   i If MEDCs did more to control palm oil production greenhouse gas emissions *might/must* decrease.

**16** Read the following statements and decide which support sustainable development in rainforests and/or desert environments. Copy your answers into your notebook.

**KEY WORD**

**Sustainable development** to meet the needs of the present without harming the needs of the future

   a Logging companies replant hardwood trees as they chop them down.
   b The land cleared by logging companies is turned into pasture for large scale cattle farming.
   c Local people are encouraged to plant trees to reduce water and wind erosion.
   d International organisations control the number of new oil palm plantations.
   e The indigenous people abandon their land and their traditional way of life to work in factories and mines and services.
   f Tourism brings wealth and employment to the indigenous people.
   g Tourist interest in the culture and way of life of the indigenous people helps to preserve their traditions
   h Large hotels are built in previously unspoilt areas to meet the tourist demand.
   i Local farmers are encouraged to grow drought-resistant crops that do not need so much water.
   j Plantations of oil palms are restricted to areas of rainforest that have already been cleared.
   k Nomadic tribes are forced to stay in one place so groundwater supplies dry up because of the increased demand all year round.
   h The growth of settlements near waterholes and oases drives animals away.
   i When oil or other minerals are discovered townships and modern infrastructures develop.
   j Hunting endangered species is made illegal.

# Ecosystems and resource management 12

**17** Complete the crossword using the clues below

### Across:
1. Something that eats something else
5. Groundwater is brought to the surface by digging a _____
6. Someone who moves from place to place in search of food and water
7. When animals eat all the vegetation in an area so that nothing regrows
10. Deserts have a large _____ range in temperature
11. A covering or layer
12. A _____ belt is a line of trees planted to prevent soil erosion by the wind

### Down:
2. A tropical hardwood
3. Plants that can survive in very dry climates
4. Plants that remain dormant until it rains
8. Rising above the canopy layer of trees
9. An animal that comes out mostly at night

157

## 12 • Ecosystems and resource management

### Talking points

Why should the biodiversity of rainforests be protected?

Why is land becoming desert?

Who benefits most from the exploitation of the rainforests?

Should LEDCs use their rainforests to make money?

How can the international community best help to protect the rainforests?

### Extension

**Internet search: Find out about…**

Oil palms

Deforestation

Desertification

Think about the questions from the start of the chapter. Can you answer these now?

- Why do some trees have buttress roots?
- Who lives in hot deserts?
- Where is desertification happening?
- What is sustainable development?

# Glossary

Translate these key words into your first language
Listen to the glossary pronunciation at www.oxfordsecondary.co.uk/oclssupport

**Aid** Help or assistance

**Alleviate** To reduce the effect of something unpleasant

**Altitude** The height above sea level

**Anemometer** An instrument to measure the speed and strength of the wind

**Annual range** The difference between the highest and lowest average temperatures

**Anti-natalist** A policy which aims to reduce birth rates

**Arable** Growing of crops

**Arch** A narrow 'bridge' of rock made by waves in a headland

**Atmosphere** The gases which surround the Earth

**Atoll** A coral reef circling an extinct volcano

**Attraction** A place or feature which draws people to visit

**Attrition** Rocks and stones hitting against one another, becoming smaller and smoother

**Background** At the back of a picture

**Backwash** Waves moving down a beach

**Bankfull** Water in a river is up to the top of the banks

**Bar** A barrier of sand or shingle which blocks a river mouth or bay

**Bar chart** A type of graph using bars of varying lengths to illustrate quantities

**Barometer** An instrument to measure air pressure

**Barrier reef** A coral reef which grows off a tropical island or coast separated by a deep channel of water

**Barter** Exchanging goods or services in return for other goods or services

**Bay** A curve on the coast line where soft rock has been eroded

**Beach** A gentle slope of sand or shingle where land meets the sea

**Bedding plane** A horizontal line of weakness between layers of sedimentary rock

**Bedload** The heaviest material carried by a river: boulders, rocks and large stones

**Biodiversity** All the different species in a particular environment

**Biogas** Gas which comes from decaying plant material

**Biological weathering** The effect of plants on rocks causing them to break up

**Birth rate** The number of babies born each year per 1000 people

**Breach** To break through

**Buffalo** A type of cattle; water buffalo are used for pulling machines in Asia

**Bulb** A type of plant root that stores nutrients after flowering and which produces new flowers each year

**Buttress root** A wide base to a tree trunk to keep a tall tree stable

**Cancer** A condition which causes the growth of tumours and the destruction of healthy tissue

**Canopy** The uppermost layer of vegetation in a forest

**Capital investment** Using money to make a profit

**Carbon dioxide** A colourless odourless gas

**Carbonation** A chemical reaction between rainfall and limestone rock

**Carbonic acid** A weak corrosive chemical compound

**Carnivore** A meat eating animal

**Cash crop** A crop that is grown to be sold, not for one's own use

**Cave** A hollow in the base of a cliff

159

# Glossary

**CBD** Abbreviation for Central Business District

**Cereal** Grain eg corn, oats, wheat, barley, maize, rice

**Chalk** A soft sedimentary rock composed of calcium carbonate

**Chemical weathering** Changing the minerals in a rock so that it breaks up

**Cirrus** Wispy, high altitude clouds

**Cliff** A steep rock face

**Cliff retreat** The wearing away of a cliff by marine erosion so that it is further inland

**Climate** The average weather for a place over a long period of time

**Combine harvester** A farm machine that cuts grain

**Commercial** Relating to buying and selling for money

**Commute** To travel daily to and from work

**Composite volcanoes** Steep sided volcanoes at convergent plate margins

**Composition** All the elements which come together to form something

**Condensation** The conversion of gas to liquid (ie water vapour to water)

**Confluence** The point where rivers join

**Conservation** Protection of natural and cultural resources

**Constructive waves** Gentle waves which carry material onto the coast and deposit it

**Consumer** Someone or something that eats, uses or takes up something else

**Contaminate** To make impure/pollute/poison

**Contamination** Pollution

**Continental climate** Climate in the middle of large land masses: cold winters and hot summers

**Continental crust** Thick but light crust forming land

**Conurbation** A large urban area where towns merge with each other

**Convection currents** Movement in a circular pattern as heat causes the current to rise; cold causes the current to fall

**Convergent** Moving towards one another

**Coral bleaching** The whitening of coral which can cause death to the organisms

**Coral reef** An underwater ridge of coral

**Core** The centre of the earth

**Corrasion** The weakening of cliffs/river bed and banks by water throwing rocks at them

**Corrosion** Rocks being dissolved in seawater or river water

**Crisis** A very difficult time when things can go completely wrong

**Cross contamination** When two or more separate varieties of plant are changed because of their proximity to one another

**Cross section** A slice of the river showing the shape of the river channel

**Cruise** A holiday on board a boat, ship or liner, usually calling in different ports

**Crust** The solid surface of the earth

**Cultural** The shared knowledge, customs and beliefs of a community

**Cumulonimbus** Tall thunder clouds

**Cumulus** Large fluffy white clouds

**Cyclone** Large scale storm system in the Pacific Ocean

**Dairy** Produce that comes from cows-cheese, cream milk

**Dam** A barrier built across a river to control the flow. A reservoir is often created on the upstream side

**Death rate** The number of deaths each year per 1000 people

**Death toll** Number of people killed

**Debt** Something that is owed to someone else

# Glossary

**Decomposition** Changing the chemicals which make up a rock so that it breaks up

**Deficit** An amount which is less than is needed

**Deforestation** The clearing of forests

**Delta** A triangular river mouth where the river breaks up into smaller channels before reaching the sea

**Demography** The study of populations

**Demultiplier effect** How certain conditions cause something to decrease

**Density** The number of people living in a particular area

**Dependant** A person who relies on others for food, care, money and support

**Deposit** To put down or drop something

**Deposition** The putting down or dropping of the load

**Desert** A very dry area with little vegetation

**Desertification** The process by which land becomes so dry that no vegetation grows there

**Destination** The place that you are travelling to; the intended end of the journey

**Destitution** Extreme poverty

**Destructive waves** Powerful waves which pull material away from the coast

**Dilemma** A problem which has no obvious solution

**Discharge** The amount of water in a river at a certain place and at a certain time

**Disintegration** Breaking into smaller pieces

**Dispersed** Scattered over a large area

**Distributary** Small water courses of a river delta

**Distribution** The way in which a population is spread across an area

**Divergent** Moving apart

**Domestic** Based at home, not in another country

**Donor** Someone who gives

**Dormant** Inactive, sleeping

**Downstream** The part of the river near its mouth

**Drainage basin** The area from which all rainwater and tributaries run to one river

**Drip tip** The pointed end to a leaf which directs water down to the roots of the plant

**Drought** A severe shortage of rainfall over a long period

**Dry-point site** A place that is not likely to flood

**Dust storm** Dust carried by a strong wind

**Earthquake** Shaking of the crust as a result of the sudden movement of plates

**Earthquake proof** Able to resist the force of an earthquake

**Ecology** Study of the environment and organisms

**Economic migrant** Someone who moves to get more money and a better standard of living

**Economically active** Someone who works and earns money usually aged 16–65 years

**Ecotourism** Tourism which aims to cause no damage to the environment that is visited

**Emergency** A desperate situation that needs to be addressed urgently

**Emergent** A tree which is taller than the surrounding trees

**Emigrate** To move out of one's country to live somewhere else

**Employment structure** The distribution of people working in the primary, secondary and tertiary sectors

**Energy** Power

**Environment** Surroundings

# Glossary

**Ephemeral** Something that lasts for only a short time and leaves no trace

**Epicentre** Point on the earth's surface directly above the focus of an earthquake

**Equator** Imaginary circle around the Earth equidistant from the North and South Pole

**Erosion** The process of wearing down something

**Eruption** Explosion; something breaking out

**Evacuate** To move people from a dangerous place to somewhere else

**Exfoliation** Pieces of the outer layer of rock break away

**Exploit** To take advantage of something or someone for one's own benefit

**Export** Something sent away to be sold

**Extensive** Spreading over a large area

**Extinct** Having died out

**Facilities** Arrangements that are provided so that people can easily find comfort, enjoyment and entertainment. eg. swimming pools, hotels, parks, restaurants

**Factor** Reason or element which influences people or situations and has an effect on outcomes

**Famine** Widespread decline in the amount of food per person for a large number of people

**Fell** To cut down

**Fertilise** To improve the growing conditions by adding nutrients to the soil

**Finite** Limited

**Float** To rest on the surface of the water

**Flood** When water overflows its normal course and covers the surrounding land

**Floodplain** Flat land on either side of a river channel formed by a river flooding

**Focus** The point within the crust where two tectonic plates suddenly move

**Fold mountains** Mountains formed by the crushing and compacting by convergent plates

**Food chain** A sequence or hierarchy showing how living things feed and are eaten by others

**Footloose industry** An industry that can locate almost anywhere

**Foreground** At the front of a picture

**Foreign exchange** The changing of one national currency (money e.g. US dollars) into another national currency

**Fossil** Plant or animal remains which have been buried for thousands of years, and which have been preserved in rock.

**Freeze thaw** Fluctuating temperatures above and below 0°

**Friction** The resistance between two moving objects

**Fringing reef** A coral reef which edges the coast or an island separated by a shallow channel of water

**Fuel** Something that is burned to provide energy

**Function** The use or purpose of something

**GDP** abbreviation for Gross Domestic Product (a country's income minus foreign investments)

**Geothermal** Heat that comes from beneath the earth's surface

**Global** Worldwide

**GM (genetically modified)** When the genes of an organism have been manipulated to cause changes in it

**Gradient** The steepness of an area of land

**Granite** Large-grained igneous rock

**Grant** Money given by a government to enable a person or a company to do something

**Gravity** The force pulling objects down to the earth's surface

# Glossary

**Green Revolution** A change from traditional to modern methods of farming which greatly increased the productivity of some LEDCs

**Greenhouse** Literally a glass house that retains the sun's heat and helps plants to grow. The term is now also used to describe the way $CO_2$ and other gases e.g. methane trap the sun's heat and cause the average temperature of the Earth to rise: the greenhouse effect

**Groundwater** The water that is stored in rocks beneath the earth's surface

**Hamlet** A group of houses but with no services

**Hardwood** Wood from very slow growing broad leaved trees

**Harvest** To pick or gather produce

**Headland** Part of the coastline consisting of hard rock which sticks out into the sea

**Headquarters** Main base from which directions are given

**Hemisphere** Northern or southern half of the Earth

**Herbicide** A substance that kills plants

**Herbivore** A plant-eating animal

**Hierarchy** A group organised according to importance or size

**High pressure** Atmospheric condition when cold air sinks leading to calm, dry weather

**Higher order services** Services to which people travel and which serve a large area e.g. cinema, secondary school, hypermarket

**Holiday** Time taken off from work or usual activity when you can enjoy a different way of life, often away from your home

**Honey pot** A huge attraction that draws great numbers of tourists

**Humidity** The amount of moisture in the air

**Hurricane** A large scale storm system in the Atlantic Ocean

**Hybrid** A plant produced from crossing two different plants

**Hydraulic action** The power of water hitting cracks in cliffs or a river bed and the banks

**Hydro-** A prefix meaning water. Hydroelectric power means power generated by water pressure

**Hygrometer** An instrument to measure humidity

**HYV** Abbreviation for high yielding variety

**Igneous** Rock formed from cooling magma as it rises to the earth's surface

**Immigrate** To come to a new country to settle there

**Impact** The effect something has on something else

**Import** Something brought into a country or region from another country or region

**In situ** In the same place

**Incentive** Something that encourages others to do something

**Indigenous** Originating and naturally living or growing in a place

**Industry** A commercial activity that involves many people

**Inequality** Differences between groups which affect their status

**Infant mortality rate** The number of children who die before they reach one year old per 1000 per year

**Infiltrate** Water moving from the ground surface into the soil

**Infinite** Without any limits

**Infrastructure** The basic organisation of public services

**Inner zone** Residential area nearest to the CBD

**Inorganic** Not animal or vegetable but composed of minerals

**Input** Something being put into a process

**Intensive** Concentrated into a small area

**Inundate** To flood

163

# Glossary

**Investment** Money put into a venture or a business to make more money

**Involuntary migrant** Someone who moves because of reasons beyond his/her control

**Irrigate** To supply water so that crops will grow

**Irrigation** The supply of water to an area

**Joint** A vertical line of weakness in rock

**Lag time** The time between the peak rainfall and the peak discharge of a river

**Lagoon** A lake formed by a bar or a reef cutting off the sea

**Landslide** A large movement of rock and soil down a slope

**Latitude** The distance from the equator in degrees

**Lava** Magma when it erupts from a volcano

**Leakage** The unintentional loss of revenue from tourism going to TNCs

**Leisure** Free time when you do not have to work

**Levee** Banks formed by flooding at the edge of the river channel

**Life expectancy** The average number of years a person is expected to live

**Limestone** Sedimentary rock composed of calcium carbonate

**Linear** Arranged in a line

**Litter** Rubbish which has been dropped on the ground

**Livelihood** Source of income

**Location** Where something is situated

**Long profile** A description of the changes in gradient of the land a river crosses

**Longshore drift** The movement of beach material along the beach

**Low pressure** Atmospheric condition when warm air rises leading to windy and wet weather

**Lower course** The part of the river near sea level

**Magma** Molten rock beneath the crust in the mantle

**Mahogany** Reddish brown hardwood

**Malnutrition** When a person does not eat enough of a certain type of food e.g. protein

**Management** The care, organisation and control of a business, an area or resources

**Mantle** The layer of molten rock beneath the earth's crust

**Manual** Done by hand

**Marine erosion** The wearing away of the coast by the sea

**Maritime climate** Mild climatic conditions because of the effect of the sea

**Market** A place where goods are bought and sold

**Marram grass** A grass with long roots which grows on sand dunes

**Marsh** Low-lying wet land often beside a body of water

**Maximum-minimum thermometer** A thermometer which records the highest and lowest temperatures

**Meander** A large bend in a river

**Meander neck** The area of land between two meanders

**Mid-ocean ridge** The line of hills or mountains on the sea bed at a constructive plate margin

**Migrate** To move from one place to another

**Migration** Movement of people oranimals from one place to another

**Mixed farm** A farm with crops and livestock

**Model** A pattern which shows complex influences in a simple format

**Molten** Melted; in hot liquid form

**Monitor** To check the progress of something or someone

# Glossary

**Monoculture** The cultivation of just one crop

**Monsoon** A wind that reverses direction seasonally and which brings heavy rain

**Mouth** The point where a river meets the sea

**Multiplier effect** How certain conditions cause something to increase

**Natural increase** The growth of the population caused by the birth rate being greater than the death rate

**NIC** Abbreviation for Newly Industrialising Country

**Nomadic** Moving from place to place according to the season

**Nuclear reactor** A power station or plant where splitting atoms (nuclear fission) produces heat energy

**Nucleated** Clustered together around a central point

**Oasis** Fertile place in a desert where fresh water can be found

**Ocean currents** The movement of water in the sea

**Oceanic crust** The surface of the earth beneath the sea

**Offset** To compensate for the effects of another factor

**Okta** Measure of cloud cover

**Omnivore** An animal that eats everything

**Orchard** A field with fruit or nut trees

**Organic** Something living that develops naturally

**Oriented** Directed towards/dependent on

**Output** Something produced by a process

**Over fishing** Fishing so much that fish stocks do not recover

**Overcultivation** The continuous farming of the same piece of land which removes the nutrients and makes it infertile

**Overgrazing** Animals feeding on an area so that all the vegetation disappears

**Overhang** Rock extending over the waterfall

**Ox/oxen** Cattle used for pulling heavy loads and for ploughing

**Oxbow lake** An old meander which has been cut off from the river channel

**Oxidation** A chemical reaction with oxygen which turns substances reddish brown

**Oxygen** A colourless odourless gas which is essential for life

**Pacific Rim** The countries around the Pacific Ocean

**Package** A type of holiday where everything is organised for you in advance by the travel company

**Pastoral** A farm with livestock

**Peak** The highest point

**Per capita** For each person

**Perish** To die

**Perishable** An item that is likely to deteriorate after a short time

**Permanent** Lasting for ever

**Pesticide** A substance that kills pests

**Photosynthesis** The process by which green plants turn carbon dioxide and water into oxygen and sugars

**Physical weathering** The effect of rain and temperature on rocks causing them to disintegrate

**Plantation** A large farm where trees are grown for their produce such as tea, coffee, bananas

**Plate** A large section of the earth's crust

**Plate margins** Lines at which plates meet

**Plough** To break up the soil

**Plunge pool** A deep pool at the bottom of a waterfall

**Policy** A formal plan of action which a person, a group or a government follows

# Glossary

**Pollution (air noise visual environmental water)** Making something dirty or impure

**Population** The number of people who live in a place such as a village, town, region, country or continent

**Population pyramid** A type of graph to show the number of males and females alive in a country

**Pot hole** A hole caused by erosion on the river bed

**Poverty** The state of being poor

**Primary industry** An industry that removes raw materials from the earth e.g. mining, fishing forestry farming

**Process** A series of actions which has a particular aim

**Profit** The income after all costs have been paid

**Profit margin** Measure of how much profit is made after all expenses have been paid

**Proportion** A part and its size relative to the whole amount

**Prosperity** Having money, success and doing well

**Pull factor** A reason which attracts people to a place

**Push factor** A reason which makes people want to leave a place

**Pyroclastic flow** Violent eruptions of lava, with hot ash and hot gases

**Quad bike** A four wheeled bike suitable for rough terrain

**Radioactivity** The nature of a substance such as uranium or plutonium that emits high energy particles which can be harmful

**Rain gauge** An instrument to measure rainfall (in millimeters)

**Rainforest** A thick evergreen tropical forest

**Ranch** A livestock farm which covers a large area

**Rate** How fast something happens; how often it happens

**Ravages** Damaging effects

**Raw material** A natural material e.g. rock, soil, vegetation

**Recipient** Someone who receives something

**Refugee** Someone seeking safety from war or persecution

**Relentless** Constant and without any respite

**Renewable** Something that can last indefinitely as there is an endless supply

**Resource** A supply of a material that can be used by people.

**Richter Scale** Measure of the intensity of an earthquake (0 weakest – 10 strongest)

**River bank** The side of the channel

**River bed** The bottom of the channel

**River load** The material carried by a river

**Rural** Relating to the country

**Rural-urban fringe** The area where town becomes country

**Rural-urban migration** The movement of population from the country to the town

**Sahel** The area of Africa south of the Sahara Desert

**Salt marsh** Flat areas of plants and mud which are covered by water at high tide

**Saltation** The action of bouncing along

**Sand dune** A heap or hill of sand found on coasts or in deserts

**Season** Period of the year. A peak season means that at this time of year a place or activity is very popular. A low season means that there is little interest in the place or activity at this time of year. Seasonal attractions are e.g. snow; festivals; botanical gardens

**Seasonal distribution** The difference in temperature and rainfall in each of the 4 seasons

**Secondary industry** An industry that uses raw materials to manufacture new items

**Sector** A part of a whole system

**Sedentary** Staying in one place

# Glossary

**Seed drill** A hollowed out shallow channel prepared for planting seeds

**Seismic** Relating to earthquakes

**Service** Something that providing goods or help for the population e.g. Bus service

**Settlement** People living in a particular place

**Shanty town** Poor quality housing on the outskirts of large towns in LEDCs and where many people live

**Shear** To cut the hair or fleece or leaves from something

**Shelter belt** A strip of land planted with trees to give protection against erosion by wind and rain

**Shield volcanoes** Gentle sided volcanoes at divergent plate margins

**Shingle** Small pieces of stone on a beach

**Shoddy** Badly constructed

**Shortage** Lack

**Silt** Lighter material in river water; it is deposited on the flat land when the river floods

**Site** The land on which a settlement is built

**Situation** The characteristics of the area around a settlement

**Slash and burn** Traditional agricultural method of cutting down trees in a small area, burning them and then cultivating the land

**Slip-off slope** Gently sloping beach on the inside bend of a meander

**Slump** A sudden drop in value

**Smog** Thick fog caused by pollution

**Soil erosion** The wearing away of the top layer of earth

**Solar energy** Energy from the sun

**Soluble** Able to be dissolved in water

**Source** The starting point or origin

**Sphere of influence** The area served by a settlement or service

**Spit** A beach that sticks out into a river mouth or bay

**Squalid** In poor and dirty condition

**Stack** A pillar of rock that is no longer joined to the mainland

**Stalactite** A pillar hanging from the roof of a limestone cave built up from deposits of rainwater dripping through

**Stalagmite** A pillar rising from the floor of a limestone cave built up from deposits in rainwater dripping through the roof and onto the floor of the cave

**Staple food** Basic food

**Starvation** Not having enough food to live

**Sterilization** Stopping a person being able to reproduce

**Stevenson screen** A shelter for thermometers and hygrometers which protects the instrument from direct sunlight

**Store** A place to keep something safe

**Strain** Stress caused by demand on resources

**Stratus** Low-lying flat grey clouds

**Stricken** Badly affected

**Structure** The way in which different elements fit together to form a whole

**Subduction** The process by which oceanic crust moves beneath continental crust and into the mantle

**Subsidence** Sinking of the land surface

**Subsidy** A contribution of money by the government to help a company or organisation to function

**Subsistence** Growing enough food to survive with little or none to sell

**Suburb** Residential area on the edge of a town

**Succulents** Plants with thick fleshy leaves and stems which can store water

167

# Glossary

**Suspension** Fine particles carried along in the river water without sinking to the bottom

**Sustainable** Meeting the needs of today without harming the needs of people in the future

**Sustainable development** The management of a resource that meets the needs of the present without harming the ability of future generations to meet their own needs

**Swash** Waves moving up a beach

**System** Several parts which come together to make a whole

**Tectonic plates** Large pieces of crust which float on magma

**Tertiary industry** An industry that provides a service to a population

**Thermal** Producing heat

**Thermal power station** A power station which uses fossil fuels to produce energy

**Threshold population** The minimum number of people needed to keep a service working

**Tide** The rise and fall of the sea against the coast, usually over a 12 hour period

**Timber** Wood for building or for furniture

**TNC** Abbreviation for Transnational Company

**Tor** A rocky mass of granite at the top of a hill

**Tourism** Travel to different places for pleasure

**Tourist** Someone who travels away from home for pleasure

**Traction** Large rocks rolling along the river bed

**Trade winds** Winds which blow warm air from the Tropics towards the equator

**Traditional** A way of life or a style which has not changed over the years

**Transform plate margins** Plates moving alongside one another, sliding past one another in opposite directions or moving in the same direction

**Transnational** Crossing international boundaries

**Transnational Company** A company with its main base in one country but which has factories and stores in other countries

**Trawling** Fishing by dragging a net

**Tributary** A river which joins a larger river

**Tropical** Relating to the area between the Tropic of Cancer and the Tropic of Capricorn

**Trough** The low hollow area between waves

**Tsunami** A wave caused by an earthquake on the ocean bed

**Turbine** A machine with blades that are turned round by water, air or steam to produce electricity

**Typhoon** Large scale storm system in the Indian Ocean

**Undercanopy** The lower layer of trees in a forest

**Upper course** The part of the river near the source, usually high land

**Upstream** The part of a river near the source

**Urban** Relating to the town

**Vaccination** An injection for a person or an animal to give protection against an infection

**Velocity** Speed

**Village** A small settlement with a small number of low-order services

**Volcano** A mountain formed by magma being released at the earth's surface

**V-shaped valleys** Shape of river valleys in upper river courses

**Water vapour** Water as a gas in the air

**Waterfall** A shelf in a river bed where the water falls vertically down to a lower level

**Wave** Movement of surface water caused by the wind

# Glossary

**Wave cut notch** A large crack caused by wave erosion at the base of a cliff

**Wave cut platform** Flat solid rock at the base of a cliff

**Wave height** The distance between the peak and a trough of a wave

**Wave length** The distance between the peaks of two waves

**Weather** The state of the atmosphere-temperature, rainfall, wind, sunshine and cloud cover-for a short period of time

**Weather station** A place which measures the weather for reports and forecasts

**Weathering** The break down of rocks in situ by the action of rain and temperature changes

**Well** A hole dug to get to fresh water, gas, oil

**Wet** A site with a good fresh water supply

**Wind vane** An instrument which indicates the direction of the wind

**Windmill** A building with revolving sails which are driven round by the wind to produce energy

**Xerophytic** Plants suited to desert conditions

**Yield** The amount produced or grown

**Zigzag** A diagonal movement repeatedly going one way and then the other

# Answers

**Chapter 1** Population

1. More babies being born = rise in birth rate
   More babies dying = increase in infant mortality
   More people dying = rise in death rate
   People living longer = increase of life expectancy
   The number of babies being born is more than the number of people dying = natural increase

2. high; changing; clean; death; high money; little; drop; birth; high; rising; death; decline; birth; fall; growing; low; careers; slower; are lower;

3. a to increase, to rise, to soar, to grow, to accelerate,
   b to tumble, to drop, to dwindle, to decline, to fall, to decrease
   c to stabilise, to stay
   d to fluctuate, to change

4. pyramid; base; 20–24; economically; dependents; old; stage; demographic; higher; growing

5. a larger, b greater, c lower, d higher, e older, f faster, g smaller, h lower

6. a 1979, b the country was in danger of not being able to support its people with food, jobs and energy, c a system of financial and social rewards, d workers are more closely monitored by their employers, e yes – population is 400million lower than predicted before 1979, f one child has responsibility of four grandparents and two parents; aging population; women prefer careers to starting families; ratio of men to women makes it harder for men to find wives

7. 

| Noun | Adjective | Noun | Adjective |
|---|---|---|---|
| wealth | wealthy | poverty | poor |
| prosperity | prosperous | affluence | affluent |
| riches | rich | comfort | comfortable |
| need | needy | misery | miserable |

8. a 50 year old widow, b a female graduate, c a doctor in a rural community, d a farmer, e an only child, f a young couple with one child

9. Immigration: d, g
   Emigration: b, e, f
   Tourism: a, c, h

10. a true, b not given, c false, d true, e true, f true, g not given, h true, i not given, j true, k false, l true

11. a Juanita, b Manuel, c Sergei, d Tomo

12. 

| 1 b | We arrived in Hong Kong at 13h00. |
|---|---|
| 2 a | The coach came into the station fifteen minutes early. |
| 3 a | He entered the country illegally. |
| 4 a | They got to the border at nightfall. |
| 5 a | She went from her village to the city. |
| 6 a | I set off from my hiding place at dawn to avoid the enemy patrols. |

13. a The lowest population densities are found in the **west** of China.   b The highest population densities are found in the **south** and **east** of China.   c The population densities in the **south/east** are higher than in the **north/west**.

14. a The land to the west is **higher** and **steeper** than in the east.
    b It is much **drier** in the west and **wetter** in the east.
    c In January it is **warmer** in the east than the west.
    d n June the east is **hotter** than the north and west of China.
    e The **colder** and **drier** climate in the west makes life there much **harder**.
    f It is **easier** to grow crops in the east as it is **wetter** and **warmer**.

## 15

```
Flatter land                Higher rainfall          Less extreme             Very hot or very          Very dry so            High and steep
so easier to                so better                temperatures so          cold temperatures         hard for crops         land hard for
build on                    farming                  more comfortable         do not make life          and people             buildings and
                                                     to live                  easy for people           to survive             roads
                    ↓                                                                            ↓
              SOUTH AND EAST                                                              NORTH AND WEST
                    ↓                                                                            ↓
More accessible    Bigger cities and     High population          Low                Lack of large           Landscape too
for roads,         more industries       density                  population         industries and large    difficult to build
airports etc       provide more                                   density            cities so few jobs      roads, railways or
                   jobs so attract                                                   available               airports so area
                   more people                                                                               is inaccessible
                                              ↓
                                           CHINA
```

## 16

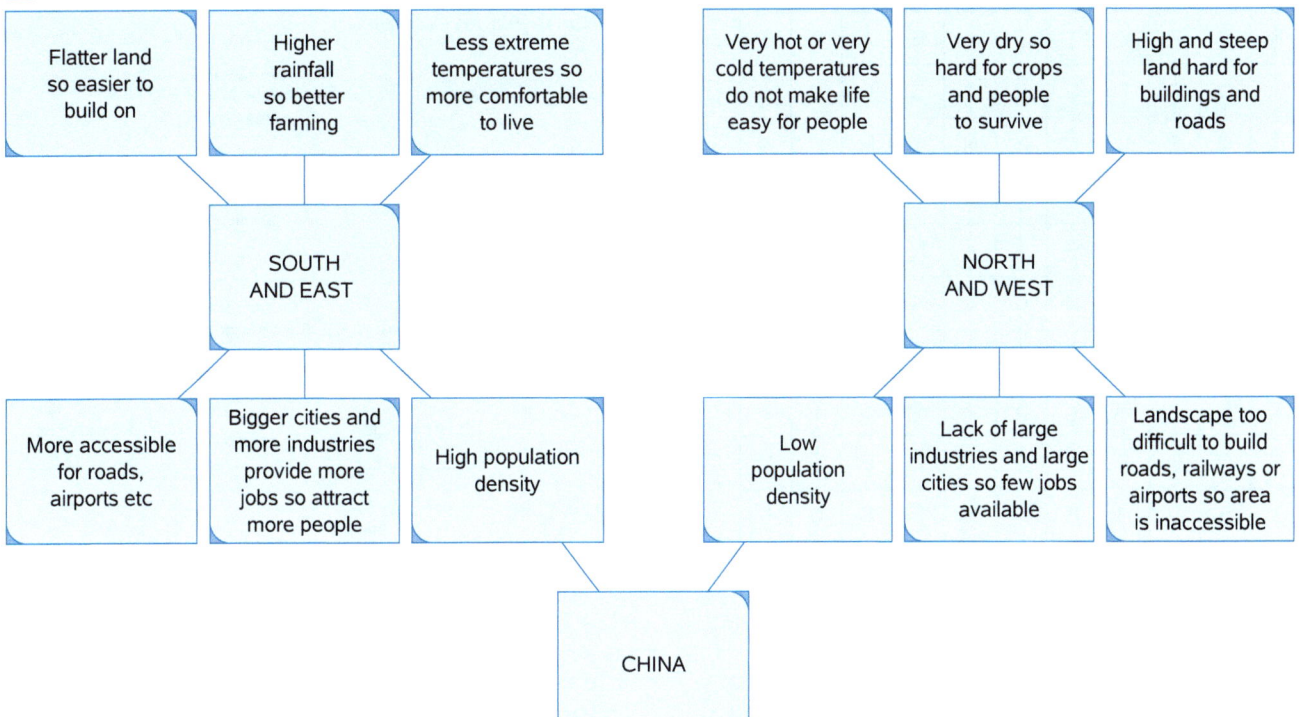

| Events | Rise or fall in birth rate | Rise or fall in death rate | Total population growth or decline? |
|---|---|---|---|
| a A period of economic growth. | Rise | Fall | Growth |
| b A period of political stability | Rise | Fall | Growth |
| c An earthquake | Fall | Rise | Decline |
| d An epidemic of flu. | Fall | Rise | Decline |
| e Several years of **drought** | Fall | Rise | Decline |
| f Forest fires which devastate crops and settlements | Fall | Rise | Decline |
| g Improved health care. | Fall | Fall | No change |
| h The outbreak of war | Fall | Rise | Decline |
| i The provision of wells to supply clean water | Fall | Fall | No change |

**17** a Involuntary – push factor, b Economic/voluntary – pull factor, c Involuntary – push factor, d Voluntary – pull factor, e Economic/voluntary – pull factor, f Voluntary – pull factor, g Voluntary – pull factor

**18** a The number of people living in a town, an area, a country or a continent is called its **population**. b How people are spread across an area is known as **population distribution**. c How many people live in a given area is known as **population density**. d The study of population is known as **demography**.

## Chapter 2 Settlements

**1** Pyramid (top to bottom): Conurbation, City, Town, Village, Hamlet, Farm

**2** a hamlet, b farm, c village, d town, e conurbation

**3** a C, b D, c B, d A

**4** It is following a road and a river

**5** a hamlet, b town, c village, d city

**6** a A, b B, c D, d E, e F, f G, g I

**7**

| situation | The characteristics of the area surrounding a settlement |
|---|---|
| site | The natural characteristics of the actual location of the settlement |
| function | The purpose of a settlement |
| threshold population | The minimum number of people needed to keep a service running |
| sphere of influence | The area served by a settlement or service |

171

# Answers

**8**

| D | N | P | U | T | S | L | E | I | R | I |
|---|---|---|---|---|---|---|---|---|---|---|
| I | U | O | S | H | E | I | C | E | U | I |
| S | C | P | E | R | R | N | T | R | U | A |
| P | L | U | T | E | V | E | C | O | F | A |
| E | E | L | T | S | I | A | N | E | U | L |
| R | A | A | L | H | C | R | S | M | N | F |
| S | T | T | E | O | E | R | N | T | C | T |
| E | E | I | M | L | S | I | T | E | T | I |
| D | D | O | E | D | O | L | P | E | I | N |
| I | S | N | N | R | S | N | L | S | O | L |
| C | S | I | T | U | A | T | I | O | N | T |

**9** Busy, crowded, noisy, expensive, polluted, modern

**10**

| mountains | chalet |
|---|---|
| suburbs | detatched; semi-detatched; |
| inner zones | terraced house; apartments/flats |
| countryside | farmhouse |

**11** a true, b false, c false, d false, e true

**12** a pressure on the infrastructure and quality of life; air pollution; congestion, b they reduce the flow of air so allowing smog to build up over the city, c days lost from work due to congestion; commuters spending hours each day in traffic jams; deaths from respiratory diseases and road accidents, d commuters – fewer cars on the roads, quicker travel to and from work; people using buses and metros pay just one fare; local population breathe better air

**14** a Mexico City is surrounded by high mountains, b High levels of air pollution are caused by the 4 million private cars, c The city's drinking water is contaminated by waste water and sewage, d The health of its inhabitants is improved by better air quality, e $CO_2$ emissions have been reduced, f Time will be saved by travelling on the metro bus, g Tickets will be bought in advance

**15** a Private cars used to cause traffic congestion, b Diesel buses used to emit $CO_2$ gas.  c Factories and vehicles used to pollute the air.  d Smog used to hang over the valley.  e People used to suffer from respiratory diseases.  f Children used to die in traffic accidents.

**16** Please note: No two mind maps need to look the same, this is just an example.

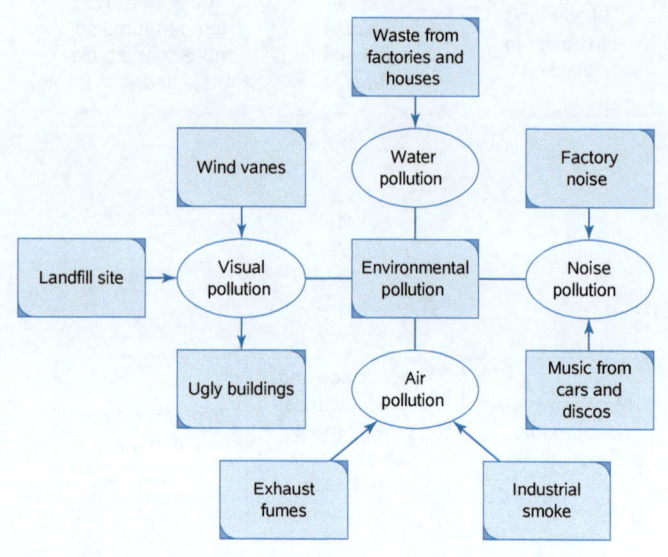

**17** g, c, h, a, d, i, b, e, j, f

**18** a nucleated, b rural, c central business district, d shanty town, e transition zone, f inhabitant, g urban sprawl, h infrastructure, i commuter, j linear, k conurbation, l congestion

Mystery word: urbanisation – the growth in cities and towns as more and more people live in urban areas.

## Chapter 3 Agriculture and Food

**1** Across: 1. Commercial  6. Sedentary  7. Nomadic  8. Dairy  9. Crops  10. Subsistence

Down: 2. Mixed  3. Pastoral  4. Orchard  5. Intensive

**2**

| To plough | To mix up the soil to prepare it for sowing crops |
|---|---|
| To irrigate | To add water to the soil |
| To fertilise | To add nutrients to the soil |
| To harvest | To collect up the crops when they are fully grown |
| To shear | To cut off the wool off a sheep |
| To sow | To put seeds into the soil |
| To herd | To collect together livestock such as sheep |
| To weed | To pull up unwanted plants from a field |
| To thresh | To remove the unwanted husks from the grains of cereal |
| To feed | To give nutrients to livestock |

**3**

| Inputs | Stores | Processes | Outputs |
|---|---|---|---|
| sunshine | barn | feeding | wool |
| rainwater | shed | mowing | meat |
| grass | farmhouse | fertilising | profit |
| labour | fields | washing | |
| sheepdog | | herding | |
| quad bike | | shearing | |
| money | | | |
| machinery | | | |

**4** a false, b true, c true, d false, e true

172

# Answers

**6**

| Large areas of flat land ......... | ......... allow machinery such as combine harvesters to be used easily |
|---|---|
| Fertile prairie soil ......... | ......... produces high yields of crops |
| Warm, dry summer climate ......... | ......... provides good conditions for the growing and ripening of the wheat |
| Modern machinery such as combine harvesters ......... | ......... helps farmers produce and harvest more cereal to make more profit |

**7** is grown; is flooded; is fertilised; are used; are ploughed; is drawn; are sown; is harvested; is dried; is threshed

**8 a** Canadian wheat farm, **b** Kenyan coffee farm, **d** New Zealand; India, **e** Canada, The Netherlands, Kenya

**9**

| Farm location | Commercial/ Subsistence | Extensive/ Intensive | Pastoral/Arable/ Mixed/Plantation |
|---|---|---|---|
| Canada | Commercial | Extensive | Arable |
| Kenya | Commercial | Extensive | Plantation |
| New Zealand | Commercial | Extensive | Pastoral |
| Netherlands | Commercial | Intensive | Arable |
| India | Subsistence | Intensive | Arable |

**10**

| verb | noun naming the process | noun | adjective |
|---|---|---|---|
| To industrialise | industrialisation | industry | industrial |
| To purify | purification | purity | pure |
| ............... | desertification | desert | desert |
| To irrigate | irrigation |  |  |
| To contaminate | contamination |  |  |
| To modernise | modernisation | modernity | modern |
| To fertilise | fertilisation | fertility | fertile |
| To diversify | diversification | diversity | diverse |

**11 a** lush, **b** scorched, **c** glut, **d** fertile, **e** stunting, **f** debt, **g** abundance, **h** neglect

**12 a** Drought has reduced output from farms in Ethiopia and Australia. **b** The wheat farmers in Australia are extensive, arable, commercial farmers. **c** The people in Ethiopia are facing food shortages as they do not have enough food in storage. **d** In both Ethiopia and Australia the rural communities are suffering most. **e** Drought is more likely to lead to starvation and malnutrition in Ethiopia than Australia.

**13**

| Noun | Verb | Adjective |
|---|---|---|
| starvation | to starve | starving |
| exhaustion | to exhaust | exhausting |
| nourishment | to nourish | nourishing |
| malnourishment | to malnourish | malnourished |
| undernourishment | to undernourish | undernourished |
| food | to feed | fed |
| consumption | to consume | consuming |

**14 a** true, **b** false, **c** true, **d** false, **e** not given, **f** true, **g** true

**15 a** The increase in grain production in Asia and Central America through the introduction of new farming technologies. **b** A crop variety that has been developed by cross-breeding of varieties of the same crop. **c** Adding water to crops from river or groundwater through canals, sprinkler systems or wells.

**16** 2000; 309 million; irrigated; hectares; increased; tractors; 0.2 million; fertliser

**17**

| a | Donor | recipient |
|---|---|---|
| b | Flood | drought |
| c | Shortage | glut |
| d | Irrigation | drainage |
| e | Revolution | continuation |

**18**

| Advantages | Disadvantages |
|---|---|
| "Food aid provide essential help to those people in greatest need" | "Food aid only leads to corruption and supports bad governments so they do not have to invest in agriculture" |
| "Food aid may not help a country get richer but it may allow people to live longer, healthier lives" | "Food aid helps countries but it cannot overcome their long term problems" |
| "Without food aid millions of people would die. Any other way would take too long" | "Food aid does not always go to the people who need it most" |
|  | "It would be better to provide the means to grow crops rather than provide people with cheap food" |
|  | "Providing continuous food aid simply stops people and governments having the incentive to make progress" |

**19 a** drought, **b** flood, **c** starvation, **d** malnutrition

**20**

| Condition | Suggestion |
|---|---|
| a drought | irrigation |
| b flood | drainage |
| c starvation | emergency food aid; providing seeds and infrastructure |
| d malnutrition | emergency food aid; education; providing seeds and infrastructure |

**21** Arable, plantation, pastoral, mixed

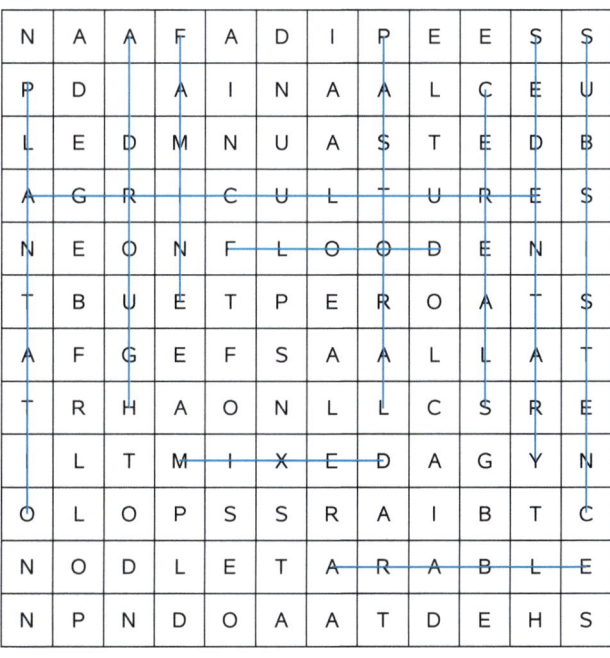

**22**

| N | A | A | F | A | D | I | P | E | E | S | S |
|---|---|---|---|---|---|---|---|---|---|---|---|
| P | D |   | A | I | N | A | A | L | C | E | U |
| L | E | D | M | N | U | A | S | T | E | D | B |
| A | G | R | C | U | L | T | U | R | E | S |
| N | E | O | N | F | L | O | O | D | E | N |
| T | B | U | E | T | P | E | R | O | A | T | S |
| A | F | G | E | F | S | A | A | L | L | A | T |
| T | R | H | A | O | N | L | L | C | S | R | E |
|   | L | T | M | I | X | E | D | A | G | Y | N |
| O | L | O | P | S | S | R | A | I | B | T | C |
| N | O | D | L | E | T | A | R | A | B | L | E |
| N | P | N | D | O | A | A | T | D | E | H | S |

173

# Answers

## Chapter 4 Industry

**1**

| To remove | To make | To provide |
|---|---|---|
| to mine<br>to take out to extract | to use<br>to manufacture<br>to process<br>to create<br>to construct | to give<br>to supply |

**2**

| Primary industry | The removal of raw materials from the earth. |
|---|---|
| Fishing | An industry where fish are caught from seas, lakes and rivers for food |
| Forestry | An industry involving cutting down trees |
| Farming | An industry which extracts nutrients from the soil to grow crops and livestock |
| Mining | An industry which extracts minerals from rocks eg. coal, oil, gold, limestone. |
| Secondary industry | An industry using raw materials to manufacture a finished product. |
| Tertiary industry | An industry providing a service to a population |

**3**

| Primary industries | Secondary industries | Tertiary industries |
|---|---|---|
| Gold miner<br>Lumberjack<br>Farmer<br>Fisherman | Steel worker<br>Car maker<br>Engineer | Doctor<br>Banker<br>TV presenter |

**4**

| Inputs | Processes | Stores | Outputs |
|---|---|---|---|
| Sunshine<br>Sheep<br>Rain<br>Grass<br>Fodder<br>Farm hands | Shearing the **fleeces** from the sheep<br>Sewing the pieces into boots<br>Preserving the skins with salt<br>Packaging the boots<br>Cutting the wool from the skins<br>Gluing soles on to the boots<br>Applying the boot patterns to the skins | Warehouse for the finished boots<br>Farm | Sheepskin boots |

**5** a false, b true, c true, d false, e true, f false, g false

**6** employment; proportion; tertiary; agriculture; primary; proportion; small; tertiary; population; secondary

**7**

| 1 | A steel industry has inputs of heavy coal, iron ore and limestone so it is a raw material oriented industry |
|---|---|
| 2 | Governments encourage industries to locate in certain places by offering incentives. |
| 3 | Raw materials are imported to factories to make the finished products. |
| 4 | It is cheaper to locate an industry in the countryside than in the middle of a city. |

**8** transnational; Tokyo; Singapore; New York; 12; Asia; labour; Malaysia; infrastructure; tax-free; USA; skilled; Europe; markets

**9** a East Malaysia, b West Malaysia, c West Malaysia, d oil, rubber, timber, palm oil, tin, e agriculture, f more money is invested in education and skills development, g tertiary

**10** a due to, b thanks to, c The resulting from, d as a result of, e on account of

**11**

|  | Advantage / Disadvantage |
|---|---|
| The TNCs take business away from small local companies | disadvantage |
| The TNCs provide more employment for the country | advantage |
| The TNCs encourage governments to improve infrastructure such as roads, airports and electricity | advantage |
| The country can become too dependent on the foreign business | disadvantage |
| The TNCs bring more money to the country | advantage |
| A lot of the money made by the TNC will go back to its headquarters in a different country (**leakage**) | disadvantage |
| The TNCs train local people to learn new skills | advantage |

**12**

| Secondary industry: | Processing of raw materials<br>Manufacturing goods from raw materials |
|---|---|
| Tertiary sector: | Nursing<br>Teaching |
| Export: | Selling tin to the USA<br>Supplying DVD players to European market |
| Incentives: | Grants to attract new industry<br>Subsidies to help new companies |

**13** a *tertiary*, b *primary*, c *secondary*, d *more*, e *reduce*, f *attract*, g *on the Pacific Rim*, h *works*, i *more*, j *independent*, k *expands*, l *exports*

**14** a Tertiary, b Footloose, c Export, d Primary, e Infrastructure, f Transnational, g Raw materials, h Secondary

## Chapter 5 Leisure and Tourism

**1** increased; million; 1950; 25.3; steady; greatest; 1985; 320.1

**2**

| Getting bigger | Getting smaller |
|---|---|
| to expand<br>to grow<br>to rise<br>to increase | to contract<br>to decrease<br>to drop<br>to fall<br>to plummet<br>to shrink<br>to slow<br>to lower |

**3** suddenly, dramatically, steeply

**4** a domestic tourism, b short break, c cultural tourism, d long haul travel, e eco-tourism, f adventure tourism

**5** d There are more European countries in the top 10 tourist destinations than any other continent. f There are no African countries in the top 10 tourist destinations.

**6** a Location, b Landscape, c Climate, d Colonisation, e Sugar, f Independence, g Tourism, h Economy, i Future

# Answers

**7**

| Primary resources | Secondary resources |
|---|---|
| white sandy beaches | deep harbour |
| tropical climate | water sports |
| clear turquoise blue sea | hotel complexes |
|  | restaurants and entertainment |

**8** a surrounded by; b fringed with; c situated in; d lined with; e located on

**9** a used to cultivate; b used to import; c used to be; d used to cover; e used to work; f used to be

**10** a Although; b Despite; c However; d despite; e On the other hand; f Although; g however

**11** Negative: International hotels allow leakage; Mangrove swamps are being cleared for hotels to be built; the economy becomes overdependent on tourism (the rest are positive).

**12** a Lemans-caraholics, b Black-Sheep, c Cleopatra-cruises, d City-shopping, e Oriental escapes, f Zambia-adventure, g Welsh-hideaway-cottages, h Costa Rica experience, i Villas-in-Italy

**13**

| The free time when someone is not working | Leisure time |
|---|---|
| Tourism where people try to limit their impact on the local people and natural environment | Eco-tourism |
| Travel more than 5 hours flying time from home. | Long haul |
| A holiday booked through an agent which includes accommodation, travel, food and activities | Package holiday |
| Holidays within the home country | Domestic tourism |

**14 Across:** 1. Ecotourism  3. Seasonal  8. Package  9. Honeypot  10. Leisure  11. Litter  13. Sustainable  14. Adventure

**Down:** 2. Infrastructure  4. Leakage  5. Tertiary  6. Domestic  7. Tourist  12. Urban

## Chapter 6 Energy and Water

**1**

| finite | non-renewable |
|---|---|
| renewable | infinite |
| fuel | energy source |
| to run out | to exhaust |
| thermal | heat |
| absorb | soak up |
| to generate | to produce |

**2** are burned; are produced; is used; are turned; is generated; is absorbed; is heated; are extracted

**3** 1 = wind turbine, 2 = geothermal power station, 3 = hydroelectric power station, 4 = dam, 5 = reservoir, 6 = magma, 7 = steam, 8 = windmill, 9 = wind power

**4**

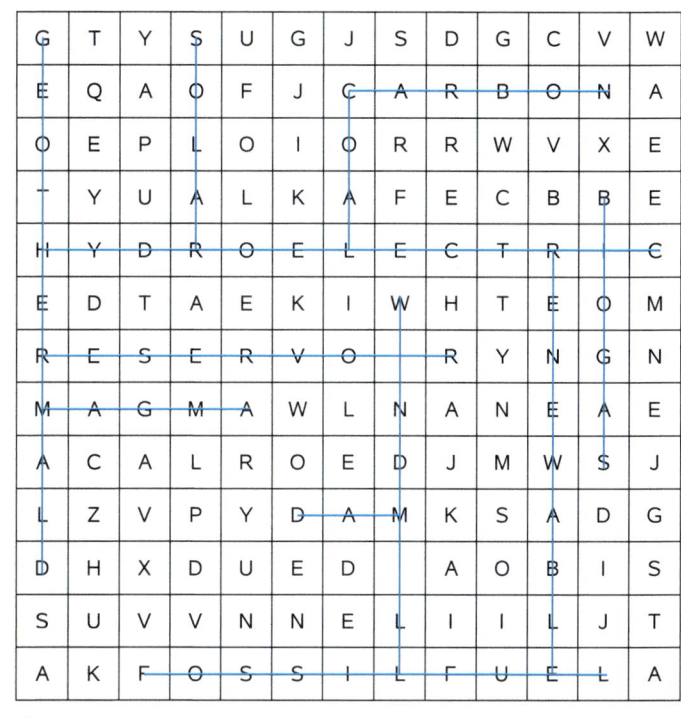

| G | T | Y | S | U | G | J | S | D | G | C | V | W |
|---|---|---|---|---|---|---|---|---|---|---|---|---|
| E | Q | A | O | F | J | C | A | R | B | O | N | A |
| O | E | P | L | O | I | O | R | R | W | V | X | E |
| T | Y | U | A | L | K | A | F | E | C | B | B | E |
| H | Y | D | R | O | E | L | E | C | T | R | I | C |
| E | D | T | A | E | K | I | W | H | T | E | O | M |
| R | E | S | E | R | V | O | I | R | Y | N | G | N |
| M | A | G | M | A | W | L | N | A | N | E | A | E |
| A | C | A | L | R | O | E | D | J | M | W | S | J |
| L | Z | V | P | Y | D | A | M | K | S | A | D | G |
| D | H | X | D | U | E | D |   | A | O | B | I | S |
| S | U | V | V | N | N | E | L | I | I | L | J | T |
| A | K | F | O | S | S | I | L | F | U | E | L | A |

**6** a, e, b, g, f, d, c

**7** a oil, gas, coal, b radioactive waste, c inviting people to visit the power stations; emphasising benefits to the community, solving the problem of waste disposal, emphasising prospect of cheap electricity, d they began to question the idea of nuclear power filling the energy gap, e waste was stored so parts could be recycled and further research undertaken, f 58, g it exports electricity to its European neighbours

**8**

| Nuclear power stations can produce more energy than thermal power stations | A |
|---|---|
| Waste material is radioactive and very dangerous | D |
| No gases are given off when energy is produced | A |
| Storing the waste materials is very expensive | D |
| It is a clean fuel | A |
| A lot of attention is paid to safety and security. | A |

**9** a true, b false, c true, d true, e false, f false, g true, h true, i false

**10** a which; b what; c Who; d Which; e whom; f Which; g Whose

175

## Answers

**11**

| Source | Renewable/non renewable | Non-polluting/ polluting | Reliable/unreliable | Plentiful/Scarce | Cheap/expensive |
|---|---|---|---|---|---|
| fuelwood | non-renewable | polluting | reliable | scarce | cheap |
| water | renewable | non-polluting | reliable | plentiful | cheap |
| wind | renewable | non-polluting | unreliable | plentiful | cheap |
| biogas | renewable | non-polluting | reliable | plentiful | cheap |
| solar | renewable | non-polluting | unreliable | plentiful | |
| geothermal | renewable | non-polluting | reliable | plentiful | |
| nuclear | renewable | polluting | reliable | | |
| oil | non-renewable | polluting | reliable | | cheap |
| natural gas | non-renewable | polluting | reliable | | cheap |
| coal | non-renewable | polluting | reliable | plentiful | cheap |

**12** c on the rural-urban fringe
**13** b less accessible than water in rivers
**14** a too much carbon dioxide in the atmosphere
**15** c stores of water are not refilled by rainfall and melting snow
**16** a coal, b nuclear power, c hydroelectric power, d geothermal power, e natural gas
**17**

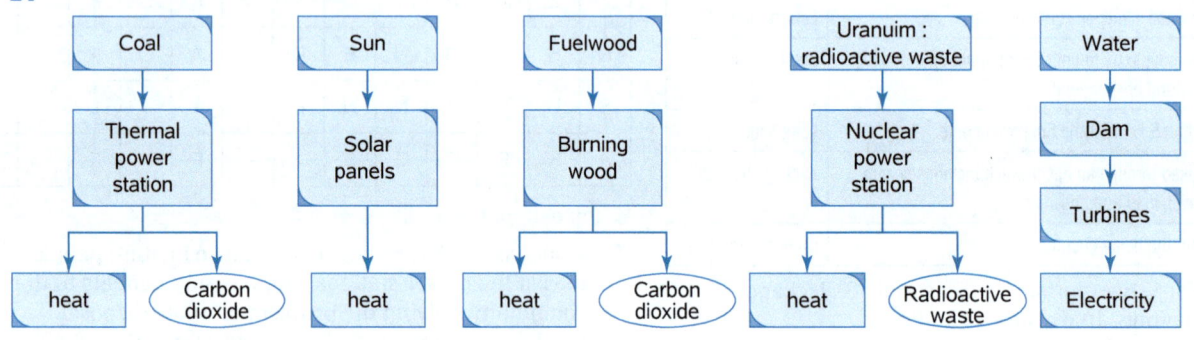

- Coal → Thermal power station → heat, Carbon dioxide
- Sun → Solar panels → heat
- Fuelwood → Burning wood → heat, Carbon dioxide
- Uranuim: radioactive waste → Nuclear power station → heat, Radioactive waste
- Water → Dam → Turbines → Electricity

## Chapter 7 Plate Tectonics

**1**

| verb | noun | adjective |
|---|---|---|
| converge | convergence | convergent |
| diverge | divergence | divergent |
| erupt | eruption | eruptible/eruptive |
| subduct | subduction | _____ |
| transform | transformation | transformable/transformative |

**2**

| plate | a large section of the earth's crust |
|---|---|
| crust | the solid surface of the earth |
| magma | molten rock beneath the crust |
| convection current | movement of hot magma within the mantle |
| core | the centre of the earth |
| divergent | movement away from each other |

**3** a centre, b diverge, c converge, d smooth, e whole
**4** Anagrams
1 = crust, 2 = mantle, 3 = magma, 4 = volcano, 5 = convection current
Diagram
1 = magma, 2 = crust, 3 = convection current, 4 = mantle, 5 = volcano.

**5** 1 = oceanic crust, 2 = mantle, 3 = magma, 4 = continental crust, 5 = volcano, 6 = subduction, 7 = fold mountains

**6**
1 If oceanic crust is pushed beneath continental crust, (subduction) — b fold mountains form with violent volcanic eruptions and earthquakes.
2 If tectonic plates slide past one another, (transform) — d earthquakes occur but no volcanic eruptions
3 If tectonic plates move apart, (diverge) — a magma is released from volcanoes forming mid-ocean ridges
4 If continental crust is pushed against continental crust, (converge) — c fold mountains form and major earthquakes.

**7** a heavier; denser; b steeper; c runnier; d louder; more explosive; e higher
**8** b At a subduction zone the oceanic crust sinks beneath the continental crust. c Plates move towards each other at convergent plate margins. f A volcano erupts when magma from the mantle rises through the earth's crust.

176

# Answers

## 9

1 If a pyroclastic flow occurs, — **b** areas on the slopes of the volcano will be covered in hot ash.
2 If warnings of volcanic activity are given, — **e** people will evacuate their homes.
3 If the epicentre of an earthquake is in a large city, — **d** there will be a large amount of damage to buildings.
4 If an earthquake occurs in the middle of the night, — **c** most people will be asleep.
5 If the epicentre of an earthquake is in an area of low population density, — **a** there will be very little damage and few deaths.

## 10

| Description of the effects | Richter Magnitude |
|---|---|
| 1 Tremors hardly felt | Less than 3.5 |
| 2 Tremors just noticeable and recorded | 3.5–5.4 |
| 3 At most slight damage to well constructed buildings. Windows rattle, plaster cracks, bricks fall. Over a small area poorly constructed buildings can suffer serious damage. | 5.5–6.0 |
| 4 Can cause destruction in areas up to 100 km from the epicentre. Chimneys fall, houses move, walls crack. | 6.1–6.9 |
| 5 Major earthquake causing destruction over larger areas. Bridges twist, buildings collapse | 7.0–7.9 |
| 6 Great earthquake causing devastation in areas several hundred kilometres across. Most buildings collapse or are seriously damaged, objects are thrown in the air, earth's surface moves | 8 or greater |

**11** **a** mountains and river valleys; convergent plate margins; earthquakes; urban areas, **b** Sichuan, **c** Sichuan, **d** Sichuan, **e** both agreed to give funding for rebuilding and improving infrastructure, **f** strengthening buildings; setting and following building guidelines

**12** **a While** Beichuan has been abandoned, L'Aquila is being rebuilt.  **b Like** the survivors of L'Aquila, the survivors from Beichuan had to move to temporary accommodation.  **c Both** the inhabitants of L'Aquila and the inhabitants of Beichuan felt angry about the shoddy construction of many modern buildings.  **d** Volunteers **not only** from Italy and China **but also** from abroad rushed to help rescue people from the ruins of the devastated towns.  **e Whereas** the damaged dams threatened the lives of the inhabitants of Sichuan after the earthquake, the dangerous state of the buildings was the major threat in L'Aquila.

**13** **a** destroyed/damaged/wrecked; **b** injured/killed; **c** damaged; **d** demolished; **e** injured

## 15

1 If London lay on a transform plate margin, — **d** it would experience earthquakes
2 If people were warned of an earthquake, — **a** they would be able to move to a safer place
3 If an earthquake under the sea bed caused a tsunami, — **b** coastal regions would be in danger.
4 If buildings were reinforced with steel and rubber, — **c** they would sway but should not collapse.

## 16

1 If Beichuan had not been situated in such a dangerous location, — **b** the town would have been rebuilt.
2 If L'Aquila's monuments had been reinforced, — **a** they would have withstood the earthquake better.
3 If people had been warned, — **d** they would have left the danger zone.
4 If the dams had not been damaged, — **c** there would not have been a danger of flooding.

## 17

| Earthquake planning | Volcano planning |
|---|---|
| **b** Put wide open spaces in towns and cities where the public can meet where they would be safe from falling buildings and debris | **a** Do not build in river valleys running down the mountain as they are the likely paths of pyroclastic flows |
| **c** Restrict the height of buildings as tall buildings are most likely to collapse | **d** Put in land use zoning. Build urban areas a good distance from the mountain and agriculture or forest closer to it |
| **e** Dig deep foundations for buildings so they are less likely to fall over | |
| **f** Reinforce the building structure with steel frames and rubber counterweights so allowing them to sway without falling over | **g** Set up early warning sirens in the area so people know when they should evacuate |
| **h** Earthquake drills in schools and at workplaces so people know what to do | **i** Identify and inform people of safe evacuation routes |
| **i** Identify and inform people of safe evacuation routes | |

# Answers

**18**

| Location | Plate boundary | Types of crust: oceanic/oceanic continental/continental oceanic/continental | Subduction Yes/no | Potential Hazard volcano/earthquake/tsunami |
|---|---|---|---|---|
| Kobe | convergent | oceanic/continental | yes | volcano/earthquake/tsunami |
| Sichuan | transform | continental/continental | no | earthquake |
| Iceland | divergent | oceanic/oceanic | no | |
| Los Angeles | transform | oceanic/continental | no | earthquake |
| Sumatra | convergent | oceanic/continental | yes | volcano/earthquake/tsunami |
| Pinatubo | convergent | oceanic/continental | yes | volcano/earthquake/tsunami |

**19**

| Reasons based on fact | Reasons based on personal feelings |
|---|---|
| Living in the mountains is cooler and the rivers provide water. There has not been a disaster for a very long time. The soil in the valley is very fertile so I can earn a good living. The town's buildings have been reinforced to withstand violent tremors. The scenery is lovely and the climate is good. The government has introduced measures to make our town safe. | My family has always lived here. The ability to predict volcanoes and earthquakes will surely improve. I would lose everything if I moved away from my home. Nowhere is safe from natural disasters so there is no point in moving. |

**20** A = divergent margin, B = Convergent margin, C = transform margin, D = transform margin

**21** **a** i) have steep, **b** ii) plates colliding, **c** ii) plates moving apart, **d** ii) oceanic crust is forced beneath continental crust

## Chapter 8 Weathering

**1**

| Noun | Verb |
|---|---|
| disintegration | **to disintegrate** |
| **composition** | to compose |
| decomposition | **to decompose** |
| integration | **to integrate** |
| erosion | to erode |
| exfoliation | **to exfoliate** |
| **fluctuation** | to fluctuate |

**2** a expands; crack; b thawing; weaker; c fluctuates; freeze-; d widens; e temperature; water; f rock; g night; freezes; drops; h melts

**3** c, e, a, h, g, d, b, f

**4**

| a | Chalk and limestone dissolve in rainwater _____ | d | _____ because rainwater contains a weak carbonic acid |
|---|---|---|---|
| b | Oxidation turns iron minerals a brown-red colour _____ | e | _____ because the minerals react with oxygen in the air. |
| c | The cracks in rocks get wider _____ | a | _____ because water expands when it freezes. |
| d | Exfoliation occurs in deserts _____ | b | _____ because there is a big difference between night and daytime temperatures. |
| e | The mineral composition of rocks may change _____ | c | _____ because chemical weathering has occurred. |

**5** a False, b True, c False, d True, e True, f True, g False

**6**

| Phrasal verb | One word verb |
|---|---|
| To work together | To combine |
| To break up | To disintegrate |
| To change the make up | To decompose |
| To make up | To compose |
| To make unstable | To destabilize |
| To lose a layer | To exfoliate |
| To absorb into liquid | To dissolve |
| To spread out | To expand |

**7** a expands/spreads; b dissolved; c decomposes; d disintegrate; e combine/work together; f made up/composed; made up/composed; g disintegrate/break up

**8** a = Rock of Gibralter, b = Uluru, c = Enchanted Rock

**9**

| Location | Rock type | Appearance | Weathering processes? |
|---|---|---|---|
| **Enchanted Rock, Texas** | Granite | Sheets of rock breaking up on the surface | exfoliation |
| **Uluru, Australia** | Sandstone | Red isolated mound | oxidation |
| **Rock of Gibralter** | Limestone | Sheer rock faces; caves | carbonation |

**10** Physical weathering: A, D Chemical weathering: B Biological weathering: C

**11** a Into a crack in the rock, b The water freezes, c The ice expands, e The rock is weakened and will disintegrate, f Freeze-thaw weathering

**12** a carbonation, b the rock is dissolved, c warm, wet tropical climates

**13** a the cracks get larger, b biological, c chemical

**14** a rapid, b deserts, c the bedding planes and joints, d exfoliation, e sedimentary and igneous

# Answers

**15** a rainwater, b dissolve, c limestone, d physical, e exfoliation, f horizontal, g vertical, h oxidation, i igneous, j groundwater, k decomposing

**16** a speeds up chemical weathering, b freeze- thaw weathering when it fluctuates around 0°C, c exfoliation when there is a large difference between day and night

## Chapter 9 Rivers

**1**

| narrow | wide |
|---|---|
| shallow | deep |
| fast | slow |
| full | empty |
| large | small |
| rough | smooth |
| gentle | steep |

**2**

| narrow, shallow channel | F | Long Profile | A |
|---|---|---|---|
| flat land at sea level | D | rough river bed with large rocks | G |
| Cross Section of a river near the source. | E | gentle gradient of lower course | C |
| steep gradient of upper course | B | river banks | H |

**3** a narrow; shallow; b large; c gentle; d fast; e rough

**4** a wider; deeper; b slower; c smoother; d steeper; e smaller

**5**

| discharge | The amount of water in a river at a certain place and a certain time |
|---|---|
| mouth | Where the river meets the sea |
| corrasion | Rocks in the river hitting the river bed and banks so wearing them away |
| drainage basin | The area drained by a river and its tributaries. |
| attrition | Rocks hit each other so become smaller and smoother |
| river bed | The bottom of the river |
| corrosion | The river water dissolves rock |

**6** hard; waterfall; erodes; river; plunge; hydraulic; corrasion; undercut; Gravity; plunge pool; corrosion; larger

**7** a 5, b 2, c 8, d 3, e 9, f 7, g 6, h 10, i 4, j 1

**8** a 3, b 1, c 4, d 2

**9** a False, b True, c False, d True, e True, f False

**10** a basin/bowl, b course/channel, c to deposit/to put down, d to erode/to wear away, e flood/inundation, f lake/pool, g meander/bend, h velocity/rate of flow, i vulnerable to/prone to, j waterfall/cascade

**11** a inundates/floods; b basin; c waterfall; d meanders; e lakes; wears away/erodes; f channel

**12** a Despite; b Although; c despite; d however; e on the other hand

**13** a subsistence farmer, b school child in Dhaka, c emergency aid worker, d member of medical team, e international ecologist, f Bangladeshi politician

**14** a The schoolchild said that she/he couldn't go to school when the floods came, and her/his mother wouldn't even let her/him go out to fetch food because of the snakes.  b The farmer said that when the waters rose he could do nothing but watch all his hard work being destroyed. If the rice crop failed he would have nothing to eat.  c The international ecologist said that global warming could no longer be ignored as natural disasters such as the 1998 floods in Bangladesh were occurring more and more frequently.  d The Bangladeshi politician said that their country needed and deserved international aid to help them survive the effects of deforestation.  e The member of the medical team said that it was not the depth of the flood that was the greatest cause of death but the contamination which spread diseases such as cholera and typhoid.  f The emergency aid worker said that the waters stretched as far as he could see, and the bodies of dead animals floated past the aid station as they gave food and water to the hungry people."

**15** a to predict, b to state, c to complain, d to announce, e to assert, f to fear

**16**

| Emergency measures | Preventive measures | International measures |
|---|---|---|
| The provision of food, drinking water and medicines. | Early warning systems to alert population to future flood Construction of flood shelters on concrete pillars for the delta dwellers Crop storage in shelters above the water level Education about the importance of clean water and the avoidance of disease Construction of levees to stop rivers overflowing their banks | Construction of dams to control the water flow in the delta Agreements with neighbouring countries to protect the natural flow of transnational rivers Control of chemical waste from factories Controls on irrigation and extraction of groundwater Support for policies to reduce global warming |

**17**

| It is a large, deep area of water into which a waterfall pours water. | plunge pool |
|---|---|
| A steep rise in the river bank on the outside bend of a meander. | river cliff |
| The area of low-lying, flat land near the coast with a large number of small rivers flowing into the sea. | delta |
| There is not much water in the channel here and there are many large rocks on the river bed. | river at its source |
| A curved, shallow pool of water which lies on flat land beside a meandering river. | oxbow lake |
| A bowl carved out of a large rock which forms part of the river bank. | pot hole |
| Two rivers meet at this point causing the discharge and the power of the river to increase. | confluence |

**18** a Waterfall – B, b Tributary – D, c Source – A, d Meander – E, e Delta - J, f Flood plain – G, g Levee – I, h Oxbow lake – H, i Plunge pool – C, j Slip-off slope – F

179

# Answers

## Chapter 10 Marine Processes

1. 1 = Long wave length, 2 = Low wave height, 3 = Strong swash, 4 = Constructive waves, 5 = Weak backwash, 6 = Short wave length, 7 = High wave height, 8 = Weak swash, 9 = Destructive waves, 10 = Strong backwash

2. a False, b True, c False, d False, e True, f True, g True, h True

3. 

| | |
|---|---|
| Steep walls of rock at the coast | cliff |
| The movement of surface water caused by the wind | waves |
| The movement of the sea against the coast caused by the moon | tides |
| Waves throw stones at the cliffs and break pieces off | corrasion |
| The distance between two wave peaks | wave length |
| Where the land meets the sea | coast |
| The pressure of breaking waves on cracks in a cliff | hydraulic action |

4. a weak, b lump, c strong, d sand, e gentle

6. eroded; made; formed; broke; collapsed

7. a Cracks in the arch will be made larger by hydraulic action. b The collapse of the arch will be caused by gravity. c The headland was made weaker by corrasion. d this headland was eroded by corrasion and hydraulic action. e The stack has been eroded by breaking waves to form a stump.

8. a False, b True, c False, d True, e True, f False, g True, h False

9. a minimum; lowest; b at least; c optimum; ideal; d maximum; greatest; e at the most

10. a highest; c lowest; d coldest; d largest; e smallest; f weakest

11. a to move into/to encroach/to spread, b to put down/to deposit/to drop, c to break up/to collapse/to crumble, d to build up/to accumulate/to grow, e to drag away/to remove/to displace

12. 

| | |
|---|---|
| slowly | over a long period |
| rapidly | in a short space of time |
| constantly | all the time |
| suddenly | without any warning |
| gradually | little by little |

13. a constantly; b slowly; c suddenly; d gradually; e in a short space of time

14. hydraulic action; corrosion; backwash; attrition; swash; longshore drift; deposition; saltation

15. a 6, b 5, c 7, d 11, e 3, f 4, g 1, h 2, i 9, j 10, k 8

## Chapter 11 Weather and Climate

1. 

| | |
|---|---|
| hygrometer | An instrument used to measure the humidity of the air |
| weather | The characteristics of the atmosphere for a particular place |
| barometer | An instrument used to measure air pressure |
| humidity | The amount of water vapour in the air |
| climate | The average weather for a place over a long time |
| anemometer | An instrument used to measure the speed of the wind |

2. a 11.2, b 11.1, c 11.3

3. a False, b True, c True, d False, e False, f True, g False, h True

4. a wispy thin high feathery, b fluffy puffy individual heap

5. a West, b low pressure area, tropical depression, tropical storm, severe tropical storm, typhoon, c heavy rainfall, d It was the heaviest rain for 40 years; rivers flooded, people were killed, power and telephone lines were broken, villages were submerged in mud, e Badly – power and telephone lines were broken, roads became rivers so people were completely cut off, f diseases and infections from the dirty water

6. a President, b An old couple, c Villager, d A Filipino hospital worker in Hong Kong, e Medical aid worker, f Business man, g Rice farmer, h Young schoolgirl

7. a President = optimistic, b An old couple = grateful, c Villager = critical, d A Filipino hospital worker in Hong Kong = anxious, e Medical aid worker = exhausted, f Business man = angry, g Rice farmer = pessimistic, h Young schoolgirl = sad

8. a A survivor asked why the water didn't drain away, b He asked how much rain had fallen in 24 hours, c He asked why we had no help, d He asked what the worst consequence of Typhoon Ketsana was, e He asked if the country would recover

9. a The President declared that his country was in a state of disaster but they would recover. b An old couple describes how they had been too weak to swim and his wife had started to panic but their dear neighbour had pulled them out of the water to safety on his rooftop. c A village questioned why none of the emergency services had reached them for days although there had been pictures from eye witnesses on the Internet of the terrible impact of Ketsana. d The Filipino hospital worker said he could not get any news about his parents and all flights to Manila from Hong Kong had been cancelled. He didn't know what to do. e The medical aid worker said her team was working day and night in a temporary clinic. They were doing their best but the queues just got longer. f The business man complained that he had lost his

home and his business beneath the layer of stinking mud and the water was not draining away. **g** The rice farmer said that his rice crop had been ruined so his family faced poverty and hunger". **h** A young schoolgirl explained how her parents had been at work when water started streaming into the house so she had carried her little brother upstairs to the roof. They had stayed there until the water level had dropped and waited for her parents but they hadn't come back.

10 **a** trickling, **b** rescued, **c** succumb, **d** tsunami, **e** continue, **f** emerge, **g** surrender, **h** luck

11

| Dry conditions | Wet conditions |
|---|---|
| arid | saturated |
| parched | wet |
| scorched | soaked |
| dry | humid |
| dehydrated | moist |
| desiccated | damp |
|  | sodden |
|  | soggy |
|  | drenched |

12 **a** a woman dragging her cow
13 **b** dried up paddy fields
14 **a** hazy mountains
15 **b** cloudless
16 **c** barren
17 **a** ruined
18 **c** emaciated
19 **a** bar graph, **b** line graph
20 **a** Manaus, **b** Riyadh, **c** Manaus, **d** Riyadh, **e** Manaus, **f** Riyadh
21 **a** desert dry seasonal arid hot, **b** rainforest warm wet humid
22 coldest; hottest; greater; warmest; hotter; coldest; smaller; drier; wettest; drier; driest
23 **a** False, **b** True, **c** True, **d** False
24 warm, wet; 25–28°C; low; 3°C; high; annual total; heats; rises; rises; condenses; heavy; low; latitudes; equator; high; clear, dry; Deserts

25, 26

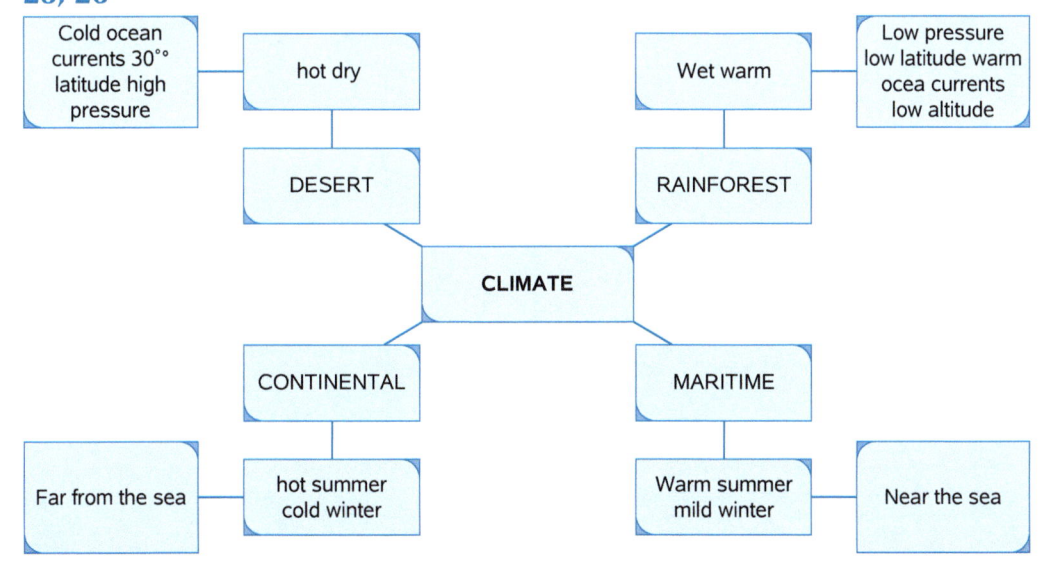

```
Cold ocean
currents 30°°                                            Low pressure
latitude high  →  hot dry        Wet warm  ←  low latitude warm
pressure                                                 ocea currents
                                                         low altitude
        ↓                                   ↓
     DESERT                              RAINFOREST
           ↘                           ↙
                    CLIMATE
           ↙                           ↘
     CONTINENTAL                      MARITIME
        ↓                                   ↓
Far from the sea — hot summer     Warm summer — Near the sea
                   cold winter    mild winter
```

27 **a** 5, **b** 1, **c** 7, **d** 4, **e** 3, **f** 6, **g** 10, **h** 8, **i** 2, **j** 9

## Chapter 12 Ecosystems and Resource Management

1

| Producers | Herbivores | Carnivores | Consumers |
|---|---|---|---|
| Leaf | Ant | Frog | Ant |
| Grass | Beetle | Mouse | Beetle |
|  |  | Eagle | Frog |
|  |  | Snake | Mouse |
|  |  |  | Eagle |
|  |  |  | Snake |

2 **a** True, **b** True, **c** False, **d** False, **e** False, **f** False, **g** True, **h** True, **i** False

3

| Leaves have drip tips to .............. | .............. allow heavy rainwater to run off the leaves |
| Large leaves in the shrub layer .............. | .............. allow plants to make use of the small amount of sunlight |
| Large trees have buttress roots to .............. | .............. support them as they grow so tall |
| The canopy layer of trees .............. | .............. reduces the amount of sunlight reaching the forest floor |
| The soil of the rainforest is .............. | .............. quite infertile as nutrients are stored in the vegetation |

4

| canopy layer | the layer of tall trees which blocks out sunlight from the forest floor |
| biome | an ecosystem found across continents |
| buttress roots | roots which spread out at the base of a tall tree to support it |
| emergents | tallest trees which reach above the canopy for sunlight |
| drip-tips | pointed ends to leave to help rain run off |
| herbivores | animals that eat plants |
| biodiversity | the number of different species |

5 **a** honesty, **b** global, **c** pessimistic, **d** conserve, **e** overseas, **f** industrial, **g** survival, **h** destruction, **i** leaves

# Answers

**6** a destroyed; b extinct; c Logging; d inhabit; e global/local; saved/conserved.

**7** a 5, b 1, c 7, d 2, e 3, f 4, g 6

**8** a B: south-east Asia, b C: timber, rubber, minerals, c A: it is renewable and offsets $CO_2$, d B: soaps and margarine, e A: low wages and lost land, f B: biodiversity has decreased

**9** Wildlife faces extinction; Infertile soil cannot be used for growing crops or rainforest; Monoculture is a risk; Carbon dioxide is released when the forest is cleared and burned; Indigenous population are exploited

**10**

| To close the stable door when the horse has bolted | To act too late to save the situation |
|---|---|
| To make hay while the sun shines | Acting promptly saves a lot of problems and extra work |
| The end of the line | Nothing else can be done |
| Too many cooks spoil the broth | If too many people are involved little is achieved |
| To turn a blind eye | Intentionally to ignore the real state of affairs |
| To have all one's eggs in one basket | To depend on just one thing |
| A rosy future | A future where things will go well |
| To be left high and dry | To be left helpless and without resources |

**11** 4 = To have all one's eggs in one basket 5 = The end of the line 7 = A rosy future

**12** bare; vegetation; clear; high; sparse; xerophytic; spines; Succulents

**13**

| desertification | Turning an area into desert |
|---|---|
| irrigation | To supply an area with water |
| deforestation | To remove trees from an area of land |
| conservation | To protect and care for the natural environment or traditional life style |
| exploitation | To use natural resources often belonging to others for one's own benefit |
| urbanisation | Turning an area into a town |

**14** a desertification, b deforestation, c irrigation, d conservation, e exploitation, f desertification, g deforestation, h desertification, i conservation

**15** a must; b should; c may; d can; e should; f could; g should; h could; i might

**16** a Logging companies replant hardwood trees as they chop them down.  c Local people are encouraged to plant trees to reduce water and wind erosion. d International organisations control the number of new oil palm plantations.  f Tourism brings wealth and employment to the indigenous people.  g Tourist interest in the culture and way of life of the indigenous people helps to preserve their traditions.  i Local farmers are encouraged to grow drought-resistant crops that do not need so much water.  j Plantations of oil palms are restricted to areas of rainforest that have already been cleared.  j Hunting endangered species is made illegal.  k MEDCs give money to developing nations as long as they do not allow further damage to the natural environment.  l The import of tropical hardwood is banned.

**17 Across:** 1. Consumer   5. Well   6 Nomad 7. Overgrazing   10 Diurnal   11. Canopy   12. shelter

**Down:** 2. mahogany   3. xerophytic   4. ephemeral 8. emergent   9. nocturnal

# Index

agriculture 37, 49–50
   advantages of the Green Revolution 47
   aims of farmers 37
   disadvantages of the Green Revolution 47–8
   effects of food shortages 45
   Farmers' Forum 41–2
   farming systems 39–40
   food aid 43, 45–6
   food shortages 43
   Green Revolution 43, 46–7
   human causes of food shortages 45
   natural causes of food shortages 44
   scale of farming 37–8
altitude 144
Andes 89
attrition 111, 124
Australia 44, 129

Bangladesh 116–17
Barbados 64–6, 68
bars 126–7
bays 124
beaches 122, 126
biodiversity 147, 151
biogas 76
birth rate 11

carbon dioxide 75, 103
carbonation 102–3
chalk 102–3, 104
Chile 89, 92
China 15–16
chloropleth maps 20
cities 24, 28, 29, 31, 33–4, 36
cliffs 122
   cliff erosion 124
climate 103–4, 134, 142, 146
   altitude 144
   climate graphs 142–3
   distance from the sea 144
   latitude 134, 143–4
   ocean currents 144
   pressure systems 144
   tropical rainforest and desert climates 144–5
   wind 144
clouds 136
coasts 122
   coastal sand dunes 127, 128–9
colour 5
contraception 11
conurbations 24
coral reefs 122, 127–8, 129–30

corrasion 111, 124
corrosion 111, 124
cyclones 44, 137

dams 76, 78
   South Eastern Anatolia Development Project, Turkey 82
data 6–7
death rate 11
decomposition 101, 102
deforestation 150, 151
deltas 115, 116–17
Demographic Transition Model 12–13
dependants 13
deposition 109, 114
deserts 144–5, 147, 148, 153–4
   desertification 154–5
diagrams 6–7
dictionaries 9
disintegration 101, 102
drainage basins 109
drought 44, 81, 140–1

earthquakes 86, 91–2
   distribution 88
   magnitude of earthquakes 92–6
   prediction and preparation 96–7, 98
eco-tourism 62, 69
ecosystems 147, 156–8
   desert ecosystems 153–4
   desertification 154–5
   distribution of rainforest and desert ecosystems 148
   food chains 147
   management of desertification 155
   rainforest ecosystems: animals 149
   rainforest ecosystems: deforestation 150
   rainforest ecosystems: humans 149–50
   rainforest ecosystems: plants 148–9
   sustainable development 147, 150–3, 156
   use of deserts by humans 154
emigration 17
employment structure 52–4
energy resources 74, 83–5
   energy crisis 81
   fuelwood 75
   greenhouse gases 75–6
   locating a hydroelectric power station 78

   locating a nuclear power station 78–80
   locating a thermal power station 75
   non-renewable energy sources 74
   nuclear power 78
   renewable energy sources 76–7
Equator 143
erosion 101
   marine erosion 123–5
   river erosion 109, 111–12
   soil erosion 154, 155
essay writing 8
Ethiopia 44
Euphrates 82
examination techniques 10
exfoliation 102

famine 43, 45
flooding 44, 109
   river floodplains 115, 116
fold mountains 89
food aid 43, 45–6
food chains 147
food shortages 43–5
fossil fuels 74, 75, 81
France 79–80
freezing 102

Ganges-Brahmaputra 116–17
geothermal energy 76, 84
global warming 74, 75, 84
glossary 159–69
granite 104, 105–6
Great Barrier Reef, Australia 129
Great Dune of Pyla, France 128
Green Revolution 43, 46–8
greenhouse gases 74, 75, 75–6
groundwater 81, 84, 103, 140, 154

Hawaii 88
headlands 124, 125–6
Himalayas 89, 93, 117
humidity 134
hurricanes 137
hydraulic action 111, 123
hydroelectricity 76, 78

Iceland 88
igneous rock 103, 104
immigration 17
industry 51–2, 59–60
   change in employment structure over time 53–4
   employment structure 52–3
   footloose industries 55
   industrial location 54–5

183

# Index

industrial systems 52
   newly industrialising countries (NICs) 56–8
   transnational companies 55–6
infant mortality rate 11
Internet 9
Iraq 82
irrigation 81, 154

L'Aquila, Italy 93, 95
latitude 134, 143–4
LEDC (less economically developed country) 31
leisure 61–2
libraries 9
life expectancy 11
limestone 102–3, 104, 106
London, UK 66
longshore drift 122, 126
Los Angeles, USA 24, 90, 96

Malaysia 57–8
Maldives 129–30
map reading 7–8
marine processes 122, 130–3
   coastal sand dunes 127, 128–9
   coasts 122
   coral reefs 122, 127–8, 129–30
   landforms of marine deposition: beaches 122, 126
   landforms of marine deposition: spits and bars 122, 126–7
   landforms of marine erosion: bays and headlands 124
   landforms of marine erosion: cliff erosion 124
   landforms of marine erosion: headland erosion 125–6
   longshore drift 122, 126
   marine erosion 123–4
   salt marshes 127
   tides 122
   waves 122–3
meanders 114
MEDC (more economically developed country) 30
memory training 8–9
Mexico 89
   Mexico City 31–2
mid-ocean ridge 88
migration 17–19, 23
   rural-urban migration 17, 18, 31, 34–5
mineral composition 103, 104
mnemonics 8

National Parks 62, 66, 69
NICs (newly industrialising countries) 56–8
Nile 154
nomads 37, 154
nuclear power 78–80

oases 154
ocean currents 144
organisation 5
oxbow lakes 114–15
oxidation 103
oxygen 103

Pacific Rim 55, 56
Pacific Rim of Fire 88
palm oil cultivation 151–2
Peru 89
Philippines 137–40
plate tectonics 86, 99–100
   convergent plate margins 87
   convergent plate margins and fold mountains 89
   convergent plate margins and subduction 89
   crust 86, 87
   distribution of earthquakes and volcanoes 88
   divergent plate margins 87, 88
   earthquake prediction and preparation 96–7, 98
   earthquakes 91–2
   magnitude of earthquakes 92–6
   plate margins 87–8
   structure of the Earth 86–7
   transform plate margins 87, 90
   tsunamis 96, 130
   volcanic eruptions 90–1
   volcano prediction and preparation 97–8
pollution 31–2, 33–4, 67
population 11, 23
   Demographic Transition Model 12–13
   Government influence on population growth 15–16
   influences on population distribution 22
   movement of people 17
   population density and distribution 20–1, 37, 78
   population pyramids 13–14
   population structure 13
   settlements 28
   threshold population 24, 29
   types of migrants 18
pot holes 112
poverty 15
power stations 75
prosperity 15

rainforests 144–5, 147, 148–50
reading 5–6
research 9
revision 9–10
Richter Scale 92, 93, 94
rivers 109, 118–21
   change in river load 113
   cross sections 109–10
   deltas 115, 116–17
   deposition 109, 114
   drainage basins 109
   floodplains 115, 116
   landforms of river erosion: pot holes 112
   landforms of river erosion: waterfalls 112
   long profile 109
   meanders 114
   oxbow lakes 114–15
   river erosion 109, 111–12
   river load 109, 113
   source 110–11
   transnational rivers 82
   transporting river load 113
rock type 103, 104
rural settlements 24, 26
rusting 103

Sahara Desert 154
Sahel, Africa 154
salt marshes 127
San Francisco, USA 90
sand dunes 127, 128–9
sandstone 106
sedimentary rock 103, 104
settlements 24–5
   central business district 29–30
   function of a settlement 28
   industrial areas 31
   managing urban problems 31–3
   population 28
   rural settlement patterns 26
   rural-urban migration 31, 34–5
   services in settlements 29
   site of settlements 26
   situation of settlements 26–7
   urban residential areas in LEDCs 31
   urban residential areas in MEDCs 30
   urban sprawl 33
   urbanisation 31
shelter belts 155
Sichuan, China 93–4, 95
solar power 76
South Eastern Anatolia Development Project, Turkey 82
spits 122, 126–7
storms 44, 137–40
study skills 5–10
subduction 89
suburbs 30, 31
sustainable development 147, 150–3, 156
Syria 82

tectonic plates *see* plate tectonics
thawing 102
tides 122
Tigris 82
Tokyo, Japan 24, 31, 96
tourism 61, 71–3

# Index

different types of tourism 62–3
growth of leisure and tourism 61–2
honeypots 66
matching travellers with destinations 69–71
negative impacts of tourism 67–8
positive impacts of tourism 66–7
sustainable tourism 69
tourist destinations 63–6
transnational companies 55–6
transnational rivers 82
tributaries 109
Tropics 134, 137, 143
tsunamis 96
    2004 tsunami 130
Turkey 82
Typhoon Ketsana 137–40

urbanisation 31
    managing urban problems 31–3
    urban settlements 24, 30
    urban sprawl 33

vaccinations 11
visualisation 5
volcanoes 86
    distribution 88
    prediction and preparation 97–8
    volcanic eruptions 88, 90–1

water 81, 83, 84, 85
    competition for water 82
    groundwater 81, 84, 103, 140, 154
    hydroelectricity 76, 78
    water shortages 81
    water vapour 134
waterfalls 112
waves 122–3
weather 134, 142, 147
    clouds 136
    extreme weather: drought 140–1
    pressure systems 144
    tropical storms 137–40
    weather data 135–6
    weather stations 134–5

weathering 101, 105–8
    biological weathering 103
    carbonation 102–3
    chemical weathering 102
    climate and rate of weathering 103–4
    exfoliation 102
    freeze-thaw weathering 102
    oxidation 103
    physical weathering 102
    rock type and lines of weakness 104
    rock type and mineral composition 104
    types of weathering 101–2
wind 144
    wind power 76